Forces of Production, Climate Change and Canadian Fossil Capitalism

Studies in Critical Social Sciences Book Series

Haymarket Books is proud to be working with Brill Academic Publishers (www.brill.nl) to republish the *Studies in Critical Social Sciences* book series in paperback editions. This peer-reviewed book series offers insights into our current reality by exploring the content and consequences of power relationships under capitalism, and by considering the spaces of opposition and resistance to these changes that have been defining our new age. Our full catalog of *SCSS* volumes can be viewed at https://www.haymarketbooks.org/series_collections/4-studies-in-critical-social-sciences.

Forces of Production, Climate Change and Canadian Fossil Capitalism

Nicolas Graham

Haymarket Books
Chicago, IL

First published in 2020 by Brill Academic Publishers, The Netherlands
© 2020 Koninklijke Brill NV, Leiden, The Netherlands

Published in paperback in 2021 by
Haymarket Books
P.O. Box 180165
Chicago, IL 60618
773-583-7884
www.haymarketbooks.org

ISBN: 978-1-64259-621-2

Distributed to the trade in the US through Consortium Book Sales and Distribution (www.cbsd.com) and internationally through Ingram Publisher Services International (www.ingramcontent.com).

This book was published with the generous support of Lannan Foundation and Wallace Action Fund.

Special discounts are available for bulk purchases by organizations and institutions. Please call 773-583-7884 or email info@haymarketbooks.org for more information.

Cover design by Jamie Kerry and Ragina Johnson.

Printed in the United States.

10 9 8 7 6 5 4 3 2 1

Library of Congress Cataloging-in-Publication data is available.

Contents

PART 2
Canadian Fossil Capitalism, Climate Change and Productive Forces

Acknowledgements

This book grew out of my dissertation and is therefore the final step in a research and writing project that has spanned several years. The book would not have been possible without the support I received as a doctoral student at the University of Victoria. My upmost gratitude goes to my doctoral supervisor, Bill Carroll, who encouraged this project from its earliest incarnation and provided invaluable intellectual input and guidance throughout the entire process. I am grateful for the comments and insights from my doctoral committee members, Martha McMahon and Jamie Lawson, as well as from Greg Albo. I also benefited greatly by participating in the Corporate Mapping Project, through which I was exposed to cutting edge research on the political economy and ecology of fossil capitalism.

I thank the editors of this series, David Fasenfest and Alfredo Saad-Filho, for their feedback and for giving a platform for my work as a part of *New Scholarship in Political Economy*.

Countless friends and family have provided me with the intellectual stimulation, engagement and emotional support that allowed me to complete this book. Special thanks goes to my Mother, Trish, for her sharp proofreading and insight. Most importantly, I would like to thank my partner and best friend Claire for her love and support.

Figures and Tables

Figures

Tables

Forces of Production and the Climate Crisis

The twenty-first century is one of profound recognition that the conditions for friendly human life are being eroded in pursuit of unending economic growth. Anthropogenic climate change represents the most dangerous and threatening of contemporary interlinked ecological crises. It is a particularly flagrant form of "mismanagement" of our metabolic relation to the rest of nature and makes clear the need to transform productive practices, process and relations in a fundamental way.

A scientific consensus on anthropogenic climate change has existed for over three decades. In 1988, leading climate scientist James Hansen delivered a testimony before the United States congress declaring that "global warming has reached such a level that we can ascribe with a high degree of confidence a cause and effect relationship between the greenhouse effect and the observed warming. ... it is changing our climate now" (as cited in Tangley, 1988, p. 538). Climate change, as Hansen asserted, is driven primarily from burning fossil fuels, which amplifies the greenhouse effect, leading directly to increased temperatures. The consequences include sea level rise, extreme weather (droughts, heat waves, floods and super storms), ocean acidification, losses in biodiversity and the spread of diseases (Intergovernmental Panel on Climate Change, 2014). Certain of the effects "feedback", amplifying and intensifying the original change (see Derber, 2010, pp. 34–46). For instance, melting glaciers reduce the planet's reflective capacity, trapping more heat; forest fires (of increasing severity and intensity) release carbon dioxide, while decreasing the forests capacity to absorb carbon; ocean acidification reduces the ocean's capacity to absorb carbon from the atmosphere, accelerating the warming trend.

Three decades after James Hansen's testimony, global warming has become a climate emergency. In 2018 the United Nations Intergovernmental Panel on Climate Change after issuing increasingly urgent warnings since 1990 – warned that we now have less than twelve years to reduce greenhouse gas emissions by half and get on target to reach zero emissions by 2050 (Intergovernmental Panel on Climate Change, 2018). Failing that, global temperatures will exceed a 1.5 degrees Celsius increase since preindustrial averages. The implications for human lives are dire. They are already witnessed today in crop failures and famine, deaths from heat waves, wildfires and extreme storms and climate refugees (Harlan et al., 2015). The future effects, if we do not radically reduce emissions soon, will be catastrophic for many living things, including most of the world's poorest people.

Marxist approaches have contributed powerfully to understanding the roots of ecological crises, including climate change, providing commanding analyses as to how capitalism works through and degrades planetary ecosystems, while simultaneously illuminating possibilities for radical political economic and ecological transformation. Building from this body of literature and aiming to contribute to it, this work offers a reinterpretation of the concept of forces of production, from an ecological standpoint. The reinterpretation tilts towards the present climate crisis and contemporary fossil capitalism.

1   An Ecological Reinterpretation of the Productive Forces

I suggest that it is most helpful to define forces of production in expansive and ecologically focused terms, namely in the following way: as *the practices, objects, techniques and knowledges through which we are purposefully linked to and transform the rest of nature.* Such a conceptualization clearly situates human beings as a part of nature, while drawing attention to the various means and mediations by which our metabolic interchange with extra-human nature takes place. It also contrasts with interpretations that tend to reduce the concept to technology (or technological "hardware"), pointing instead to a broader set of capacities and powers through which we transform nature to meet needs and support social reproduction.

Such a conceptualization, I argue, can enable a further integration of ecology and Marxist political economy. Understood dialectically, it leads us to consider how under capitalism, forces of production substantially take the commodity form and are embroiled within its (ecological) contradictions. This interpretation challenges certain inherited Marxist views surrounding the progressivity attributable to advancements in productive forces. Recognition of the forms of environmental destructiveness (and social domination) that are woven into productive forces complicates the notion that such forces can be "unleashed" from capitalist shackles and directly provide the foundations of a sustainable future. It provokes a rethinking of the material foundations of a socialism for our times; indeed, it points to the need for a green socialism that would, in decommodifying the forces of production, detach them from capital's growth imperative, and highlight the ecological use-value aspect of their development.

Simultaneously, a broad and ecological conceptualization, drawn from Marx, allows us to consider aspects of productive forces that are critical to sustainability and "rift-healing" in the 21st century. I argue that ecological knowledge, including recognition of the need to restore and maintain the indispensable metabolism between humanity and nature, represents an advancement in the productive forces. Marx himself could not have possibly foreseen the present climate crisis. But the concept of the forces of production includes associated contemporary counter-practices and counter-technologies, such as the growth of renewable energy, "green" infrastructures (e.g., low-carbon transportation, energy efficiency measures) and agroecology. Together with ecological knowledge and science these aspects of the productive forces are what I term "green forces of production". These are all vital for restoring balance in the carbon cycle. The further use and development of such practices is crucial to enabling the restoration and maintenance of our metabolic interchange with the rest of nature. A rational regulation of the socio-ecological metabolism requires that they *massively grow*.

Yet ecological knowledge, including deepening knowledge of the Earth system and of the unintended consequences of our actions, is unfulfilled. While ecological and earth science insights are today employed in efforts to limit ecological debasement (provoking a thin greening of capitalism), any application of this potential beyond profit-making is sharply constrained. Current obstructions and blockages in developing renewable energy[1] and green infrastructures point simultaneously to the inability to have ecological (and thereby human and other species') well-being or any wide measure of sustainability itself prioritized in advancing productive forces, within the confines of current relations of production.

On these terms, the reinterpretation offered here aims at rethinking the notion of a contradiction between relations and forces of production in terms that bear on contemporary ecological issues, particularly the climate crisis. To recall, Marx argued that in class societies, including capitalist social formations, a key contradiction surrounded the drive to develop forces of production within production relations that come to act as obstacles to their further

---

1   While technical barriers remain (particularly surrounding the intermittency of renewables and associated storage capacity challenges), more "optimistic" technical assessments find that due to recent developments in renewable technology and energy efficiency, all energy needs today could be met by wind, water and solar power within two decades (Jacobson et al., 2018, 2019; Jacobson and Delucchi, 2011; Schwartzman and Schwartzman, 2013). Despite emphasizing the development of renewable energy as a vital component of climate mitigation, other approaches, which are emphasized in this study (Laxer, 2015b; Malm, 2013; Trainer, 2012, 2014), argue that achieving climate stability will also require a significant scaling back of the production of goods that are consumed in the Global North and especially among the wealthiest of the population.

expansion. In a famous passage from the Preface to the *Critique of Political Economy* (a preparatory work for *Capital*) he wrote:

> At a certain stage of development, the material productive forces of society come into conflict with the existing relations of production or – this merely expresses the same thing in legal terms – with the property relations within the framework of which they have operated hitherto. From forms of development of the productive forces these relations turn into their fetters.
>
> 1976a, p. 21

Adapting this argument in present circumstances and through a reconstructed concept of forces of production, I argue that today green productive forces are fettered by capitalist relations of production.[2] This reinterpretation builds on contemporary eco-Marxist scholarship. Several works and bodies of literature are central.

2   Marx's Ecology: John Bellamy Foster and Paul Burkett

First are John Bellamy Foster and Paul Burkett's kindred reconstructions and "rediscoveries" of Marx's ecology (Burkett, 1996, 2005, 2014; Burkett and Foster, 2006; Foster, 2002, 2013; Foster and Burkett, 2016). Foster has done the most to demonstrate the ecological foundations of Marx's thought by developing and extending his concepts of the universal metabolism of nature, social metabolism and metabolic rift. Together these intertwined concepts are seen to provide a broad basis for a materialist and dialectical understanding of the human productive relation to nature. They are also shown to undergird Marx's definition of socialism as entailing the rational regulation of the metabolism by the associated producers (Marx, 1993a, pp. 958–959).

As Foster suggests, the social or socio ecological metabolism – a complex, dynamic interchange between human beings and nature, resulting from human labour – can be ecologically sound and sustainable, but it can also be

---

2 Relations of production can be defined as "relations of ownership by persons of productive forces or persons *or* relations presupposing such relations of ownership" (Cohen, 2000, pp. 34–35). They include the distribution of the means of production and subsistence, along with the relations between the immediate producers and those who appropriate their surplus product. They also include, as a specific aspect, the *objective of production* – i.e., production for the accumulation of surplus value. Therborn (1980, pp. 375–386) succinctly demonstrates the interconnection between these dimensions or aspects of Marx's concept.

disrupted and generate distinct "metabolic rifts" or ruptures in natural cycles and processes. Marx developed this approach most fully in regard to how industrial capitalism created an ecological rift in the soil nutrient cycle, while Foster and others have drawn upon this work to examine a broad array of ecological contradictions, including the carbon cycle and climate change (Clark and York, 2005; Foster et al., 2011a). Drawing from this work, I position productive forces as the (largely alienated) "mediations" – or capacities and powers – through which that socio-ecological metabolism takes place. I then highlight how capital's appropriation of productive forces and their development in pursuit of maximum exchange-value and surplus value generates and sustains metabolic rifts, most pressingly the carbon rift.

The latter argument is informed by Paul Burkett's (2014, 2005, 1996) reconstructions of the ecological basis of Marx's value analysis. With Marx, Burkett locates capitalism's tendency to degrade the biosphere in its basic relations of production and corresponding "law of value". As he suggests, extra-human natures, in their diversity, comprise a key part of society's endowment of wealth in quantitative and qualitative terms. Yet he argues that within capitalism nature is valued only in quantitative exchange-value terms, particularly in terms of labour productivity in commodity production (the average labour-time objectified in the average commodity). There is an ecological contradiction built into the value form, as capital is unable to recognize the wealth and use-value of ecological systems (their contribution to need satisfaction, or their intrinsic value). Capital abstracts from the natural processes that sustain life and values nature only according to the socially necessary labour-time for its appropriation and utilization in production.

Furthermore, Burkett points to how the "productive powers of socialized labour and nature" (1996, p. 354) are broadly organized for this valorization – for objectifying labour into commodities in the shortest period of time possible. His work thereby provides a broad foundation for analyzing how both individual corporations and capital as a whole, value and develop quantitative dimensions of the forces of production (those aimed at improving productivity and shortening necessary labour-time for the appropriation and development of objects of nature) and conversely underutilize and undervalue aspects of productive forces that are oriented to social and ecological needs (those that appropriate aspects of non-human nature in ways that sustain and enhance rather than degrade eco-systemic health).

Burkett's reconstruction challenges Promethean interpretations of Marx, pointing towards his awareness of the wastefulness and destructiveness inherent in capitalism's development of the productive forces, rooted in his theory of value. At the same time, he offers an alternative view of Marx's belief in the progressive potentiality of capitalism, from the perspective of human development. I draw extensively from Burkett, and revisit and extend his insights regarding knowledge and cooperation in particular, while developing the implications in regard to the current climate crisis.

3   Fossil Capitalism

Second is the lively fossil-capitalism literature, which analyzes the key role of fossil fuels in mediating capitalism's relation to nature and the necessary role of extractive industries to that relationship (Altvater, 2007, 2016; Angus, 2016; Huber, 2009, 2013; Malm, 2016). Historically, it argues that the consolidation and diffusion of capitalism is closely bound up with the shift from energy "flows" (energy from rivers, the sun or wind) to mineralised energy "stock" (condensed inanimate energy contained in the crust of the earth) (Malm, 2016, pp. 17–18). Indeed, the onset of fossil-fuel driven production and transportation, beginning in the late eighteenth and early nineteenth century, is bound up with the competitive struggle to increase labour productivity and reduce the worktime necessary to produce commodities. This development, which enables the acquisition of "relative surplus value", in turn produced a massive growth in forces of production, via large capital-intensive corporations.

The "making" of fossil capitalism of course did not end in the 19th century and the symbiosis between capital accumulation and fossil fuels has only deepened in the stages of the system's development. Following came the emergence of monopoly capitalism and its associated 'scientific-technical revolution' of late 19th century (Braverman, 1998; Mandel, 1999); in the period after the Second World War, we see the development of "organized capitalism", and its production of vast petrochemical and oil-auto complexes (Angus, 2016; Huber, 2013). This was rapidly followed by contemporary neoliberal globalization, which entailed the geographical relocation of industrial production and a massive expansion of fossil-powered transport and infrastructure networks (Altvater, 2007; Malm, 2012). In little more than two centuries the fossil fuel regime has become embedded in the entire economic structure, from industrial production to plastics and petrochemicals, to the agro-industry, to transportation, and all else. Furthermore, as this literature makes clear, the system of fossilized production and reproduction ensures a concentrated production of waste and pollution and the degradation of natural processes – soil fertility, hydrological cycles and especially the carbon cycle.

4   Green Productive Forces

Third is the recent work of Belgian eco-socialist, Daniel Tanuro. In a series of articles and books, Tanuro argues that Marx's view of rational regulation by the associated producers of the metabolic relation between society and nature would require a shift in the energetic basis of society, from fossil fuels to renewable energy (Tanuro, 2005, 2010, 2012, 2014). In the face of the deepening climate crisis, this is understood as an urgent priority, and one that can form the basis of a wider transformation to a sustainable economy. However, Tanuro argues that a rapid and comprehensive energy transition is impeded by corporate control over capital and technological change (and by corporate investment decisions driven by short-term profitability) and neoliberalism's adherence to market fundamentalism, rather than conscious planning. While these are common themes in recent eco-Marxist and green left theorizing, in *Green Capitalism: Why it Can't Work* (*2014*), Tanuro provokes a re-thinking of the concept of productive forces by arguing that renewable energy and energy efficiency represent "ecologically progressive" aspects of those forces.[3] While pointing to the need to re-think the concept today and offering helpful and suggestive formulations, Tanuro's perspective is underdeveloped. His analysis of the obsolescence of capitalist productive relations for renewable and green transition remains very general. Meanwhile, the notion of ecologically progressive productive forces is asserted without any close discussion of the concept and for him appears to have little basis in Marx's own thought.

In fact, according to Tanuro, there are two "blueprints" in *Capital,* which express contradictory logics (2014, p. 143). One is a cyclical, ecologically grounded vision, starting from issues of the soil and based on the idea of regulation of the exchange of matter, and the rational management of natural cycles modified by human impact. The second involves a "productivist ambiguity" – growth in productive forces, freed from shackles of capitalist development (2014, p. 144). For Tanuro, because the cyclical approach that is applied to the soil is never extended to the field of energy, there is a major blind spot or "shadow zone" in Marx's thinking (2014, p. 143). Failure to extend the ecological viewpoint to energy matters stems from a central failure: Marx and Engel's treatment of energy as "neutral", and their failure to distinguish between fossil fuels and renewables (Tanuro, 2010, 2014). For Tanuro, the treatment of both fossil

---

3   David Schwartzman (2012, 2016) has made similar arguments, suggesting that when we think of the development of the production forces we think of industrial energy systems based on cleaner and renewable fuels.

fuels and renewables as a single "amalgam", in addition to the fact that there could have been little knowledge of the atmospheric impact of carboniferous growth (since the conditions of the carbon cycle had not yet been adequately and broadly understood), created inconsistencies and flaws in Marx's thought. This confusion, or "major ecological flaw", left unattended in subsequent Marxist analyses, has had serious consequences; it has caused "linear", "utilitarian" and "productivist" notions to infect or contaminate historical materialism as a whole (2014, pp. 144–148).

By pointing to ecologically progressive productive forces, Tanuro invites us to "green Marx's conclusions", grafting green thought onto his thinking from the outside.[4] My reading of Marx in Chapter 4 challenges Tanuro's assertion that Marx saw fossil fuels as neutral, or treated all energy sources as an amalgam. More fundamentally, however, by rethinking the concept of forces of production with and through Marx, we reconstruct Marxism more internally and immanently, while showing the consistency of the "two logics": advancement of productive forces, restoration and rational regulation of natural cycles.

5   Fettering and Productive Forces

Finally, the analysis of the fettering of green productive forces is enhanced by the work of Johnathan Hughes (2000). While Marx himself never clearly defined the term, fettering entails restraint or shackling; it involves keeping something within limits and stopping it from progressing. It is taken here to be synonymous with barriers, blockages, obstacles and path dependency. In addition to basic definitions, Hughes (2000, pp. 243–246) provides a helpful and textured interpretation of types of fettering. In his typology, he differentiates *absolute* from *relative* fettering. "Absolute fettering" refers a situation of absolute stagnation, involving zero development (or even a regression) of productive capacities, potentials or powers. By contrast, "relative fettering" can involve a slower *rate of development* in productive forces, or it may be that a *smaller proportion* of existing capacity is *used*, relative to the rate and proportion to which they would develop or be used under alternative relations of production. Relative-proportional fettering then points to a situation of sub-optimal or ineffective *use* of productive forces, while relative-developmental fettering points to a slow rate in their *development*.

---

4   This point is also made by Foster and Burkett (2016, pp. 4–15). They label Tanuro's work as "first-stage" eco-Marxist scholarship, in that it attempts to create a hybrid theory in which Green theory is overlaid on certain Marxian conceptions.

Anticipating our findings, in the case of ecological knowledge, I argue that the fettering we observe largely consists in the "misuse" of an existing productive capacity. Therefore, while ecological knowledge continues to develop and deepen today (partially as an outgrowth of the ecological contradictions of capitalism), it is *underutilized,* languishing at the margins of an anti-ecological system. In so far as today we witness a thin greening of capitalism, whereby ecological knowledge is applied to production, yet within narrow confines and limits (for predominately strategic and commercial purposes), the fettering is relative-proportional. While this is observed at a broad level, the predominance of exchange over use-value also leads to the under prioritization of specific ecological insights needed for sustainable development, including at the level of basic research (see Adkin, 2020; Saed, 2011). Thus, there is an underdevelopment of research and knowledge vital for energy transition and sustainability more broadly and thereby a need for new knowledge.

On the other hand, I argue that the fettering observed in relation to renewable energy is relative-developmental. Despite technological advances that increase the potential and capacity of renewables and powerful movements for energy transition, its development has been slow.

6   The Structure of This Book

In making these arguments, the work develops in two parts. Part 1 is devoted to reinterpreting the concept of forces of production. In Chapter 1, I identify the need for such a reinterpretation, outlining the still-common reproach (outlined here via de-growth, materialist feminist, and Indigenous scholarship) that Marx harboured a Promethean view of extra-human nature, based on his faith in the growth of productive forces. I admit a certain "industrialist" position

TABLE 1   Types of fettering

Fettering (absolute)	Absolute stagnation, involving zero development (or even a regression) of productive capacities, potentials or powers
Fettering (relative-proportional)	A smaller proportion of existing capacity is used than under alternative relations of production
Fettering (relative-developmental)	Productive forces develop more slowly than under alternative relations of production

SOURCE: ADAPTED FROM HUGHES (2000, P. 244).

in Marx – his believe in the progressive potentiality of capital's advances in productive forces along the lines of large-scale industry – but point to the historical context of his writing and the human developmental nature of his arguments, challenging the assertion this commits him to a productivist or Promethean vision. At the same time, I identify ambiguities and difficulties in Marx's own conceptualization, pointing to the need to reconstruct the concept, and contextualizing it, given changed historical circumstances.

Chapter 2 begins this reconstruction. I first consider how the productivist interpretation has been bolstered from within the Marxist tradition, focusing particularly on Gerald Cohen's influential work. In contrast to Cohen, I point to the more qualitative side of Marx's concept and to the enthusiasm he shows for the growth of capacities and powers such as ecological knowledge. Next, I contrast the neutral view of forces of production implied by theorists like Cohen with more open, dialectical and political treatments of the concept, located especially in the work of Mao and in late 20th century labour process and autonomist-Marxist approaches. While the latter work understood the development of the forces of production as a social process largely independent of the "web of life", the environmental implications are brought to the fore in the 1960s and 1970s by left ecological thinkers, such as Rachel Carson, Barry Commoner and later, Ernest Mandel.

The longer Chapter 3 then demonstrates the basis for an expansive and ecologically grounded definition in Marx's own work, while drawing out and advancing its implications through recent scholarship. As we see, Marx analyzes how capital (via primitive accumulation) expropriates and then reshapes productive forces in a manner "adequate to its form". This occurs within a work process that is internally organized by capital and derives its character via commodity production, hence, from the dominance of the value form. The types of knowledge that are subsequently pursued, the networks of productive collaboration that are instantiated and the technologies and infrastructural networks that are developed, increasingly revolve around the quest for exchange-value. Under the "whip of competition", firms (increasingly large monopolistic corporations) are compelled to increase the productivity of production processes, which entails and presupposes rising matter and (at a system level) energy throughput. Such an account, I argue, provides us with an indispensable foundation for understanding the deep structural relations and processes driving contemporary ecological crises, including the climate crisis. While Marx analyses the destructiveness of capital's development of productive forces, he does not foreclose other positive potentials bound up with their advancement. The latter include qualitative capacities, such as ecological knowledge and cooperation, which today are vital to sustaining ecosystem health.

Chapter 4 puts the renewed conceptualization in dialogue with prominent contemporary eco-Marxist approaches, namely Serge Latouche's variant of the "de-growth" perspective, James O'Connor's notion of a "second contradiction" and Jason Moore's "world ecology". I consider the explicit and implicit conceptualization of productive forces at work in them, clarifying and distinguishing the approach taken here. While the latter offer numerous insights into the ecological costs and consequences of capitalist development, I suggest that the green-dialectical understanding of productive forces developed here offers some advantages, particularly in understanding and coming to terms with the contemporary climate crisis.

Part 2 moves from an "abstract-simple" analysis based on reconceptualising the forces of production, to a "concrete-complex" examination of the development and especially fettering of forces of production within contemporary fossil capitalism.[5] Focusing on the Canadian context, I analyze the growth of fossilized and fossil-fuelled productive forces and the simultaneous obstruction of green alternative forces by relations of production. The latter includes the power of corporations and especially of carbon capital.[6]

This investigation of fossil capitalism in action advances and applies the granular view of fettering offered by Hughes, while pointing to social and political transformations necessary to "unshackle" green productive forces. As we move to a concrete-complex analysis, a greater number of agencies and actors, both economic (fractions of capital, corporations and their networked relations), and "extra-economic" (state bodies, as well as civil society organizations) are introduced, producing a more complex picture. For while the "law of value" is understood to shape broad and durable patters of our relation to the rest of nature, acting as a kind of "gravitational field" (see Moore, 2014, pp. 248–249), the concrete dimensions of that relation involve considerable contingency

---

5   The movement from abstract to concrete involves the increased concretization of a given phenomenon (i.e., fettering of green productive forces by capital as a mode of production in general to fettering within contemporary fossil capitalism), while the movement from simple to complex introduces further dimensions of a given phenomena (i.e., features and aspects of relative-developmental and use fettering within the current period of fossil capital development). The spiral movement is not purely theoretical; it involves empirical studies into actual tendencies. For a further discussion of methodological principles informing the movement from abstract-simple to concrete-complex accounts, see Jessop (2002a).

6   Carbon capital is a "fraction" of capital embedded within wider structures of corporate power. It is linked to other fractions (including financial capital) via commodity chains and financial flows.

and are the result of many determinations. Three distinct but overlapping case studies make up this component of the work.

Building from Marx and recent literature on the "industrial metabolism", Chapter 5 examines the path dependency and carbon footprint of large-scale fixed capital, focusing on energy production networks and energy intensive infrastructure, such as transportation and buildings. Focusing on Canada, it analyzes fossil fuel infrastructure networks, including key pipelines that are currently contemplated to facilitate the expansion of the fossil fuel regime. Employing a "networked" lens, it provides insights on the deep path dependencies of sunk fossil capital infrastructure, while also identifying fractions of capital (not only carbon capital, but also financial firms) whose interests and modalities of power are expressed and embedded in them. Both the lock-in of physical infrastructures and the constellation of interests and forms of power that underscore them, reinforce a carboniferous social metabolism, while obstructing the growth of renewable energy and low-carbon infrastructures.

In Chapter 6, I examine the prospects of a green or "climate capitalist" energy transition, focusing on Canada. Climate capitalism points to a capital-driven process of renewable energy development (leading to industrial-scale renewable energy installations under the control of big energy companies, especially fossil fuel corporations), that is in some tension with the notion of fettering of green productive forces. While carbon capital continues to expand its carbon networks, here I examine the strategies employed by fossil fuel firms in relation to alternative energy, considering whether we are simultaneously witnessing signs of "transition capture" as some oil, gas and coal corporations invest in a gradual shift towards climate capitalism. While I find little evidence of a such a transition in the Canadian context, the study deepens our analysis of the fettering of these productive forces. It makes the case that accomplishing a transition within the current "carbon budget" will *require* incursions into capitalist property, shifting us away from the logic of private capitalist accumulation.

Chapter 7 examines the way in which science and ecological knowledge are integrated into contemporary fossil capitalism. I mark the importance of this knowledge as a force in carbon-extractive processes through its incorporation into the production of "unconventional" oil and gas (tar sands, fracked oil and gas) in Canada and more recently as a means of greening that process via the production of "clean technologies". This research provides a focused case of the underutilization or relative-proportional fettering of ecological knowledge, elucidating how its colonization and co-optation supports a thin greening of fossil capitalism, but which is of marginal ecological benefit. By showing how such knowledge is appropriated in service to the ongoing accumulation of fossil capital, the research simultaneously points to how a system of production organized to directly produce use-value would further support and prioritize the growth and development of knowledge critical to ecological sustainability, including energy transition.

The final chapter brings out the implications for transformative practice of a more dialectical, green-Marxist take on forces of production. It brings together the empirical findings from case studies with the theoretical issues raised in earlier chapters, considering how these point toward effective strategies for a just transition to an ecologically sustainable future.

PART 1

Forces of Production and Ecology

∵

CHAPTER 1

Development of the Productive Forces and Critiques of Marx

Despite longstanding efforts to undo such an interpretation, Marx continues to be dismissed as an archaic 19th century European steeped in the ideology of "progress", achieved through the ever-advancing domination of the rest of nature. This understanding often stems from his optimism in the emancipatory potential of developing productive forces. This chapter outlines this interpretation of Marx, engaging recent environmental, materialist feminist and Indigenous perspectives. I dispute the reading of Marx as having endorsed an energy- and resource-intensive future "automated paradise", as critics aver, while pointing to enduring tensions surrounding his argument that through its increases in productive output and the productivity of labour, capitalism creates material conditions for future flourishing. I defend a weak version of this argument, while placing it in historical context and alongside his prescient ecological critiques of capitalism, which have been illuminated by recent eco-Marxists (e.g., John Bellamy Foster and Paul Burkett). This establishes the need to rethink the concept of productive forces in contemporary circumstances. While my focus is on ecological questions, the reading also points to the compatibility of the concept with feminist and de-colonial politics.

1 De-growth and the Green Critique of Marx

Hans Jonas' *The Imperative of Responsibility* (1984) is an influential text in green thought and a key early work informing contemporary "de-growth" politics. In the *Imperative,* Jonas argues that in an approaching era of nuclear disaster and ecological catastrophe, we need to break with "present-oriented ethics" and advance an ethic of responsibility geared to the survival of future generations. On this basis, much of Jonas's text is devoted to weighing the pros and cons of "capitalism versus Marxist socialism" with respect to their ability to provide a future oriented ethic and practice based on salvation from disaster, rather than "fulfilment of mankind's dreams" (Jonas, 1984, p. 144). The treatment is aimed at popular rather than academic audiences; nevertheless, it captures in broad outline the green critique of Marx based on the notion of the development of forces of production.

Jonas begins his assessment by working to establish that Marx and Marxism have been "progressivist" from the beginning and like capitalism, thoroughly participate in the "cult of technology". In fact, according to Jonas, Marx and Marxists see capitalism as the crowning achievement of history to the present day, and conceive of revolution as a breaking of the fetters that hinder the development of forces of production, or technology. The fetters inhibiting the forces of production amount mainly to one fetter: capitalist ownership of the means of production, which is the cause of anarchy and fragmentation in overall production and the unequal distribution of social surpluses.

This reading is confirmed mostly by appeals to the experience of 20th century Soviet socialism, which sought to establish a framework for "catch-up" industrialization and produced models of development that largely mimicked capitalism in terms of its productivism. For Jonas, as witnessed in the Soviet Union, the goal of socialism is not only to deliver the fruits of capitalist industrialization (hitherto reserved for a minority in class society), but to be yet more productive than capitalism. This is to be achieved by unleashing the productive forces, through planning not only at the level of the factory but also the social level. Jonas provides little discussion of the historical circumstances surrounding the Soviet experience, raising it only to argue that a productivist impulse, which has been ruinous for the environment, is built deeply into Marxism.

The position appears to accord closely with Marx and Engels in *The Communist Manifesto*. As they wrote: "The proletariat will use its political supremacy to wrest, by degree, all capital from the bourgeoisie, to centralize all instruments of production in the hands of the State, i.e., of the proletariat organized as the ruling class; and to increase the total productive forces as rapidly as possible"(Marx and Engels, 2004, p.81). The productivism underscoring socialism appears to be put in even sharper terms by Engels in a chapter in the *Manifesto* on "the Principles of Communism":

> Once liberated from the pressure of private ownership, large-scale industry will develop on a scale that will make its present level of development seem as paltry as seems the manufacturing system compared with the large-scale industry of our time. The development of industry will provide society with a sufficient quantity of products to satisfy the needs of all.
>
> MARX and ENGELS, 2004, p. 151

Despite its deep productivist impulse, Jonas considers whether Marxism can renounce this vision and form the "condition of humankind's survival". He begins by gesturing to the affirmative, registering certain positives to Marxist socialism. Chief among them are first, the development of an economy governed by real needs and the removal of the profit motive, which he notes could remove one compulsion to extravagance – the (artificial and unending) market creation of needs and the goods and means to satisfy them. Second, socialism's apparently authoritarian character – its "vanguardist authoritarianism" and "centralized power and command structure" – would allow it to impose unpopular decisions, which Jonas believes the threats of the future require (Jonas, 1984, p. 146). Relatedly, he suggests that socialist societies are better able to stimulate devotion to a cause and a spirit of sacrifice as a life-style.

Yet these potential advantages are ultimately outweighed by the negatives; hence Jonas concludes that socialism would ultimately be worse. The reason is that the formal essence of the Marxist utopia lies in leisure and leisure can only exist in comfort, with an assured supply of material goods and a minimum of toil in achieving them. Jonas again mostly reads the Soviet record onto Marx and Marxism, but he does (partially) quote one passage from *Capital Volume III* on the "realm of freedom" in support of this conclusion. In the full passage, where we find one of Marx's few overt discussions of an alternative future, he wrote:

> The realm of freedom really begins only where labour determined by necessity and external expediency ends; it lies by its very nature beyond the sphere of material production proper. Just as the savage must wrestle with nature to satisfy his needs, to maintain and reproduce life, so must civilised man, and he must do so in all forms of society and under all possible modes of production. This realm of natural necessity expands with his development because his needs do too; but the productive forces to satisfy these expand at the same time. Freedom, in this sphere, can only consist in this, that socialised man, the associated producers, govern the human metabolism with nature in a rational way, bringing it under their collective control, instead of being dominated by it as a blind power; accomplishing it with the least expenditure of energy and in conditions most worthy and appropriate for their human nature. But this always remains a realm of necessity. The true realm of freedom, the development of human powers as an end in itself, begins beyond it, though it can flourish with this realm of necessity as its basis. The shortening of the working-day is the basic prerequisite.
>
> MARX, 1993a, pp. 958–959

For Jonas, the vision presented by Marx in this statement is clearly one of super abundance and its toil free command, which could only be achieved through a "perfected technology". The vision would require in his view the magnification of industrialization first, through the reconstruction or production of the earth itself – the raising of nature to a "higher state" via fertilizers, agrarian maximization strategies and so on – and second, through the mechanization and automation of the labour process, which had in the past been consumed by human strength and time. To come anywhere near this utopia an "increased global production and heightened, more aggressive technology must be the order of the day – and *a fortiori* for the universal "leisure-cum-plenty" economy envisioned by [this] utopia: an altogether enormous enhancement by several orders of magnitude of both technology and its onslaught on resources" (Jonas, 1984, p. 187).

Jonas' treatment both reflected and helped further entrench a productivist interpretation of Marx in contemporary green thought. In *Farewell to Growth*, Serge Latouche (2010), one of the leading proponents of today's de-growth movement, approvingly sites Jonas and finds that Marx's own and subsequent Marxian critiques of capitalist modernity remain "terribly ambiguous" (p. 90). He finds that with the Marxist critique, the capitalist economy is criticized and denounced for every scourge (from the proletarianization of workers, to their exploitation and impoverishment, to imperialism, wars and so on), while at the same time the growth of the forces it unleashes (seen in terms of the production/jobs/consumption trio) are seen as a great virtue and described as "productive", even though they are as destructive as they are productive. Echoing Jonas, Latouche finds that capitalism and productivist socialism are therefore, "both variants on the same project for a growth society based upon the development of the productive forces, which will supposedly facilitate humanity's march in the direction of progress" (2010, p. 89).

Reproductive and eco-feminist work, while dealing much more carefully and dialectically with Marxian categories and concepts, has often advanced a similar reading of Marx connected to the concept of productive forces. I turn to this in the following section.

2   Materialist Feminisms and Marx

At the centre of reproductive feminist critiques of Marx is the argument that he advanced a gendered theory of value and work (Arruza, 2014; Federici, 2012; Fraser, 2013, 2014; Mies, 1986). Critically, Marx's analysis of capitalism is hobbled by its blindness to the crucial nature of social *re*productive labour to the process of capital accumulation. To understand the accumulation process or the extended reproduction of capital, these theorists make clear that it is necessary to go "behind the "hidden abode"" of production (Fraser 2014, p. 61) and to bring into view the largely untheorized practices of reproduction, which are essential to the existence of wage labour and surplus productive activity.

In a classic essay, "The Power of Women and the Subversion of the Community" (1975), autonomous feminists Mariarosa Dalla Costa and Selma James, were among the first to analyze how unpaid domestic work (largely performed by women) underpinned paid (largely male) wage work. As they argued, talk about work as factory production tells only part of the story of working life under capitalism. The other part consists of unpaid labour-intensive domestic activity: cooking, cleaning, caring for one's family and one's self. Dalla Costa and James argued that this activity, which can operate much like work in the factory, is not ultimately outside of surplus value production, but the very foundation of its eventual realization.

Contemporary reproductive feminist work draws on these rich insights, while seeking to also analyze individuals and institutions that perform paid caring labour (e.g., paid domestic workers, maids, personal home care assistants), and more fully theorize care work. This work, which continues to be overwhelmingly performed by women and especially immigrant women and women of colour (Federici, 2012; Teeple Hopkins, 2017) is understood as an essential condition of labour power (and immediate life) and a critical component of capital accumulation (Mies, 1998; Arruza, 2014). Care work, affective activity, and provisioning form capitalism's human subjects, sustaining them as natural beings, while also constituting them socially. Wage labour could not exist in the absence of child raising, housework, affective care, and a host of other activities pertaining to societal reproduction more broadly (those such as public education, health care systems, leisure facilities in the community), which help to produce new generations of workers, as well as replenish existing ones (Arruza, 2014).

Yet, as these theorists argue, in capitalist societies, the pivotal role of social reproduction is *disguised* and *disavowed*. Far from being valued in its own right, "people making" within capitalism is largely treated as a mere means of making profit and this relegates those who perform social-reproductive labour to a position of subordination. As Arruzza, Bhattacharya and Fraser write in regards to the deep connection between gender oppression and capitalism: "the key move was to separate the making of people from the making of profit, to assign the first job to women, and to subordinate it to the second" (2019, p. 21). Through an analysis of the subordination of social reproduction to production for profit, this literature produces a simultaneous political-economic and *ethico-political* critique of the things and relations that capitalism does and does not value.

Most Marxists recognize that Marx had an insufficient analysis of reproductive labour. The direction of much work in this area has therefore been to revise and update Marx through a rethinking or immanent critique of the category of labour power (see Lebowitz, 2003). However, for autonomous and ecofeminists such as Federci, Mies, Salleh and Odih, Marx's blindness to reproductive labour speaks to a larger issue with his political and social theory. According to these authors, reproductive work fell below Marx's theoretical horizon largely or partly *because* of his underlying techno-Prometheanism.

Scarcity, as Silvia Federici notes (2012), was for Marx a major obstacle to human liberation and thus he anticipated that the expansion of the forces of production in the form of large-scale industrialization and its increases in the productivity of labour would create the material conditions for the transition to socialism. Subsequent to this understanding, Marx apparently viewed "the capitalist organization of work as the highest model of historical rationality, ... [he] accepted the capitalist criteria for what constitutes work, and believed that waged industrial work was the stage on which the battle for humanity's emancipation would be played" (2012, p. 95). The privileging of the waged industrial proletariat as the main contributor to capital accumulation and as the key revolutionary subject, and the associated tendency to ignore reproductive work, originate largely from his "technologistic conception of revolution", whereby freedom comes through the machine and its increases in labour productivity (2012, p. 95).

The early Ariel Salleh concurs. Marx, she writes, was "entranced by the qualitative shift from tools to production by machine technology, and he impatiently waited on the large-scale industrialisation of agriculture" (1997, p. 77). Salleh, more than many readers of Marx, historicizes his views to some degree, arguing that his belief in the liberatory potential of capitalist technology emerged from his desire to transcend the immense suffering that he witnessed in the nineteenth-century factory system. His was therefore "wishful thinking, in the very best sense" (1997, p. 79). Had Marx been writing in another era, Salleh suggests he might have developed different vantage points, and that a critical view of technology is implied by his dialectic of internal relations.[1] Nevertheless, she argues that his "case for technology" remained largely argued

---

1   A dialectic of internal relations suggests that the only way we can understand the qualitative and quantitative attributes of "things", including physical objects such as machines, or the physical articles produced through them, is by understanding the practices and relationships which constitute them and which they internalize (see Ollman, 1976, pp. 26–40). The implication is that instruments of production internalize dominant social relationships and a bundle of associated contradictions.

outside of any ecological (or gendered) context and was not sufficiently conscious of its implications on these fronts.

In her *Patriarchy and Accumulation on a World Scale* (1986), Maria Mies extends the critique of Marx's blindness in regard to women's work to his perceived blindness of other types of human and non-human production that continue to form the foundation for the accumulation process. In making this argument, she draws on Rosa Luxemburg's *The Accumulation of Capital* (2015), which argued that "primitive accumulation" is co-existent with capitalist accumulation, rather than, as Marx intimates, a period prior to industrial capitalism. While Marx's model of accumulation appears to be based on an assumption of a closed system involving only wage labourers and capitalists, Luxemburg argued that capitalism always depends on an "outside", or non-capitalist "milieu and strata", for the extension of the labour force, resources and the expansion of markets. These non-capitalist milieu and strata were initially peasants and artisans and later colonies.

Mies connects this insight to the materialist feminist analysis of women's labour (and simultaneously moves beyond the focus on industrialized societies and domestic labour in those countries) by arguing that the appropriation of nature and subsistence production (mainly performed by women, contract workers and people in the Global South) constitutes the perennial basis and precondition for capitalist wage labour and surplus value extraction. Capital accumulation, she asserts, is based on and requires the subordination, exploitation and appropriation of "women, nature, colonies" (1986, p. 48).

For Mies, the apparent invisibility of these foundations in Marx are again related to a productivist view of emancipation. Citing the same above passage in *Capital Volume III* on the realm of freedom, Mies argues that for Marx "labour is considered as a *necessary burden,* which has to be reduced, as far as possible, by the development of productive forces, or technology" (1986, p. 212). The reclaimed free time enabled by shortening necessary labour-time (defined as that aimed at satisfying basic human needs of clothing, food, shelter) forms the material basis for freedom, which is categorically excluded from the realm of work and possible only in the realm of "leisure". Subsequently, under socialism the replacement of human labour by machines and automats remains the main social goal and will be accelerated rather than slowed down. However, this paradise for some is hell for others: the bondage of nature, women, colonies is the base for his (the White Man's) "unlimited development of forces of production, for the unlimited satisfaction of his unlimited wants (or rather addictions)" (1986, p. 216).

As suggested in the above accounts, Marx argued that the development of forces of production along the lines of large-scale industry created conditions of possibility for future flourishing. This is seen in statements from earlier works, along with passages in *Capital*. In the next section I examine Marx's arguments surrounding the "quantitative" aspects of the development of forces of production under capitalism, seeking to place them in historical context, while asking if this commits him to the Promethean vision suggested by his critics (albeit one that is in clear tension with his ecological views, which are increasingly well established). If the critiques above are correct, there would be little grounds for an ecological reconstruction of the concept of forces of production.

3   The Development of Forces of Production: A More Historical and
         Human Developmental View

Along the lines suggested by Salleh, it is critical to provide a more historically grounded view of Marx's arguments concerning the emancipatory potentiality he ascribes to the quantitative development of forces of production under capitalism (i.e., increasing productivity and material output enabled by fossil powered technological development). The priority that Marx placed on both the shortening of the working day and the satisfaction of material needs in *Capital* reflected the conditions of the working class in England in the mid-19th century and the political struggles he was involved in. His arguments were made in a context of scarcity (i.e., where working classes lacked access to basic material goods) and where the capitalist appetite for surplus value appeared as the drive towards the "unlimited extension of the working day" (Marx, 1976b, p. 346). This extension, combined with the low level of consumption among the workers in his time, was to render the working class virtually unable to reproduce itself, averaging a life expectancy as low as 25 and dying in its youth from overwork.[2] Given the condition of the working class in England at this time (and the majority of the earth's workers today), it seems hard to fault Marx for this argument.

---

2   As Federici also notes (2012, pp. 94–95) the fact workers in England in the early 19th century were barely being reproduced and that capital's pursuit of absolute surplus value required little investment in the conditions of (re)production, helps explain the absence of an analysis of reproductive labour in Marx. Therefore, as she suggests, paralleling the transition from formal to real subsumption of labour is the formal subsumption of reproductive labour to capital, which Marx had only begun to witness. The point does not excuse Marx for an insufficient analysis of gender.

While Marx's arguments necessarily reflect the political circumstances that he was embroiled in, as suggested by Federici, he made a wider argument in *Capital* and elsewhere that socialism is made more feasible by a certain material foundation or "base" in productive forces. The capitalist development of the productive forces along the line of large-scale industry lays the "material conditions" for a society beyond capital:

> But in so far as he is capital personified, his motivating force is not the acquisition and enjoyment of use-values, but the acquisition and augmentation of exchange-values. He is fanatically intent on the valorization of value; consequently he ruthlessly forces the human race to produce for production's sake. In this way he spurs on the development of society's productive forces, and the creation of those material conditions of production which can alone form the real basis of a higher form of society, a society in which the full and free development of every individual form the ruling principle.
>
> MARX, 1976b, p. 739

The expanded productivity and diminished absolute scarcity resulting from capital's constant revolutionizing of means of production (under heavy competitive pressures) helps make socialism more feasible, based on social control over the material conditions of life (and the radical egalitarian distribution of those conditions, including the social surplus and access to free time).

In a section from *Capital Volume III* preceding his discussion on the realm of freedom Marx argued more sharply that by developing productive forces, capital negates any material-scarcity rationale or justification for class monopolies over the disposition of society's surplus and labour time:

> It is one of the civilising aspects of capital that it enforces this surplus-labour in a manner and under conditions which are more advantageous to the development of the productive forces, social relations, and the creation of the elements for a new and higher form than under the preceding forms of slavery, serfdom, etc. Thus it gives rise to a stage, on the one hand, in which coercion and monopolisation of social development (including its material and intellectual advantages) by one portion of society at the expense of the other are eliminated; on the other hand, it creates the material means and embryonic conditions, making it possible in a higher form of society to combine this surplus-labour with a greater reduction of time devoted to material labour in general.
>
> 1993a, p. 958

It is worth noting that in this passage Marx highlighted the bourgeoisie's monopolisation of "intellectual advantages" alongside more strictly "material" ones. Nevertheless, capitalism's monopolization of social development and subsequent development of large-scale industry provides the potential for the elimination of much arduous human labour and the possibility for everyone, rather than just a ruling class minority, to live comfortably off the social surplus. Socialism, Marx intimated, may entail more development of industry and be more productive that capitalism, in terms of both the productivity of labour and the growth of material surpluses.

Such arguments also need to be approached in light of the broad historical context of his writings. Marx, like Engels, considered industrialization necessary to the point at which it would be possible to "satisfy the material needs of all". However, in the context of mid-nineteenth-century industrial capitalism, Marx stood with most observers in assuming that use-values were produced to conform to genuine human needs. As Foster suggests (2013), it is only under monopoly capitalism, beginning in the last quarter of the nineteenth century, and more sharply with the emergence of the post-war "organized" monopoly capital, that we began to see the production of "negative use-values" in the form of the growing output of useless and wasteful commodities and the non-fulfillment of human need.

Mies (1986) is right to point to the limitations of Marx's perspective that "true freedom" exists outside of the sphere of activity "determined by necessity and mundane considerations". In adopting this perspective, Marx assumed that such activity is inherently unwanted, un-creative and not enjoyable and should therefore be reduced as far as possible. Such activity, in a society not governed by the capital and value, could be pursued as an "end in itself" (creatively and enjoyably), while also being necessary. The promise of increased leisure time also sits in some tension with arguments that increased human labour power in some fields or sectors, such as in agriculture, are likely needed to support ecological sustainability (Garibaldi et al., 2017; Reganold and Wachter, 2016).

These are important considerations, pointing to shortcomings in Marx's perspective. Yet in addition, several of the above critics project onto Marx the view that the reduction of working time would entail a broadening of anti-ecological mass consumption, creating a world of super abundance and previously unknown plenty. This argument is a-historical, in that the forms of anti-ecological mass consumption they envision exist *only in contemporary capitalism*. The suggestion that expanded free time enabled by reductions in work time would be filled with mass hedonistic consumption is not only a-historical, it also glosses over what Burkett (2014) calls the "human developmental" content of Marx's arguments.

As Burkett argues (2014, pp. 163–173), when Marx speaks to the expansion of *new* needs made possible by the development of productive forces, this includes broader access to use-values denied to large sections of the working class and the enrichment of the *composition* of use-values, rather than simply increases in general levels of material consumption. Marx, as he explains, views free time as a condition for the aesthetic, cultural, political and intellectual development of individuals, quite separate from expanding physical needs. In the context of a discussion of the struggles to reduce the length of the working day, he refers to "time for education, for intellectual development, for the fulfilment of social functions, for social intercourse, for the free play of the vital forces of the body and the mind..." (Marx, 1976b, p. 375). Physical requirements must be met, but needs are social and include further, "the worker's participation in cultural satisfactions, the agitation for his own interests, newspaper subscriptions, attending lectures, educating his children, developing his taste, etc". (Marx, 1993b, p. 287). As Marx suggests, reduction of work time not only enable the further development of political consciousness, but also provides material possibilities for increased worker and popular participation in democratic discussion and management of the economy and society (LÖWY, 2020).

While Marx rarely specifies the content of future alternatives, when he does so, he emphasizes what he referred to as "real wealth" – things that truly contribute to human physical and social well being, rather than unlimited and ever-expanding material abundance (see Mann, 2013, pp. 30–33). Here he emphasizes how real wealth in form of the development of artistic, social, political and scientific capacities would be free to develop, as an extension of needs other than strictly material ones, and that this form of development could be extended *to all of society*. He points therefore to the possibility of the production of material wealth that does not have the production of exchange-value as its ultimate aim. Yet he argues that capitalist production contains no category for understanding wealth beyond its single measure for calculating value – maximum production of surplus value – and capitalist society places no intrinsic value on activities, capacities and forms of wealth outside of this foreclosure. Ascribing to Marx the notion of constantly increasing technological advancements and an unlimited access to a boundless supply of all material goods that exist in contemporary capitalism is therefore unsubstantiated and rooted in a misinterpretation.

Furthermore, while both Jonas and Mies employ the passage on the "realm of freedom" from *Capital Volume III,* as proof of Marx's productivism, neither reflects on his assertion there that freedom "in this sphere, can only consist in this, that socialised man, the associated producers, govern the human metabolism with nature in a rational way, bringing it under their collective control, instead of being dominated by it as a blind power; accomplishing it with the least expenditure of energy and in conditions most worthy and appropriate for their human nature" (Marx, 1993a, p. 958). The conclusion of the need for achieving a rational regulation of that metabolism was rooted in his analysis (based on 19th century natural science) of how industrialized capitalist agriculture and long-distance trade created a rupture in the soil nutrient cycle. Marx generalizes this rupture in developing a theory of a rift in the metabolic interchange with nature – a notion that Bellamy Foster, Burkett, and others believe to be tailor-made to analyze the present climate crisis.[3]

Moreover, by reading Marx's arguments around free time through a productivist lens, critics here miss an opportunity to think of increased free time as a possible means of *reducing* the pressure of production on the environment (see Rosnick, 2013). Indeed, reducing work time is an important means of reducing energy and matter throughput and emissions. Under conditions of present ecological overshoot, Marx's call for a rational regulation of the exchange with the rest of nature would also mean shifting human labour from the production of "things" to needs-oriented social services such as health care, childcare, education, research, nutrition, services which also entail less ecological impact. This refocusing of economies around reproductive needs could contribute to shaping gender relations in an emancipatory fashion, redefining and redistributing what we consider as "socially necessary labour".

4   Normative Developmentalism and Capitalism's "Civilizing" Mission

Along with the charge of a Promethean or productivist relation to the environment, Marx's work is sometimes characterized as advancing a crude

---

3 Most of the work we have reviewed so far occurred before so-called "second wave" eco-Marxist scholarship, especially the work of Foster (2000) and Burkett (1999/2014). First-stage ecosocialism, as Foster and Burkett (2016) have referred to it, involved various attempts to create a hybrid theory in which Green theory was overlaid on certain Marxian conceptions. Second-stage ecosocialism, in contrast, went back to the foundations of classical Marxism, attempting a major reconstruction and also rediscovery of historical materialism as a unique method of understanding the complex relationships between humanity, society, and nature. While simplistic productivist interpretations of Marx continue to be advanced in the literature, in part as a result of this work, critiques have become more nuanced. The later Salleh (2010) and Odih (2014), for example, show a deep appreciation for ecological insights in Marx (particularly the importance of his concept of social metabolism and the theory of metabolic rift), while pointing to "oscillations", "tensions" and "unresolved issues" in Marx between a more ecological position, which they suggest exists in tension with a more techno-Promethean one.

developmentalism and pro-colonial stance. Glen Coulthard's *Red Skin, White Masks* (2014) offers a nuanced view on this matter. He insists that Marx's work contains a wealth of resources and insights for analyzing the entangled relationship between colonialism and capital accumulation. Yet Marx's theoretical framework displays problematic features that hobble the development of a "more ecologically attentive critique of colonial-capital accumulation" (2014, p. 14). Key problematic features of Marx's account that are identified by Coulthard and which must be transcended are: 1) the temporal framing of primitive accumulation (its confinement to the formative stages of capitalism, as opposed to understanding it as an ongoing process); 2) the "normative developmentalism" that sometimes underscored his formulation of primitive accumulation (the portrayal of primitive accumulation as a historically inevitable process that would ultimately have a beneficial effect on those drawn into the circuit of capital); and 3) anti-ecological tendencies in Marx's thought, rooted in an ideology of productivism in relation to the environment.

These are vital criticisms that must be taken on as part of the reconstruction of Marxian theory. This study is primarily dedicated to the third feature. However, in the following section I seek to partially address the second aspect, in so far as the developmental mission that Marx ascribes to capitalism appears connected to the "historical possibility thesis" – the notion that capitalism creates conditions of possibility for future flourishing. I defend a weak version of this thesis, while countering any sense that it and the concept of forces of production is Eurocentric and hostile toward Indigenous and other ways of life.

In the *Communist Manifesto* and elsewhere, Marx and Engels recognized that the destruction of pre-capitalist social formations could imply more miserable living conditions for populations subject to colonial domination. More traditional forms of exploitation and domination[4] "veiled by religious and political illusions" are replaced with "naked, shameless, direct, brutal exploitation" (Marx and Engels, 2004, p. 64). However, the bourgeoisie was seen to have

---

4   Marx and Engels, especially in early works, suggested that pre-capitalist and "traditional" societies were often not idyllic, but rather built upon pervasive forms of social domination. The creative-destructive logic of capitalism, in particular the objective development of productive forces, would help make socialism an "objective possibility" while undermining the institutional bastions of the old order, including forms of custom, tradition, superstition and above all religion that so often served to legitimize oppressive social and political relations. While we would be remiss to deny that many pre-capitalist societies were characterized by traditional authority, as suggested below, Marx developed a more nuanced and informed approach to non-capitalist and Indigenous communities in his later works, recognizing both the tremendous diversity of forms of life and their often collective and egalitarian character (see Anderson, 2010).

a progressive historical mission to play (however unconscious it was); through its drive to revolutionize the means of production, that class would bring "barbarian nations" on the plane of world historical development and plant in them the seeds of development and change. The *Communist Manifesto* advanced this view, asserting the following:

> The bourgeoisie, by the rapid improvement of all instruments of production, by the immensely facilitated means of communication, draws all, even the most barbarian nations into civilisation. The cheap prices of commodities are the heavy artillery with which it batters down all Chinese walls, with which it forces the barbarians' intensely obstinate hatred of foreigners to capitulate. It compels all nations, on pain of extinction, to adopt the bourgeois mode of production; it compels them to introduce what it calls civilisation into their midst, i.e., to become bourgeois themselves. In one word, it creates a world after its own image.
>
> MARX and ENGELS, 2004, pp. 65–66

Though English colonialism was brutal and violent, it appeared to be justified in developmentalist terms, as liberation could only occur after or through the establishment of modern capitalist forms of production.

Marx adopted similar views in his early journalistic writings on India. English colonialism, he suggested, comprised a "double mission": "one destructive, the other regenerating the annihilation of the old Asiatic society, and laying the material foundations of Western society in Asia" (Marx, 1853b, para. 2). Marx is not complacent in describing this process: to locate the historical origins and primary dynamic of the world system in western Europe is not itself "Eurocentric". But in these writings he failed to register the injustices of colonialism on their own terms and in their own right, and again appeared to emphasize the bourgeoisie's inevitably progressive role, writing that "whatever may have been the crimes of England she was the unconscious tool of history"(Marx, 1853a, final para.). With decidedly Eurocentric overtones, he contrasted the modernizing influence of Western capitalism with an India described as "stagnant", "uninteresting and unchanging" and which "has no history at all" (Marx, 1853b, first para.).

As Coulthard (2014) argues, the support that Marx appeared to show for integration of "backward" areas and economies into the circuit of capital, was underscored by racist assumptions of non-capitalist social formations, and grounded in antiquated normative developmentalist notions. However, as Coulthard and other commentators have pointed out (Anderson, 2010; Balibar, 2014; Mauro Di Meglio and Pietro Masina, 2013), Marx moved substantially away from this position in his later life, beginning in the *Grundrisse* and espe-cially in his writings of the 1860s.

In Chapter 31 of *Capital Volume 1* Marx points to how the colonial rela-tion and its disastrous impacts on Indigenous people, underpins the capital relation:

> The discovery of gold and silver in America, the extirpation, enslavement and entombment in mines of the indigenous population of that conti-nent, the beginnings of the conquest and plunder of India, and the con-version of Africa into a preserve for the commercial hunting of black-skins, are all things which characterize the dawn of the era of capitalist production. These idyllic proceedings are the chief moments of primitive accumulation.
>
> MARX, 1976b, p. 915

In this passage we find both a clear analysis of the genesis of industrial capital-ism in the robbery of the lands, metals and bodies of Indigenous peoples and a moral condemnation of colonialism. Specifically addressing the genocidal as-pect of capitalist colonialism, Marx writes:

> The treatment of the indigenous population was, of course, at its most frightful in plantation-colonies set up exclusively for the export trade, such as the West Indies, and in rich and well-populated countries, such as Mexico and India, that were given over to plunder. But even in the colo-nies properly so called [that is, what we now call settler colonies]... In 1703 those sober exponents of Protestantism, the Puritans of New England, by decrees of their assembly set a premium of £40 on every Indian scalp and every captured [Indigenous person]; in 1720, a premium of £100 was set on every scalp; in 1744, after Massachusetts Bay had proclaimed a certain tribe as rebels, the following prices were laid down: for a male scalp of 12 years and upwards, £100 in new currency, for a male prisoner £105, for women and children prisoners £50, for scalps of women and children £50.
>
> MARX, 1976b, pp. 917–918

Although in earlier works Marx and Engels sometimes exhibited a normative developmentalist position that saw capitalism playing a violent yet historically progressive role in its relation to non-capitalist societies, by the 1850s and in *Capital* there was a much clearer condemnation of the injustices of colonial-ism on their own terms and in their own right and emphasis towards the de-fence of Indigenous and anti-colonial struggles.

Connected to Marx's analysis of colonialism is also the development of a critical perspective on uneven development and exchange and a shift away from a view, suggested in the *Manifesto,* that capitalism would create an increasingly unified world. Marx came to recognize that capitalist development in the metropolis continued to be supported by the extraction of raw materials and huge surpluses in the colonial and semi-colonial periphery. Thus, in later writings he criticized the "bleeding process" by which the British extracted resources from India for the benefit of the British ruling class, speaking of English "vandalism in India" (as cited in Kiely, 2002, p. 102). In *Capital Volume I* Marx spoke of how "the veiled slavery of wage earners in Europe needs the unqualified slavery of the New World as its pedestal" (1976b, p. 925) and in Chapter 15 of the same work he remarked on how "a new and international division of labour, a division suited to the requirements of the chief centres of modern industry springs up, and converts one part of the globe into a chiefly agricultural field of production, for supplying the other part which remains a chiefly industrial field" (1976b, pp. 579–580).[5]

This sensitivity to uneven geographical development is also attuned to ecological questions. In Marx's view, the ecological rift is exacerbated, becomes "irreparable", due to long-distance wasteful trade and the spatial disjuncture (especially the antagonistic separation of town and country) in capitalist production (see Marx, 1976b, pp. 636–638). While Marx often shows enthusiasm for the potentiality of enhanced forms of human cooperation enabled by globalizing productive networks, already in the 19th century he recognized that production chains were overstretched and wasting resources (see Tanuro, 2012).

In the last years of his writing, as Anderson details (2002, 2010), Marx provides a much closer and sustained focus on a range of non-capitalist social formations, in an effort to understand what was at that time the periphery of an expanding world capitalism. The urgency with which Marx approached the study of non-capitalist societies, along with an expansion of his ecological studies (see Saito, 2017, pp. 217–255), led him to put aside work on *Volume II* and *Volume III* of *Capital.* The effort devoted to the latter are represented by his

---

5 While Marx and Engels are often considered to have had little to say on imperialism (Ashman, 2013), these notes laid the foundation for later theories of imperialism and combined and uneven development to be developed by Lenin and Trotsky as well as Luxemburg. For a clear contemporary analysis of imperialism that explicitly centres the concept of forces of production see Kiely (2002). Kiely, in contrast to many theorists of globalization, demonstrates that notwithstanding the breakneck development of a few southern nations such as China, late 20th and 21st century moves towards global "free trade" have only intensified uneven development.

massive 1879–82 *Ethnological Notebooks*. Marx's notebook are filled with careful reflections on dozens of specific Indigenous nations (and confederacies), along with investigations of Russian and German village communities and Indian history. In these studies, Marx (and later, Engels) noted the egalitarianism, collectivism, and democratic forms of governance often found in non-capitalism and Indigenous communities. Saito (2017) meanwhile points to how Marx's studies of ecology and ethnology came together, as his investigation of German village communities found that "the first Germanic village formation always followed the law of necessity to increase the soil's power" (p. 263).

Marx regarded these pre-colonial forms as prefigurations of a possible post-capitalist future. He also considered how the Russian village communes could function as a place of resistance against capital and establish socialism without going through capitalism:

> Historically very favorable to the preservation of the 'agricultural commune' through its further development is the fact not only that it is contemporaneous with Western capitalist production and therefore able to acquire its fruits without bowing to its *modus operandi*, but also that it has survived the epoch when the capitalist system stood intact.
>
> as cited in SAITO, 2017, p. 265

In the process, he clearly moved away from any sense that all human societies were destined to follow a single path of development (that of nineteenth century capitalist England), leaving open the notion of multiple pathways for societies like Russia and India. Marx, writes Anderson (2002), shifted from a "unilinear" to a "multilinear" philosophy of history.[6]

---

6   However, see Gellner (1980) on Yuri Semyenov's defence of a "unilineal" philosophy of history. As Gellner details, Semyenov formulates a Marxist unilinealism (the notion of successive modes of production of which the concept of forces of production is integral), that effectively breaks from the idea of western-centred "progress" as the motor force in history. In contrast to the customary understanding, in the Semyenov reinterpretation unilinealism does not imply that every society is required to go through all "stages". Indeed, he shows that it is quite implausible to think that any concrete continuous society has passed through all modes of production. Therefore, rather than crediting the succession of stages to single, continuous societies, Semyenov advances what Gellner calls a "Torch Relay" theory of history (1980, p. 761). In this view, humankind as a whole is at a given stage, when the most advanced and influential area happens to be at the stage in question. The criteria for influential is partly that it exercises a great deal of influence on surrounding peripheral regions and also that it is preparing the ground for the next stage in question. As such, the torch carrying zone can only be identified after the event, after the next stage is reached, while its powerful influence is such that societies lagging behind will no longer pass through the same stages as the

Philosophies of history that imply obligatory successive stages of society must be rejected. Rejecting an outmoded normative developmentalism does not deny, however, that there are positive *potentials* that come from capitalism's material development of forces of production, or that that new *possibilities* in world history are opened by the advance of scientific-technological knowledge underlying the use of machinery in capitalism. Increases in productive capacity and reduction of absolute scarcity make a basic egalitarianism of life conditions *more feasible*, while building something resembling socialism without a certain material "base" in the productive forces is very difficult. Considering the political possibilities that exist given certain material conditions is a fundamental feature of historical materialism. Yet these material conditions are conditions of possibility, not historical inevitability.

At the same time, rejecting such a normative developmentalism should lead to a greater attentiveness to the "articulation" of non-capitalist and capitalist modes of production. Vitally, as Coulthard (2014) suggests, this should include the ways in which the former can come to inform the construction of alternatives to the latter. The knowledge and lifeways of peoples who have experience with ways of being not overdetermined by capital are important in forging alternatives.

There are aspects of Marx's work that provide some resources for this. On the important question of knowledge and skill, I believe his work falls short. Perhaps the complete publication and ongoing analysis of Marx's late manuscripts will demonstrate such an understanding. However, I agree with Tanuro's suggestion (2010), that Marx does not do justice to the creativity, skill and knowledge belonging to peasant, or Indigenous and rural communities outside of wage labour. While his perspective shifts to some degree in later works, he continues in *Capital* to refer unhelpfully to the agricultural peasant producer as the "less advanced fraction of society" (Marx, 1993a, p. 754). In rethinking the quote discussed above from *Capital Volume III*, we should recognize that

---

pioneers. The history of humankind in this way may be "unitary", while there are many types of societies in existence. Moreover, in Semyenov's view, on occasion not only is the centre essential for attaining the next stage, but so is the periphery. Indeed, at various crucial transitions (e.g., slave/feudal) the historic periphery played a crucial role in the attainment of the next historic step. In fact, the feudalism/capitalism transition is seen as idiosyncratic as a centre-preserving transition. Although not fully spelled out, the same would now be true of the capitalism/socialism transition; the torch is often passed "sideways" to peripheral regions that are essential for carrying forward progress, while dispensing of any obligation to "pass evenly through all stages". While it does not overcome all the problems facing unilealism, the Semyenov reinterpretation, as Gellner suggests, moves away from the Eurocentric and self-congratulatory customary understanding.

these rationalities also have a vital role to play in construction of ecologically sound alternatives.

Fruitful in this vein is again Ariel Salleh's work (2010, 2009). Reflecting from a global and "Third-Worldist" perspective, Salleh has highlighted the metabolic contributions of what she terms "meta-industrial labour". Meta-industrial labour denotes "workers, nominally outside of capitalism, whose labour catalyzes metabolic transformations – be they peasants, Indigenous gatherers, or parents" (2010, p. 212). The concept combines productive and reproductive labour on the basis that the non-monetized work meta-industrial labourers is fundamentally *regenerative* – it sustains everyday life. Furthermore, she emphasizes that much Indigenous work, peasant reproductive provisioning and subsistence farming are critical to the maintenance and reproduction of natural environments. This labour is often "rift-healing" (2010, p. 205) and possesses "metabolic-value" (2010, p. 212), denoting its contribution to sustaining and supporting ecological integrity.

In the process, Salleh works to (re)valorize the knowledge and skills of various meta-industrial labourers. They possess a "vernacular science" – a tacit knowledge that is embodied and rooted in practice-in-place.[7] As Salleh suggests, it is vital to recognize these diverse labourers as skilled ecological managers, and to consider how such place-based practices as associated forms of knowledge can inform alternatives to capitalist ways of relating to nature. Her work, in combination with the thesis advanced here, points to the necessary, though admittedly difficult task, of integrating place-based and Indigenous knowledges, with ecological sciences (more formally understood) in the construction of alternatives.

5   Conclusion

Despite longstanding efforts to undo such an interpretation, critics of Marx continue to see his optimism in the emancipatory potential of developing productive forces as proof of a deep-seated techno-Prometheanism. On this view, Marx's vision of socialism is reduced to an outmoded and anti-ecological

---

7   Coulthard (2014: 13) points to "grounded normativity", by which he means "the modalities of Indigenous land-connected practices and longstanding experiential knowledge that inform and structure our ethical engagements with the world and our relationships with human and nonhuman others over time". This is the "place-based foundation for Indigenous decolonial thought and practice".

"automated" paradise, which simultaneously and substantially continues rather than overcomes a patriarchal, imperialist and colonial "mode of living".

Marx, as I have outlined, demonstrated enthusiasm about the heightened productivity and increased material output enabled by the capitalist development of productive forces. This provided material conditions for a society beyond capital where the material needs of all would be met and arduous human labour would be greatly reduced. In some instances, particularly in earlier works, he implied that socialism would increase this productivity and that capitalist production was not mechanized enough. In such statements, he did not yet, as Amy Wendling puts it, "question the use-value of production's amplification in increased material output" (2011, p. 206).

While pointing to enduring tensions surrounding his argument that developing productive forces along the lines of large-scale industry would help make socialism an "objective possibility", I argued that this perspective needs to be approached with greater sensitivity to the historical circumstances of his work, as well as the human developmental content of his arguments. Marx suggested that the further development of industry may be required to "satisfy the material needs of all" from a perspective of scarcity, while he was also clear that the scientific and technological resources accumulated during the capitalist period could enable qualitative changes. These material conditions enhance the possibility of the development of forms of wealth that exceed a productivist dimension: especially the development of the artistic, social, political, scientific capabilities of human societies. While this wealth is potentiated by capitalist society, Marx argued that it is suppressed by the regime of value and could only be reached if control over society's productive powers were no longer in the hands of only one part of society (capital).

Marx's enthusiasm regarding the heightened productivity of capitalism also needs to be considered in light of his arguments surrounding the wastefulness and destructiveness inherent to capitalism's development of the productive forces. These arguments, which I have only gestured to thus far, reject the possibility of ascribing to Marx an overly positive verdict on capital's development of productive forces. Furthermore, in this chapter, I have only considered the quantitative side of Marx's concept of forces of production (i.e., those associated with increased productivity and productive output). As indicated in the introduction, forces of production include social aspects (such as cooperation) and other qualitative features (such as knowledge). These are part of the practices and processes by which we appropriate the rest of nature for human requirements, and they may also possess metabolic or ecological use-value – i.e., can contribute to mending the metabolic rift. Such an understanding, along with a fuller account of Marx's recognition of their deformation and destructiveness based on value and capital, invites us to unpack more carefully the unfulfilled potentialities he ascribed to capitalism and a consideration of what might be worth retaining from that view today. These issues animate the next chapter, where I provide a more sustained reconstruction of the concept by engaging twentieth-century Marxist approaches.

Marxism and Forces of Production: Towards an Ecological Conception

This chapter reconstructs the concept of productive forces, pointing to the importance of a more expansive understanding that moves beyond its narrow identification with technological "hardware" and increases in productivity and material output. I begin by first considering how the productivist interpretation has been bolstered from within the Marxist tradition, focusing especially on Gerald Cohen's influential *Karl Marx's Theory of History: A Defence* (KMTH hereafter). In contrast to Cohen, and drawing on Bertell Ollman (1976), I point to the more qualitative side of Marx's concept and to the enthusiasm he shows for the growth of capacities and powers such as cooperation and ecological knowledge. Next, I contrast the neutral view of technology implied by theorists like Cohen with more open, dialectical and political treatments of the concept located in the work of Mao, in late 20th century labour process and autonomist-Marxist approaches and in post-war left environmental thought. This provides the grounds for (re)-evaluating the destructiveness of capital's tendency to develop productive forces, without foreclosing the ecological and other positive potentials bound up with their advancement.

1   Productive Forces and Technological Determinism

Gerald Cohen's KMTH provides helpful definitions of the concept of productive forces, initially working against the grain of treatments (as glimpsed in Chapter 1), which tend to reduce the concept to bundles of technology or technological hardware. At the same time, he produces a powerful late 20th century defense of a more deterministic and productivist account of Marx. His work provides a helpful starting point for our reconstruction.

KMTH represents an attempt to apply the rigors of analytic philosophy to Marx's various statements on historical change, in an effort to pinpoint and tie down the specific causal mechanism(s) in Marx's interpretation of history and then to test that theory across historical epochs. This so-called "no bullshit" Marxism is pitted against dialectical thinking, which offers a relational, interdependent and more contingent understanding of change, and which for Cohen, "thrives only in an atmosphere of unclear thought" (2000, p. xxiii). In contrast to dialectical approaches, he argues that Marxists need to provide rigorous analyses and explanations of the specific micro-mechanisms through which epiphenomenal events emerge, rather than enlist teleological reasons or enter into the morass and push and pull of theories of "co-constitution".

Cohen works towards a definition of the forces of production by creating a catalogue or list of items that contribute to production. As he writes, "to qualify as a productive force, a facility must be capable of use by a productive agent in such a way that production occurs (partly) as a result of its use, and it is someone's purpose that the facility so contribute to production" (2000, p. 32). Within this understanding, Cohen treats productive forces as consisting primarily in labour power and the means of production. Labour power is defined as the productive faculties of producing agents. This includes strength, skill, and knowledge, encompassing the productively "relevant" parts of science (2000, p. 45). Scientific knowledge for Cohen is neither "superstructural" nor ideological, and in so far as it is productively relevant and "useful", and involved in the construction of instruments of labour, he includes it in his understanding of the productive forces. He defines means of production as either instruments of production, raw materials, or geographical spaces. By contrast, relations of production are framed as "[e]ither relations of ownership by persons of productive forces or persons *or* relations presupposing such relations of ownership" (2000, p. 34). In terms of ownership, Cohen clarifies that we think of this not as a legal relationship but as one of *effective control*.

In KMTH, Cohen subsequently argues that Marx was committed to the belief that history is based on the growth of human productive powers and that the economic structures that come to determine the form of society (such as slavery, feudalism and capitalism) rise and fall according to how they enable or impede that growth. Cohen exposes the reader to key statements in Marx on the forces and relations of production. He then proceeds to show analytically, that while Marx often asserts that productive forces produce changes in social relations and mental conceptions of the world, arguments suggesting a reverse dialectical movement are nowhere to be found in Marx's corpus and in any event simply do not hold. While Cohen admits some difficulty in reconciling his primacy thesis in KMTH with his recognition that capitalist property relations provide a clear stimulus to the development of the forces of production, he is able to side-step this problem and re-assert primacy. He does this via a functional explanation: phenomena are explained by their tendency to bring about certain effects. For Cohen, property relations underpinning capital clearly spur on the productive forces, but this does not contradict his primacy thesis, in so far as relations of ownership and control function to develop the forces, and exist given their capacity to do so. Put differently, the forces of production are understood to *choose* social relations and political/ideational structures and arrangements according to their capacity to promote further development.

Cohen's initial definitions of both productive forces and relations are quite expansive and insightful. The suggestion that both modern science (as instrumentalized under capitalism) and geographical space be considered productive forces, is particularly helpful. Yet, beyond this initial conceptual exegesis, in KMTH Cohen analyzes the forces of production and their positive potential almost exclusively with respect to the productivity increases they enable. Productivity for him means that less direct labour is required in order to make a larger product, such that productivity equals size of product/amount of direct labour to produce it. Most fully, the power of the productive forces refers to "the amount of surplus production [they] enable", or the amount of the day that remains after the labouring time required to maintain producers has been subtracted (2000, p. 61).

Cohen subsequently positions the drive for increased productivity as a trans-historical motor force of development.[1] In doing so, he appeals to an exogenous force behind the development of productive forces: human rationality and the basic impulse of human beings to better their life situation, reduce toil and overcome material scarcity by boosting productive forces. This enables Cohen to boil down his concept to the point where he understands technological development as an autonomous historical force that continually smashes through anachronistic forms of property ownership, creating a clear path towards socialism.

In Cohen's view, capitalist relations of production necessarily exist because they promote productivity, and they will also change because a new technological power has arisen to which they are ill-adapted. As capitalism clearly continues to stimulate some forms of technological progress, he must offer an alternative view of "fettering", which goes beyond the suggestion that capitalism will continue to exist so long as it permits *any* increase in productivity. Developing an account of fettering similar to that outlined in my Introduction, Cohen argues that relations of production fetter the productive forces when an alternative economic structure would better promote the further development

---

1 My focus in this chapter is on ecological questions. As such, an analysis of Cohen's entire theory of history is beyond the scope of this study. Miller (1981) provides an excellent critique of the notion that economic structures throughout history exist and endure by proving maximum productivity. While capitalism is driven towards and includes substantial increases in productivity, it is particularly hard to sustain the view that feudalism was maintained by its ability to promote the growth of productive forces towards this end. For a critique of functionalist explanations undergirding Cohen's philosophy of history see Agar (2003).

or use of those forces. An economic structure thereby lasts only so long as it is *optimal* for both the *development* and *use* of its accumulated productive power (2000, p. 297).

Based on this notion of fettering (which, following Hughes, I have called relative-fettering) and Cohen's focus on advancements in productivity (understood to encompass the reduction of labouring time required to maintain producers), Cohen argues that the central contradiction of advanced capitalism surrounds the priority given to the creation of exchange-value over use-value, such that "the structure of the economy mitigates against the optimal use of its productive capacity and functions to the detriment of general human welfare" (2000, p. 310). More specifically, Cohen argues that advanced capitalism displays a distinctive bias towards expanding output, as against reducing toil. The productivity improvements enabled by capitalism are in his view open to two "uses" – reducing toil and extending leisure – while maintaining output or (alternatively) increasing output, while labour stays the same. However, as he argues, a productive process oriented to exchange-values promotes only the expansion of consumptive goods, but cannot reduce toil, even when the option of greater leisure is more desirable for most people. Based on its single measure for calculating value – maximum production of surplus value – capitalist society places no value on diminishing labour. Capitalism,

> cannot realize the possibilities of liberation it creates. It excludes liberation by febrile product innovation, huge investment in sales and advertising, contrived obsolescence. It brings society to the "threshold of abundance" but locks the door. For the promise of abundance is not an endless flow of goods but a sufficiency produced with a minimum of unpleasant exertion.
>
> 2000, p. 307

In the notion of a bias towards expanding output as against reducing toil, Cohen outlines a central contradiction of contemporary capitalism. His is also not an anti-ecological vision in the end. While he, like Marx, views capitalism in an earlier historical period as an engine for producing material wealth from the standpoint of scarcity, the priority given to the creation of exchange-value over use-value renders the system reactionary in more advanced stages, characterized by a blind and boundless pursuit of (often wasteful and superfluous) consumption goods.

Nevertheless, difficulties in Cohen's work encourage the construction of an alternative and ecological view. They do so in two ways. Firstly, his exclusive focus on productivity greatly restricts a discussion of what the productive forces *are* and consequently the unfulfilled potential of their overall advancement today. While the concept is adopted from liberal political economy, the Marxist variant refers not only (or even primarily) to quantitative phenomena such as improvements in productive output or increases in labour productivity in the way Cohen suggests (Graham, 2015).[2] Instead, the concept is a tool to provide a socio-historical analysis of the growth of *human capacities and powers to use and modify natural environments purposefully, in a way that is conducive to their own sustenance and reproduction, in a given society and at a given historical interval.* Of course, capacities and powers concern surplus production and productivity increases; this dimension of their development should certainly not be discounted. Yet, to focus exclusively on this quantitative dimension is reductive; it is a form of reification, which reduces our conception of the world to quantities, on the model of money (see Lukács, 1972). It effectively forecloses a consideration of capacities and powers necessary to maintain, restore and improve ecosystem health, and an analysis of how capitalism critically denies the ecological use-value aspect of the productive forces.

2   Productive Forces and the Dialectic of Capacities and Needs

That forces of production can be understood as expressions or manifestations of historically developed capacities and powers to transform the rest of nature, is contained in Bertell Ollman's account of the dialectics of needs and capacities, found in his classic, *Alienation* (Ollman, 1976). Following Marx, Ollman makes a distinction between "natural-being" and "species-being", on the basis of capacities or powers on one hand and needs or desires on the other. Needs, as he explains, are felt desires, drives or wants, and they are attached to, or dialectically coupled with, the powers or capacities necessary for realizing them. Natural-being involves powers or capacities and needs or desires that human beings share with all living entities. They are the "processes of life devoid of human attributes" (1976, p. 83). The needs associated with natural being involve biological and corporeal requirements of human beings as living parts of nature, such as requirements for food, water, shelter and procreation, and are coupled with the powers to satisfy them, such as labour, eating and sex. Centring practices that sustain life, Ollman suggests that natural-being involves

2   Therborn (1980, pp. 353–386) provides an excellent account of the genesis of the concept through classical political economy.

powers or capacities and needs or desires that are directed toward and realized in the external world:

> Take eating as a natural power, man's impulses which drive him to eat are clear enough: he is hungry. The abilities which enable him to eat include all that he does when eating. The tendencies which direct him toward satisfactory objects are his taste and his general knowledge as to what is edible and what is not.
>
> 1976, p. 78

Because natural-being powers are directed towards the external world and realized through it, the powers together with the external world are fundamentally intertwined. Citing Marx, Ollman continues:

> If man's powers can only manifest themselves in and through objects, he needs these objects to express his powers. Hunger is an example of such a need for objects. Marx says that hunger "needs a nature outside itself, an object outside itself ... to be stilled. Hunger is an acknowledged need of my body for an object existing outside it indispensable to its integration and the expression of its essential being".
>
> 1976, p. 78

Ollman places corporeal intertwining with the world at the heart of practices that sustain life. Natural-being is an embodied, ecologically embedded experience.

Species-being, on the other hand, reflects social activities through which humans develop, alter and expand their powers, needs and a sense of self in relation to others. Species powers include a broad array of items and various senses such as seeing, hearing, touching, smelling, tasting, knowing, judging, making love, thinking, being aware, wanting, procreating and loving. Vitally, Ollman argues that species powers extend natural powers and build upon the already ecologically embedded character of human life (natural-being). As he writes: "If natural powers can be viewed as establishing the framework within which life itself goes on, then man's species powers express the kind of life which man, as distinct from all beings, carries on inside this framework" (1976, p. 83). Species powers are means by which people learn about, interact and establish particular relationships with nature (both nonhuman nature and other people as parts of nature).

Ollman suggests that the extension of species powers through the senses is captured in Marx's distinctive understanding of "appropriation". As

Ollman explains it, "appropriation" means to utilize constructively, to build by incorporating:

> For Marx, the individual appropriates the nature he perceives and has become orientated to by making it some way a part of himself with whatever effect this has on his senses and future orientation. To "capture" a sunset, it is not necessary to paint, write or sing about it. It becomes ours in the experience of it. The forms and colors we see, the sense of awakening to beauty that we feel and the growth in sensitivity which accompanies such an event are all indications of our new appropriation. To paint the sunset, or to write or sing about it, if joined by genuine emotions, would achieve an even higher degree of appropriation, would make this event more a part of us.
>
> 1976, p. 89

Appropriation here can be read as a process in which bodies interact with and are affected by sensuous engagement with the world. Appropriation affects the experiences humans can have and their stance toward the world. Moreover, appropriation transforms species powers; in the case above, it increases one's ability to differentiate colour and appreciate a sunset.

This theory of the human relationship to nature and its appropriation is exceptionally broad. It encompasses all the human capacities and powers (including the five senses and their contents, as well as other actions and functions) by which we become aware, learn about, interact with or otherwise "contact" nature (both human and non-human). As Ollman suggests, various "spheres" of life (such as art, literature, the family, politics), provide occasion and materials for the objectification and alteration of species powers.

Material production is, in this light, but one crucial area of life within which the fulfillment, alteration, and expansion of powers or capacities and life-needs take place. Conscious, purposive activity in the productive process, or as Marx puts it, "purposeful activity aimed at production of use-values", "appropriation of natural substances to human requirements" (1976, p. 290), is a key arena for the objectification and development of species-life, or humanity's powers. Moreover, the *forces* that are adopted, applied and developed within the productive process, reveal and are themselves expressions of powers and capacities to purposively transform the rest of nature and meet needs. Productive forces and species powers are as Ollman suggests but "two sides of the same relation" (1976, p. 96). The perspective finds its origins in Marx and Engels, who in the *German Ideology* wrote that, "The history of the evolving productive forces...is, therefore, the history of the development of the powers of the individuals themselves" (1976, p. 91). Later in the same text, and in view of the "re-appropriation" of the productive forces from capital under socialism, they asserted that, "the appropriation of these forces is itself nothing more than the development of the individual capacities corresponding to the material instruments of production" (1976, p. 96).

From this perspective, I argue that an adequate account of productive forces should include the capacities and powers that are collectively available to us (and reflect a need) to transform and appropriate non-human nature in a manner that *maintains, restores and improves ecosystem health*. The limitations of Cohen's view are most immediately evident in his discussion of knowledge and science. While Cohen helpfully includes science and knowledge as a productive force, commensurate with Marx who repeatedly describes them as such, they are included in Cohen's list of productive forces only in so far as they intervene in the transformation of nature in order to advance productivity.

By contrast, when Marx and Engels discuss the growth of science and its potentiality, their enthusiasm centres new forms of ecological knowledge and understanding. For example, Marx points to developments in the field of agronomy aimed at soil restoration, following from the environmental impacts of capitalist agriculture. He takes this development to be "one of the great results of capitalist mode of production" (Marx, 1976, p. 754). Such knowledge, as is the case with science more generally, is understood to be the result of vast networks of human cooperation. Marx points to how it is privately appropriated by capital and applied to the agricultural industry, yet within highly narrow confines and "in so far as this is at all possible within the conditions of private property" (1976, p. 754).

As Burkett (2014, pp. 158–163) shows, Marx also expresses enthusiasm for the growth of new and more *universal* forms of ecological understanding and awareness, which capitalism unwittingly propels by virtue of its intensive globalized appropriations of nature and accompanying ecological dysfunctions. Engels captures this succinctly:

> Thus at every step we are reminded that we by no means rule over nature like a conqueror over a foreign people, like someone standing outside nature – but that we, with flesh, blood, and brain, belong to nature, and exist in its midst, and that all our mastery of it consists in the fact that we have the advantage over all other creatures of being able to learn its laws and apply them correctly...And, in fact, with every day that passes we are acquiring a better understanding of these laws and getting to perceive both the more immediate and the *more remote consequences* of our interference with the traditional course of nature. In particular, after the

mighty advances of natural science in the present century, we are more
than ever in a position to realize and hence control even the more remote
natural consequences of at least our day-to-day production activities.

ENGELS, 1972, p. 261, my emphasis

While this passage contains problematic elements of a modernist 19th century
vision of *mastering* nature, in it and in other places, Marx and Engels show
excitement for new forms of ecological knowledge and consciousness. While
the metabolic processes they knew were more local and regional in character,
they point to the increased scale of environmental problems and to a corresponding growth in ecological understandings of the unintended consequences of our productive metabolic interaction with nature. They view this growth
in knowledge as an augmentation of collective productive powers and capacities that corresponds to or fulfills a need to sustain the natural conditions that
support friendly human life and flourishing. This knowledge should help shape
our productive activities – its conscious and comprehensive application would
form a vital component of humanity "rationally regulating their interchange
with nature".

Secondly, Cohen's intentionally undialectical and "cumulative" view of increases in labour productivity means that the political aspects of the mode of
production relate primarily to ownership of means of production, or "effective
control", while productive forces appear not to be tied to substantial variations
of a social and political kind, but rather subject to linear and purely technical
development. On this view, Cohen (like some critics as seen in Chapter 1) has
Marx endorsing capitalist industry as an altogether positive acquisition, not
contaminated by history and relations of production and power. Socialist production (including associated forms of work organization) is directly inherited
from capitalism, while activating a better use of its technological mixes.[3]

---

3 Cohen is able to sustain a neutral view of the forces of production and to see their development as an autonomous result of the effort to overcome natural scarcity, in part by also ex-
  cluding important social and relational dimensions of forces of production, such work relations and work organization. As suggested above and shown in Chapter 3, this does not fit
  well at all with Marx's classification. For example, in *The German Ideology* Marx and Engels
  wrote that "By social we understand the cooperation of several individuals, no matter under
  what conditions, in what way and to what end. It follows from this that a certain mode of
  production or industrial stage is always combined with a certain mode of cooperation, or
  social stage, and this mode of cooperation is itself a "productive force"" (1976, p. 76). Marx
  continually invoked this conception throughout his mature work. As the labour process theorists reviewed below suggest, it is clear that work organization and work relations are governed to a large extent by a concern for labour discipline and social control, rather than
  simply being the result of the drive to increase productivity.

In the next section, I bring out the limitations of this perspective by engaging more dialectical and political treatments of forces of production, located first in the work of Mao as well as in neo-Marxist work of the 1970s pertaining to work organization and technology, as forms of labour control. These perspectives point to how class relations are inscribed within forces of production, challenging the neutral view of science, technology and technique implied in analyses like Cohen's. Despite lack of attention to non-human nature, they raise questions that remain relevant to today's left and help expose the complexity and challenge of discovering and advancing those aspects of productive forces appropriate to a democratic green socialism for the 21st century.

3 Lenin, Mao(ism) and Forces of Production

As suggested in Chapter 1, 20th century Soviet socialism sought to establish a framework for "catch-up" industrialization and produced models of development that largely mimicked capitalism in terms of its productivism. This included enthusiastic support for the growth of science and technology geared towards rapid modernization and heavy industry. Therefore, Lenin's vow that "no dark power would be able to withstand the union of representatives of science, proletariat and technique" (as cited in Werskey, 2007, p. 404), understood the progressive historical force of science in terms of its practical role in advancing industrialization. The new Soviet Republic officially viewed heavy industry and technology as an expression of applied scientific knowledge. In regard to "technique", Lenin also praised the most advanced American methods of production and set up factory systems similar to those created by US corporations. In his 1918 piece, "The Soviets at Work", he suggested that:

> The possibility of socialism will be determined by our success in combining Soviet rule and Soviet organization or management with the latest progressive measures of capitalism. We must introduce in Russia the study and teaching of the Taylor system and its systematic trial and adoption.
>
> LENIN, 1918, section on Higher Productivity of Labor

Echoing the sentiment in a later speech delivered in Moscow in 1920, he famously described socialism as "Soviet power plus the electrification of the whole country" (Lenin, 1920, para. 18).

As intimated in Chapter 1, Lenin's perspective on the growth of productive forces (including his advocacy of Henry Ford's moving assembly line for mass production and Taylorist work organization) needs to be considered in view of historical circumstance. He worked in the setting of a "backward capitalism" and Soviet society's underdevelopment. Logically enough, the development of socialism implied a rapid growth of forces of production centred on increasing output and "durables". The immediate problem with capitalist production technologies was therefore not with the techniques or technological mixes, but with their use to produce surplus value for the capitalist, rather than enough output to build up the young Soviet Union and (ultimately) satisfy the material needs of all. Moreover, the exigencies of the Revolutionary moment – war and mass disruption – gave a strong impetus to the process of rapid industrialization, with priority assigned especially to heavy industry (Harvey, 2010). The leadership saw this as a means to safeguard the revolution and provide military defence against foreign aggression. Lenin was therefore partially justified in turning to the most advanced capitalist technological forms in order to revive and extend production and safeguard revolution. However, in the long-term, this was a problematic strategy.

Interestingly, Chattopadhyay (2014) has shown that the early Soviet Union from 1917–1930 developed the most advanced ecological science in the world. It revolutionized fields such as climatology, while pioneering forms of conservation, especially in the area of forestry. Werskey (2007) similarly recalls various early dissenters to soviet-style "industrialized science" within the scientific community in the Soviet Union, and the production in the 1920s of various visions and advanced practices aimed at producing a "leaner and greener" socialist society. However, once firmly under Stalin's custodianship, an "alliance of science, the proletariat and technique" that might have moved in a more ecological direction was obliterated (with violent purges aimed at its leading ecological thinkers in the 1930s and 40s) and the Soviet Union became bent on rapid industrialization in its efforts to outpace the United States in per capita production (Werskey, 2007).

While working under broadly similar conditions (in terms of levels of economic development, including relatively undeveloped capitalist industry and peripheral position within world capitalism), Mao and the other political thinkers of communist China more often presented an alternative model and method of developing productive forces. This stems from an understanding of the "transition society" and the problem of building the material foundations of socialism.

Some of Mao's best known contributions to Marxist philosophy come from his elaborations on the notion of contradictions in "On Contradiction" (1947) and later in "On Correct Handling of Contradictions Among the People" (1957). The dimension of Mao's work that is most often discussed from the former concerns his writings on the principal *aspects* of a contradiction, which challenged the Stalinist orthodoxy of the time. As he wrote:

> ...in the contradiction between the productive forces and the relations of production, the productive forces are the principal aspect; in the contradiction between theory and practice, practice is the principal aspect; in the contradiction between the economic base and the superstructure, the economic base is the principal aspect; and there is no change in their respective positions. This is the mechanical materialist conception, not the dialectical materialist conception. True, the productive forces, practice and the economic base generally play the principal and decisive role; whoever denies this is not a materialist. But it must also be admitted that in certain conditions, such aspects as the relations of production, theory and the superstructure in turn manifest themselves in the principal and decisive role. When it is impossible for the productive forces to develop without a change in the relations of production, then the change in the relations of production plays the principal and decisive role. .... When the superstructure (politics, culture, etc.) obstructs the development of the economic base, political and cultural changes become principal and decisive.
>
> 1947, Section 4

For Mao, impulses for social change often derive from a central structural contradiction between forces and relations of production, yet how these impulses are channelled, whether or not they give rise to social change, and the content and character of subsequent transformations: all these questions, in his view, were matters of political and ideological struggle. Mao here appeared to have emphasized the "subjective" factor (that is the role of theory, of consciousness, of politics), in the process of historical struggle aimed at social transformation. As Lenin also remarked in critique of central European Social Democracy, revolution is not a mechanical working out of fatalistic contradictions, which given sufficient maturity would somehow automatically lead to proletarian victory. In the face of structural contradictions, he argued for the "primacy of politics", maintaining that the outcome of struggle depends on the creativity of political leadership offered by antagonistic classes. Mao was himself a Leninist, who insisted on combining faith in the masses with a vanguard party. Additionally, he pointed to the importance of building class alliances between proletarians and dispossessed peasants and argued that revolutionary practice in China could be built around poor peasants together with an urban proletariat, which remained a relatively marginal class in China in this period (D'Mello, 2009).

However, the notion of primacy of politics or politics in command concerned not just the organization and building up of revolutionary forces, but also the long-term process of building a revolutionary socialist project. In the formation of socialism following a revolutionary rupture, Mao emphasized the continued importance of education and of transforming consciousness. This attention given to ideology and transforming attitudes has been understood and critiqued as representing a "voluntarist turn" to the superstructure (Mamo, 1981). Yet, as Rossana Rossanda (1971) suggests, the notion of politics in command is not only (or even primarily) a matter of consciousness, of ideological struggle. Instead, it concerns fundamental questions of the "transitional society" – that is of how to effect a break with the capitalist mode of production and in a manner than resolves its multiple contradictions. Such a break would need to go deep into the structure and the material base.

For Mao, the capitalist mode of production is not reducible to the relation of private ownership of the means of production; instead, he argued that this relation is embedded within the web of relations that constitute capitalist accumulation, including work organization and divisions of labour. Thus, the break with the capitalist mode of production would mean breaking not only with private ownership, but also with the capitalist form of these productive forces (or at least their radical transformation). In Rossanda's view, this understanding was precisely what was lacking in the official Soviet model from 1917, which was based on the conviction that socialism could be built only in accordance with technologies and a production model similar to the Industrial Revolution, save ownership of the means of production and the social distribution of the product. Such a model would inevitably re-produce contradictions in the relation to nature (including an increase in the gap between town and country), renew capitalist divisions of labour in the workplace, and entrench privileged position for technique and intellectual labour, in comparison with manual labour. Rossanda (1971) proposes that the Cultural Revolution too is often misunderstood – it was not primarily aimed at bringing about "ideological" changes, but rather aimed at achieving changes in the development of technology, work organization and in the relationships between labour, knowledge and authority.

This position was prefigured in the first Great Leap Forward beginning in 1958. The Great Leap was premised on a strategy of advancing productive cooperation in steps or stages, first by incorporating individual peasant households into systems of mutual aid, then into producer cooperatives, and on into larger collective economic and political units (communes) (D'Mello, 2009). The vision, as Hinton writes, was "dialectical, projecting a society in constant development, communities at different levels all moving towards higher levels of multifaceted cooperative development at speeds determined by their own potential and internal dynamism" (1994, p. 4). Mao criticized the Soviet model's bias towards heavy industry and centralization, to the neglect of light industry, agriculture and local participatory initiatives (Li, 2008). Mao thereby helped initiate the development of rural industries, premised on using "appropriate technologies", along with a more decentralized planning process that encouraged greater initiatives from localities and grassroots workers (Li, 2008).

The Great Leap Forward, which lasted until 1962, produced some initial breakthroughs and also had catastrophic concrete effects. In its first year, the strategy produced important technological advancements, led to the construction of industrial and agricultural infrastructure and enabled millions of peasants to gain preliminary experience and knowledge of modern industrial production (Li, 2008). However, the economic surge of 1958 gave way to several years of major economic turmoil and wide-spread food shortages. From 1959–1962 China experienced a massive famine in which up to 30 million people are reported to have died (Dikötter, 2011). In addition to internal political tensions that led to fundamental divisions over development strategy and policy (Hinton, 2004) and external factors (poor weather), major mistakes and failures in agricultural policy and planning under Mao's leadership contributed to the famine. The application of untested ideas of Soviet agronomist Trofim Lysenko and his followers, such as close cropping, deep plowing and applying unusual fertilizer mixtures, led to decreases in agricultural production (Hinton, 2004). Breakdown in communication also contributed to massive misallocations of resources (Li, 2008). As the government failed to recognize that grain production was much lower than reported, China remained a substantial net exporter of grain during this period (Dikötter, 2011). Grain was requisitioned from the country-side, while a large amount of labour was also diverted from agriculture to steel production and construction projects, such that harvests were left to rot uncollected in some areas (Dikötter, 2011). The problem was aggravated by locust swarm caused by a disastrous Great Leap campaign against sparrows for their toll on grain stocks and rice (Kreston, 2014).

Despite the very concrete failures of the Great Leap Forward, its initiatives are not without merit and were in some ways well conceived in their method of involving the masses in the development of the productive forces in agriculture and small industry. Contained in the initiatives is a recognition that human beings themselves are part of the productive forces – that people's skills, tacit knowledge and creativity could be "unleashed" and that human capacities for cooperation and democratic problem solving in communities and workplaces could be built up as the result of human activity and practice (as well as via investments in education and health).

A focus on matters of "labour, knowledge and authority" could also be seen in Maoist politics concerning the politicization and practical application of science and also in tensions between "reds and experts". Mao understood natural science to be inherently political. Its techniques and aims were seen to be deeply shaped by historically determinant social relations – reflective of certain economic priorities and class interests. The aims and conduct of science under socialist social relations and in the transition society, would therefore need to look quite different. Science would need to be politicized (directly through the guidance of the party), so that it could be conducted in the service of the "interest of the masses". Moreover, for Mao, the productive utilization of science under conditions of labour's subjection to capital also hampered the *diffusion* of scientific knowledge of natural conditions. It forced an extreme separation or distinction between scientists/experts and workers/lay people and separated knowledge from practice and practical experience. These separations needed to be overcome or diminished as far as possible; in Mao's view, socialist praxis would encourage people to be both red and expert.

The politics of the Cultural Revolution, which grew out of the first Great Leap Forward, were characterized by Mao's "mass science" imperative. The latter sought to undermine "elite science", and was based on the tenets of integrating experts and the masses in scientific endeavours and combining Indigenous and Western science (Brock and Wei, 2012). This included efforts to have scientists concentrate on immediately useful projects and practical problems, such as in agriculture and industry and efforts to involve uneducated masses in research work, such as plant breeding and pest control. The educative components of the Cultural Revolution therefore sought to expand the ranks of scientific and technical personnel via basic professional training programs, especially in rural areas, and were conceived as a project of human capacity building (Brock and Wei, 2012). Agronomists and geologists went to the countryside to collect information and engage peasants concerning their knowledge of crop variety, the location of useful minerals, and folk knowledge of precursors of earthquakes, such as levels of water in wells or the unusual behaviour of domestic animals (Brock and Wei, 2012).

Strong currents of anti-intellectualism also accompanied the Cultural Revolution, as the practices of natural science and the attitudes of scientists were often positioned as being as opposed to the interests of the masses. Brock and Wei (2012) thus point to an oscillation in Maoist China between science being viewed as a productive force (and scientists concomitantly viewed as "workers") and its periodic reclassification as part of the "superstructure" (with scientists subsequently viewed as belonging to the suspect intellectual camp). There was also a depreciation of scientific theory in this period, as science was directed only at immediate and practical problems and often on a trial and error basis. Indeed, the period displayed some of the dangers of "Lysenkoism", a movement in the 1930s to 1960s in the Soviet Union which was an attempt at a scientific revolution, including a political campaign against emerging genetic theory and certain forms of science-based agriculture (see Levins and Lewontin, 1987, pp. 163–196). The latter were disavowed and repressed as they contradicted the official party line (genetic theory, for example, was considered to contradict Soviet views surrounding the social malleability of human character).

The harshest excesses of the Cultural Revolution yielded to relative stability by the 1970s, as the Great Leap Strategy of advancing productive cooperation in steps or stages, was revived and proved more successful (Schmalzer, 2012). Within this approach, China's development model emphasized an ethic of "doing more with less" and subordinating technological development to human social development. In rural areas in particular, there was a focus on the development of small-scale industries, such as small dams and local irrigation systems, as well as programs to use waste materials such as biogas as an energy source, suited to using local resources and meeting local needs. Priority placed on the health of the people and healthy living conditions led to coordinated sanitation efforts aimed at cleaning up rivers, factories and eliminating pests, in combination with preventative medicine (Brock, 2012).

It is not the purpose of this chapter to conduct a careful or detailed study of what happened during the Cultural Revolution and its aftermath. This is a highly contested history, while recent work, as reflected here, suggests a more nuanced and complicated view than that found in narratives of absolute failure (Li, 2008). I point rather to how Mao's understanding of the transitional society breaks with assumptions that had dominated much Marxist thought in the period, especially concerning the construction of alternative futures. Certain aspects of this, I suggest, remain relevant to today's left in the "age of the Anthropocene".

Broadly, as Rossanda suggests, within Maoist politics, there was a critique and often "rejection, a ceaseless re-examination of the elements of historical continuity that the capitalist epoch hands on to subsequent epochs" (Rossanda, 1971, p. 76). Socialism was seen not as merely a new way of managing a society which has been inherited – a renovated version of what we already have – but also as a continuous act of "creative-destruction", and reconstruction (Rossanda, 1971, p. 77). This process of creative destruction extended to the productive forces and their conscious transformation in ways that better accord with egalitarian social relations and a restorative metabolic relation to nature. Socialism is not so much something in the distant future to arrive at, but is, as Marx and Engels described in the Communist Manifesto, a movement of the present reality that works towards a constant and revolutionary transformation.

This understanding of the transition society, as entailing a long process of transformation that is not free from contradictions, and within which a great deal of the capitalist mode of production survives, "not as a vestige of the past but as an intrinsic feature of the present" (Rossanda, 1971, p. 62), has merit. It is an insight that appears to be particularly important to uphold in a context where the ecological critique of capitalist "technoscience", often now leads to a total rejection, dismissal and disdain of the technologies, forms of knowledge and infrastructures that sustain much of modern life (as an exemplar see Ho (2013)). This radical left stance contains some quite problematic tendencies. While a transition to post-capitalism will not necessarily be smooth, it is very difficult to imagine, for example, how we can immediately shut down the vast productive networks, infrastructural configurations and built environments ("re-worked second natures") that currently support and sustain huge swaths of human life, without courting humanitarian disaster. Transforming and transitioning away from these entails some inevitable "compromise" with the forms of productive organization and social relations that produced them. It is quite dangerous and potential deadly to suggest otherwise. Any future society, to paraphrase Marx, is necessarily stamped with the birthmarks of the old one.

Concerns surrounding the politicization of science and tensions between so-called reds and experts, are also relevant today. Considering how to transform science in its prioritization is an important feature of ecological transition, given that many branches of science are today deeply implicated in the ecological problems we now face (more on this below). The politics of knowledge in Maoist China also extended to a general unease regarding the role of science in developing alternative political economic projects, for fear of the formation of a scientific-technological elite, and of institutionalized technocratic power that runs counter to democratization. The attempt to transform science in a socialist direction there, thereby extended to efforts to diminish the separation of manual and mental labour and alleviate inevitable tensions between the average worker and experts. Such concerns are also pertinent to today's projects for green transformation. If, as McKenzie Wark (2016) suggests, exiting today's climate crisis requires the participation and collaboration of workers in scientific and technical fields, it is also important to consider ways of encouraging a greater diffusion of ecological knowledge and a more bottom up approach to science. On this point, Marx himself stressed the importance of widespread technical and agricultural education and of direct producer's efforts to re-appropriate knowledge and skills fragmented and monopolized by capital (see Saito, 2017, pp. 125–129).

Challenging the content of science (as opposed to its use and institutional organization) is a more complex matter, however. The effort in Maoist China to build a science "free from bourgeois ideology" displayed some of the potential dangers of this endeavour, in the form of "Lysenkoism". This included as Levins and Lewontin write, "a one-way external interaction between philosophy and science, in which philosophers interpreted and blessed or condemned particular scientific views" (1987, p. 195). As Saed (2011) asserts, efforts at constructing an "alternative science" should involve natural scientists working extensively on developing alternative methods or epistemologies, rather than critiquing natural sciences from an external position.

4   Marxism and the Labour Process

Neo-Marxist work of the late 1960s and 1970s, particularly labour process approaches, produced similar challenges to any presumption that socialism could involve straightforwardly inheriting productive forces and putting them to new productive uses. Driven in part by the insufficient attention to class relations and the absence of social critique that often accompany more productivist understandings of Marx, they provided more systematic analyses of how the class relations and forms of power that prevail in capitalist societies not only assert themselves politically and economically, but also enter deep into the process of production and subsequently fashion science, technology and labour organization (Braverman, 1998; Noble, 1986; Panzieri, 1976, 2005).

A classic work in this area is Harry Braverman's *Labour and Monopoly Capitalism* (1998). Extending Marx's analysis of 19th century capitalism, Braverman showed how jobs that once required the worker both to conceptualize as well as to execute tasks had been reorganized into, on the one hand, a mass of jobs requiring little or no conceptualization, and on the other hand, a smaller number of elite managerial and technical-scientific jobs that require little else. Braverman referred to the overall decline in society of the number of jobs that require both conceptualization and execution, i.e., skill, or craftsmanship, as the "degradation of work".

Braverman understood, like Marx, that the labour process is a process of exploitation, as well as a struggle for control, where the outcome is shaped by social power. He illustrates this through a close analysis of Taylorism and scientific management, in which the motions of workers were broken down into the smallest possible components in order to be separated, reorganized and recombined in such a way as to *simultaneously* enhance control over workers, and increase the rate of exploitation. While evident in the 19th century, Taylorism came to be applied systematically in the twentieth century with the advancing development of monopoly capitalism.

Braverman is sometimes criticized for focusing extensively on Taylorism, which is considered to be a thing of the past, superseded by work organization methods and principles that incorporate the "human factor" neglected by Taylor (such as in post-fordist "flexible work" schemes). Yet such criticisms miss the essential contribution of Braverman's critique of scientific management (see Foster, 1998). For Braverman, Taylor's system at its strictest (before being superseded by more accommodating versions) represented the key to understanding of the labour process. Taylor broke down capitalist managerial imperatives into their most basic elements, and presented these imperatives not as a technical necessity, or as a Weberian "despotism of rationality", but as an expression of an open and undisguised concern for the steepest possible rate of the exploitation of labour. Key to Taylor's system was the disassociation of the labour process from the skills of the workers – the gathering and development of all traditional knowledge and skills of craftspeople which are classified, tabulated and a codified into "science"– and a clear-cut and novel division of manual and mental labour, or a separation of conception and execution, throughout the workshops.

Following from this control over knowledge was the ability of management to control each step of the labour process and its "mode of execution" (1998, pp. 77–82). This management also provides the basis for the process by which science is fully inducted into capital accumulation. While capitalism begins to apply science routinely to the production process during the Industrial Revolution, Braverman analyses the historical passage, along with the emergence of monopoly capitalism beginning in the last two decades of the 19th century, by which capital went from sporadically appropriating science (exploiting the accumulated knowledge of the physical sciences as a "free gift"), to the later capitalist endeavour to systematically appropriate, organize and fund science. Braverman calls this the scientific-technological revolution:

> The contrast between science as a generalized social property incidental to production and science as capitalist property at the very centre of production is the contrast between the industrial revolution, which occupied the last half of the eighteenth and first half of the nineteenth centuries, and the technical-scientific revolution, which began in the last decade of the nineteenth century and is still going on.
>
> 1998, p. 108

As he documents, invention in North Atlantic capitalist states itself became big business in the early 20th century through the creation of networks of corporate research laboratories and the extensive hiring of research scientists by large firms. While in 1920 in the US there were approximately 300 corporate laboratories, by 1940 there were over 2,200, enabling corporations to effectively "invent on demand" (1998, p. 113).

While these developments began in the late 19th century and progressed in the early 20th in the post-war era of "state organized" monopoly capitalism, science became more thoroughly enmeshed in capitalist relations of production. The R&D budgets of large corporations continued to rise, while post-war affluence was linked to the commercialization of science (see also Angus, 2016; Werskey, 2007). Through the post-war boom, General Electric for example worked to convince consumers that "in engineering, in research, in manufacturing skill, in the values that bring a better, more satisfying life, progress is our most important product", while Dupont aimed to produce "better things for better living through chemistry".

Braverman's analysis of the changing structure of the labour process under monopoly capitalism also extended to the development of unproductive or wasteful labour (1998, pp. 284–293). This was meant not strictly in Marx's original sense of labour which produces commodity value, but also in reference to labour which existed *only* to realize surplus value. Braverman argued that this labour was irrational from a wider social standpoint and did not correspond to that which a society of cooperating "associated producers" might expect by promoting worthwhile, useful and rewarding forms of labour. The forms of labour he identified were those associated especially with the sales effort and financial speculation (1998, p. 288). The latter profoundly shaped that which is produced in manufacturing industries.

While Braverman's analysis is sometimes reduced to a conception of generalized deskilling, on these terms, he did not argue that the general level of skill in society would decline as a result of the division of labour under capitalism. As he writes, "the labour processes of society have come to embody a greater amount of scientific knowledge, clearly the "average" scientific, technical and in that sense "skill" of the labour process is much greater now than in the past" (1998, p. 294). His central question, however, was whether the scientific and educated nature of the labour process tended towards polarization, to which he answered in the affirmative.

By explaining scientific managerial imperatives as a class imperative (exercised in the name of rationality) Braverman launched a powerful attack on technological deterministic approaches, which Cohen had reproduced and which Lenin also appeared to support on the assumption that work relations were technically determined and that socialism had to use Taylorism. For Braverman, however, capitalist managerial imperatives do not have their essential character in the machine logic itself, but rather in the class basis of the division of labour, logically independent of machinery. The machine on this view is then partly made possible by these tendencies, and partly brought into being in order to accelerate them.

David Noble's inquiry into the social evolution of automatically controlled machine tools in *Forces of Production: A Social History of Industrial Automation* (1986), advanced this understanding. In the above work, Noble provides a case study of the way in which the design, development and diffusion of technoscience is deeply caught up with social and political criteria. While Noble analyzes the complex social determinations of technology from many angles and levels (which I cannot adequately summarize here), perhaps the most provocative part of his analysis is to show how the concepts of "economic and technical viability" that are continually cited as the generic criteria for technological development and advancing automation are, upon close historical inspection, inherently political and deeply intertwined with social relations of production.

By carefully reconstructing the historical genesis and design of "numerical controls" (NMC's) which were widely used for automating machinery beginning in the post-war period, Noble argues that a cheaper and simpler variant for automation called "record playback", was sacrificed and never developed in the early stages of automating industrial production. Noble, echoing Braverman, suggests that "management was willing to sacrifice economy and cost in order to retain control over production" (1986, p. 185). Noble argues that record playback, which necessitated shop floor participation and programming, and which emphasized workers' skill and creativity in the labour process, was abandoned for more expensive and less efficient numerical controls. These offered management a means of breaking down the power of skilled unionized machinists by eliminating the human element and shifting programming to a separate and centralized office. According to Noble, taking up Marx's remarkable suggestion that "it would be possible to write a whole history of the inventions made since 1830 for the sole purpose of providing capital with weapons against working-class revolt" (Marx, 1976b, p. 563), capitalists are seen to be consciously constructing new technologies as weapons of class-struggle. The implication is that both work organization and technology are forms of work control and express social domination. Put differently, machines are bound to pose problems, given that they internalize and express social relations, ways of living and producing.

Such conclusions are sharply expressed in certain strands of autonomous Marxism or Italian *operaismo*, which draw heavily on Marx's notion of the real subsumption of labour to capital. Exemplary is the early work of Raniero Panzieri (1976). Here we find a potent critique of "orthodox" Marxist understandings of the development of the forces of production (and the possibilities for their immediate planning by a socialist state). Panzieri posed a direct challenge to what he called "objectivist" Marxist positions that posited technological rationality as a self-moving development of scientific innovation, as part of politically neutral forces of production.

In the so-called objectivist approach, politics is external to the technical labour process, as a movement towards the eventual assumption of technological processes, achieved through socialist planning. The conjunction of objectivist and planning positions is evident in Lenin, expressed in the passage quoted in Chapter 1 calling for the adopting the latest "progressive" measures of capitalism, including Taylorist work organization. However, as Panzieri suggests, for Marx (as for Braverman and Noble), technical forces develop not within a logic of neutral scientific progress, but as a means of consolidating a particular form of the extraction of value. The introduction of machines on a large-scale in the factory and the technical principles of the machine –"the technically given speed, the coordination of the various phases and the uninterrupted flow of production imposed on the will of workers as a "scientific necessity" – are the direct manifestation, and also naturalization, of capitalist power and control" (Panzieri, 1976, p. 9).

On this view, any socialist assumption of a more efficient planning and advancement of the technological forces of production directly inherited by capital was a misguided approach that failed to recognize sufficiently the immanence of capitalist relations to technics. Thus, for Panzieri the collective ownership of production made little difference to the continued capitalist functioning of the machine. He concludes:

> Faced by capital's interweaving of technology and power, the prospect of an alternative (working-class) use of machinery can clearly not be based on a pure and simple overturning of the relations of production (property), where these are understood as a sheathing that is destined to fall away at a certain level of productive expansion simply because it has become too small. The relations of production are within the productive forces, and these have been "moulded" by capital.
>
> 1976, p. 12

By showing that class relations are inscribed within machinery, such accounts present important challenges to inherited understandings of the progressive potential of advances in the latter. While authors championing such potential often ask us to accept continual technical growth, in so far as it carries an underlying movement towards a higher social order, labour process and autonomist theorists remind us that the assembly line and the fragmentation and division of work upon which the growth of those forces is premised, appears in large part as progress only within or against a particular socio-political background.

Braverman's analysis of the centrality that science came to occupy in the forces of production beginning under monopoly capitalism, also complicated the notion that scientific knowledge might be "liberated" under alternative social arrangements. While the early Soviets saw science being fettered under conditions of market anarchy, monopoly capitalism had given rise to the overt politicization and planning of "capitalist science". By pointing to capital's monopolization of knowledge and to the planned and increased subordination of science to the production of exchange-value, it became increasingly difficult to see it as value-free, or as a socially neutral progressive force.

Although such works maintain that a transition to socialism requires a certain base in the forces of production (that is, they seem at least implicitly to uphold that new possibilities in world history are opened by the advance of scientific-technological knowledge underlying the use of machinery in capitalism), the implication is that the technologies, forms of knowledge and other relations that could really sustain something like socialism will to a substantial degree develop in the context of social transformation, in a transition society where a great deal of the capitalist mode of production survives. While we cannot avoid adapting and making use of capitalist legacies, this work again forces a recognition that the technological mixes (including forms of knowledge, work organization and divisions of labour) that are inherited from capitalism will need to be significantly transformed in ways that better accord with eco-socialistic relations and other kindred political projects, be they feminist or de-colonial.

5   Modern Ecology and the "Forces of Destruction"

The labour process scholarship discussed above is helpful in reconceptualising the development of forces of production and critical for deepening socialist politics. Concerned as it was to renew Marx's critique of work organization and class analysis at the shop floor, it mostly stopped short of engaging the ecological content, implications and promise of his work. As such, "nature" in these accounts continued to serve as the untheorized substratum for the unfolding of social relations.

However, the emergence of modern environmentalism in the 1950s and 1960s, including the work of ecologists such as Rachel Carson and Barry Commoner, led to an increased awareness and recognition of the ecological destruction brought by capitalist development, particularly in the post-war period. As Braverman suggested, this period solidified earlier processes associated with monopoly capitalism, namely an economy dominated by large corporations and the deepening integration of science and industry.

Rachel Carson's *Silent Spring* (2002) examined growing environmental problems caused by synthetic pesticides, particularly the agricultural use of the insecticide DDT, which experienced prodigious growth following the Second World War. As Carson wrote, after only two decades of their use, synthetic pesticides had been so thoroughly distributed that "every human being is now subjected to contact with dangerous chemicals from the moment of conception until death" (2002, p. 15). Although Carson admitted that there are some situations where the application of synthetic pesticides, or what she called "biocides", could be appropriate, she argued that their indiscriminate overuse, which was driven by the "gods of profit and production" (2002, p. 11) was not only environmentally destructive, but also counterproductive in the long-term. This was the case because targeted pests would develop resistance to pesticides, making them useless in eliminating the target insect populations, while also weakening ecosystems that would fall prey to unanticipated invasive species. She thereby predicted a pesticide "treadmill" – an increased dependency on them and their use in ever greater quantities. In response, Carson called for a biotic (organic) approach to pest control as an alternative to chemical pesticides, wherever possible, and argued that eliminating pesticide use should be the goal.

While Carson is sometimes credited with launching the modern environmental movement, as Foster and Clark suggest (2008), her work is best understood as part of a larger modern ecological movement that initially arose in the 1950s and 1960s surrounding the dangers of nuclear radiation. As Foster and Clark recount (2008), the scientific community (drawing together biologists, geneticist, ecologists and meteorologists), raised concerns over the harmful effects of nuclear radiation, as they explored the movement of radioactive materials through the atmosphere, ecosystems and food chains. While Carson had focused on the problem of synthetic pesticides, the overarching theme of *Silent Spring*, is the wider and often destructive interaction between humans and the rest of nature, and her analysis drew upon and was rooted in these earlier ecological treatments.

Barry Commoner, who was a prominent researcher and activist surrounding nuclear testing and radioactive fallout, subsequently raised concerns about humanity's ability and propensity, in the post-war period, to pollute the environment and degrade ecosystems on a *scale* never before possible. In *Science and Survival* Commoner wrote that:

> Never before in the history of this planet has its thin life-supporting surface been subject to such diverse, novel and potent agents. I believe the cumulative effects of these pollutants, their interactions and amplifications, can be fatal to the complex fabric of the biosphere.
>
> 1966, p. 21

Commoner's account, along with that of other research into nuclear radiation, pointed to humanity's ability to disrupt metabolic processes at a planetary level. While his work gestured to this understanding, as Ian Angus (2016, pp. 122–124) suggests, this awareness only became evident in the 1970s, with the discovery that Chlorofluorocarbons (chemicals used in refrigeration), were damaging the ozone layer. This realization contributed directly to the birth of Earth System science, which in turn has led to a much fuller understanding of the global climate system and of global metabolic rifts (Angus, 2016).

In his *The Closing Circle* (1971), Commoner again linked the growing scale and intensity of environmental problem to the "sweeping transformation in productive technology since World War II" (p. 177), particularly the spectacular expansion of the petroleum and petrochemical industries. For Commoner, this marked the full realization of the scientific-technological revolution. In this period, advances in applied sciences (such as in chemistry, physics and engineering) that were adopted for military purposes in the war, now became thoroughly applied to industry and agriculture. In the *Closing Circle* Commoner subsequently provided a brilliant analysis of the ways in which productive technologies and transport systems with intense impacts on the environment continually displaced less ecologically destructive ones, in a process he referred to as a "counter-ecological growth pattern" (p. 177). The root of the problem, Commoner argued, laid in large corporation's seizure of technological innovation and their drive to maximize productivity and profits, over ecological and human health (pp. 258–268).

In analyzing the way in which post-war productive technologies followed a counter ecological growth pattern, both Carson and Commoner pointed to the way in which science had contributed to many of the ecological problems we now face. Their work was part of a larger "revolt" within science, arguing that these developments had nothing to do with the rational application of scientific knowledge (Foster and Clark, 2008). This challenged the assumption that the application of science to production inevitably leads to progress and advancement for society.

Writing only shortly after Cohen, Braverman and Panzieri, Ernest Mandel, reflecting a growing ecological consciousness within the post-war left, articulated a vision of a post-productivist Marxism rooted in a vision of sustainable human development. It is worth quoting him at length:

> Likewise, there is no reason to identify the growing suspicion of the risks involved in capitalist technology and the capitalist misuse of the natural sciences with a general retreat into irrationalism, mysticism, despair, and disdain for the human race. We socialists and Marxists do not share the irresponsible "productivist" credo of the 1950s and 1960s. Many social criticisms of that credo are amply justified. ...Neither has one to accept the impoverishing implications of permanent asceticism and austerity, so alien to the basic spirit of Marxism, which is one of enjoyment of life and infinite enrichment of human potentialities, in order to understand that the endlessly growing output of an endless variety of more and more useless commodities (increasingly, outright harmful commodities, harmful both to the environment and to the healthy development of the individual) does not correspond to a socialist ideal. Such an output simply expresses the needs and greeds of capital to realize bigger and bigger amounts of surplus value, embodied in an endlessly growing mountain of commodities. But the rejection of the capitalist consumption pattern, combined with a no less resolute rejection of capitalist technology, should base itself from a socialist point of view on a vigorous struggle for alternative technologies that will extend, not restrict, the emancipatory potential of machinery (i.e., the possibility of freeing all human beings from the burden of mechanical, mutilating, non-creative labor, of facilitating rich development of the human personality for all individuals on the basis of satisfaction of all their basic material needs).
>
> Mandel 1995, pp. 81–82

Echoing modern ecological thinkers, Mandel pointed to the growing output of useless and wasteful commodities, the proliferation of environmentally damaging technologies and the role of science in these developments. He emphasized how under capitalism, forces of production substantially take the commodity form and are thus entangled in its (ecological) contradictions. Elsewhere Mandel presciently observed that "growing productive forces, with growing commodity-money relationships can in fact move a society farther from the socialist goal instead of bringing it closer" (1974, pp. 20–21).

6   Conclusion

The works discussed above challenge a neutral view of technology, science and technique, found in some well-known Marxist analyses, implied at times in Marx's own work and expressed in 20th century Soviet practice. They make it clear that the technologies (including forms of knowledge, work organization and divisions of labour) that are inherited from capitalism will need to be significantly transformed and reconfigured, rather than simply reproduced.

While the climatic implications of capital's deployment and materialization of science and technology were not yet apparent, by the late 20th century, thinkers such as Mandel pointed to a situation of generalized overproduction in the Global North and accompanying ecological harms. For them, the socialist alternative no longer implied growth in the processing of natural resources and increased "output", but instead implied a retreat in aspects of forces of production dedicated to this growth. In the context of the deepening climate crisis, this conclusion is yet more inescapable. Meanwhile, the notion that growing productive forces can move us away from the socialist goal, takes on new meaning. Indeed, as Alexandre Costa warns "socialism is not possible on a scorched earth" (as cited in Angus, 2016, p. 195).

To take on these challenges a much more circumspect view of "liberating productive forces", than that implied by more "orthodox" Marxist views (and a different view of socialism and the struggles and challenges it will entail) is needed. This means looking beyond bundles of technology and increases in productivity and material output and rethinking some of the most basic of productive forces, such as ecological knowledge, which is not opposed to productive forces but part of them. It is in reference to the future enhancement and current fettering of the capacities and powers collectively available to us for the maintenance, restoration and improvement of natural conditions that it is most helpful to retain Marx's view that capital is not "the *absolute* form for the development of the forces of production...it is a discipline over them, which becomes superfluous and burdensome at a certain stage of their development, just like the guilds etc". (Marx, 1993b, p. 415, my emphasis).

In the next chapter I go back to Marx, providing an ecological reading of the concept of forces of production in his work, while drawing out and advancing its implication through recent scholarship that implies, but does not adequately develop such a renewed conceptualization. This will allow us to fully elaborate the concept of forces of production from Marx right through to recent literature, contributing greater theoretical depth to the arguments advanced so far.

CHAPTER 3

Marx and the Critique of Political Economy and Ecology

In a classic statement outlining the aims and goals of historical materialism from the *German Ideology* Marx and Engels asserted the following:

> The first premise of all human history is, of course, the existence of living human individuals. Thus the first fact to be established is the physical organization of these individuals and their consequent relationship to the rest of nature.... All historical writing must always set out from these natural bases and their modification in the course of history through the action of men and women.
>
> 1976, p. 37

Marx's "mature" political economy retains a focus on the human and societal relation to the rest of nature and its transformation through human labour. Incorporating natural scientific understandings, he conceives of this relation in terms of a socio-ecological metabolism – a complex, dynamic interchange between human beings and nature. The concept of forces of production can then be helpfully interpreted as the powers and capacities through which that metabolism takes place. Specifically, it can be taken to refer to *the practices, objects, techniques and knowledges through which we are purposefully linked to and transform the rest of nature.*[1]

This chapter provides such an ecological reading of the concept of forces of production in Marx, while drawing out its implications through contemporary literature. I begin by establishing the ecological foundations of the concept in Marx, focusing especially on his mature political economy of the *Grundrisse* and *Capital,* while also drawing on further methodological statements from his

---

1   Within this definition, I retain a focus on the process of production and analytically distinguish productive forces from the forces of societal and social reproduction. The latter also involve processes through which we are linked to and transform the rest of nature (e.g., cooking and cleaning transforms natural materials, while public transportation entails the construction of a built environment for consumption). Yet I find it necessary to separate them analytically from productive forces. Likewise, despite their ecological dimensions and implications, I do not count military operations as part of the productive forces. While I exclude these spheres from the category of productive forces and a fulsome discussion of them is beyond the scope of this study, they enter into the analysis at numerous points, particularly in the discussion of green transition.

early work. I consider how this broad usage provided him with a means of examining how capital's appropriation and development of productive forces torques them in a quantitative direction (bound up with the compulsion to increase labour productivity as a means of extracting relative surplus value), and activates epochal transformations in them. Next, I show that he did not blindly endorse the "total development" of the productive forces, as critics (and some supporters) aver. Instead, he considered how such development took place at the expense of disrupting the sustainable metabolic interaction between humans and the rest of nature, eroding the material conditions for sustainable and friendly human life. In the process, he provides vital foundations for analyzing how the productive forces are embroiled in capitalism's ecological contradictions, including the carbon rift. In the final section I return to the potentials that Marx gleaned surrounding "qualitative advancements" in our social productive powers, including ecological knowledge and (planned) cooperation, while drawing out their broad implications for coming to terms with the climate crisis.

1   Labour Process, Metabolism and Forces of Production

The fact that we are embodied, sensuous and physiologically needy, means that we have inescapable requirements for basic natural substances that reside outside of ourselves and which are, "the everlasting nature imposed conditions for human life" (Marx, 1976b, p. 493). While the appropriation of nature is characteristic of all "natural-beings", Marx and Engels developed a co-evolutionary approach to society-nature relations and insisted that we maintain a focus on the human relation to nature in its social and historical evolution.

Each understood human beings as unique among animals in our capacities to produce with foresight and intention. The capacity to modify and improve upon prevailing productive forms and techniques (to produce new forms of social organization and instruments of labour), to produce according to a plan on a grand scale over and above what is required by natural necessity and to do so through a learned history, are seen as distinctively human capabilities.[2] The development of the powers and processes by which we interact with the rest of

---

2   While Marx and Engels are sometimes accused of harbouring a "species imperialism" in light of the comparisons they draw between animals and humans (Benton, 1993, pp. 32–44), establishing qualitative differences does not imply a deficiency of animal capacities. Wilde (2000) is especially clear on this point. Moreover, as he argues, Marx's view of establishing a sensitive and responsible metabolic relation to more than human nature, includes an ethical and compassionate relation to other species. For other kindred contemporary attempts to rethink

nature are subject to a continual process of transformation. Critical to their development are the historically specific relations among the producers and among the producers and appropriators of the social product. The conception is materialist and dialectical in so far as the social form of production and the material content of human production are mutually constituted. Thus, Marx and Engels suggest in the *German Ideology* that each historical stage "contains a material result, a sum of productive forces, a historically created relation to nature *and* of individuals to one another, which is handed down to each generation from its predecessor" (1976, p. 62, my emphasis).

The relation of human beings to the rest of nature constantly evolves, while the dependence of human beings on nature is an insurmountable material fact. From this foundational position, Marx interprets historical development, at one of the most basic levels, as a process whereby in order to reproduce themselves, people enter into social relationships and work to appropriate nature. They do so in a manner that is consistent with those relationships and forms of knowledge, skills and means of production that are historically developed and available. It is from this basis that we encounter the simplest and perhaps most helpful understanding of forces of production, comprehended broadly as the practices, objects, techniques and knowledges through which we are purposefully linked to and transform the rest of nature.

Marx's later political economy continues to focus on the labour or production process with a view to the production of use-values, which he saw as constituting the main metabolic interaction between humans and the rest of nature. As Marx defined it in *Capital*:

> The labour-process is purposeful activity aimed at production of use-values. It is an appropriation of what exists in nature for the requirements of man. It is the universal condition for the metabolic interaction between man and nature, the nature imposed condition of human existence, or rather it is common to all forms of society in which human beings live.
>
> 1976, p. 290

The "process between humanity and nature" is viewed here (and since the *Grundrisse*) in terms of a socio-ecological metabolism. This notion of metabolism is more than just analogy or metaphor; it emanates from 19th century natural science, and is transformed by Marx to understand the complex material interchange between human beings and natural systems. The notion of mutual

the concept of a "species-being" that avoids any semblance of species imperialism see Harvey (2000) and Dyer-Witheford (2004).

interdependence and exchange contained in the concept breaks with the uni-directional Enlightenment idea of humanity "utilizing" nature (Schmidt, 1971).

Therefore human societies, as Marx stresses, emerge within and are depen-dent upon a wider earthly or "universal" metabolism, which in turn is ind-ependent of labour and which precedes the appearance of human life itself. The labour process, which is human action aimed at producing use-values, is a condition for the material interchange between society and the rest of nature and requires the appropriation of natural substances not produced by labour. In this definition, Marx abstracts from the social and historical character of the labour process, defining moments that are common to all such processes, in-dependent of the *form* of society. While the labour process is defined here in a trans-historical sense, production is always historically specific and the meta-bolic interaction or exchange between society and nature is necessarily social-ly and historically "mediated". As Burkett writes, "the production relation be-tween people and nature must be treated as a socially mediated natural relationship" (Burkett, 2014, p. 29) and thus human beings can be conceived as self-mediating beings of nature (Meszaros, 1986). The *forces* of production, on this view, refer to the distinctive set of powers and capacities through which that relation or exchange occurs.

The specific form and content of this "mediation" – that is of the various powers and capacities through which we are purposefully linked to extra-human nature – is again a socio-historical product. In contrast to the view of-fered by classical economists, Marx writes that, "capital did not begin the world from the beginning, but encountered production and products already present before it subjugated them beneath its process" (Marx, 1993b, p. 675). As Van der Pijl (1998, p. 28) puts it, capitalism "annihilates previous disciplines over the productive forces", while prioritizing the process of accumulation in their de-velopment over any inherent (re)productive needs of society.

In the next section, I outline Marx's analysis of the social separation of pro-ducers from natural conditions and produced instruments of production and the conversion of these into private property and into the powers of capital. The process of appropriation and conversion is seen as a vehicle and overall condition for the historically unprecedented growth of the productive forces.

2   Primitive Accumulation, Expropriation and Nature's "Free Gifts" to Capital

For Marx, one of the illusions that capital evokes is that of its own comprehen-siveness. This includes obscuring the fact that capital is rooted in violent processes of expropriation. In the final chapters of *Volume 1* of *Capital*, Marx takes up the historical processes of land enclosure and dispossession, which he viewed as integral to the establishment and reproduction of capitalism as a way or mode of life. As Marx describes, so-called primitive accumulation forcibly tears Indigenous societies, peasants and other small-scale agricultural producers from their access to means of subsistence and natural conditions of production (that is to access to land, food, shelter, clothing, tools and work, as can be obtained without having to go through labour markets). Through the agency and power of the capitalist classes (typically backed by the deployment of violent state power), collectively held lands and resources are actively enclosed and shared resources are transformed into the private property of a small minority.

In this process, we find the dissolution of people's prior, more communal relations to the land (and of their more communal forms of property) by capitalist relations of production. A decisive aspect of capitalism is therefore private property in the means of production and subsistence, which presupposes the separation between producers and the social and natural conditions of production and existence and therefore a division between workers and capitalists.[3] This separation typically compels immediate producers to enter daily the exploitative realm of the labour market as wage labourers for their survival. On Marx's view, labourers are "freed" in a double sense: firstly, in terms of a legal status, they are not enslaved, enserfed or bound to a particular master; but secondly, they are "freed" from access to means of subsistence, production and survival. This separation makes possible the exploitation of wage labour (the appropriation and extraction of surplus value from workers), the central pivot on which capitalism's peculiar production of profit and value depends.

The dispossession of collectively held lands through enclosures in England was part of a greater age of the global expropriation of wealth, as land and labour were seized through colonization, enslavement and the plundering of resources (Dawson, 2016; Foster and Clark, 2018). In Chapter 31 of *Capital Volume 1* Marx points to how the colonial relation underpins the capital relation:

> The discovery of gold and silver in America, the extirpation, enslavement and entombment in mines of the indigenous population of that

---

3   While these are the "basic" or "fundamental" classes, of course neither group is homogenous. For a more textured and elaborated sociological account of modern class formation that builds from Marx, see Wright (1998, 2015).

continent, the beginnings of the conquest and plunder of India, and the conversion of Africa into a preserve for the commercial hunting of blackskins, are all things which characterize the dawn of the era of capitalist production. These idyllic proceedings are the chief moments of primitive accumulation.

MARX, 1976b, p. 915

Primitive accumulation is ongoing and not limited to a prehistory of capitalism. The violent expropriation of land continues throughout Africa in particular, and the dispossession of peasant populations in Latin America and throughout East and South Asia is still with us (Franco et al., 2013). As Coulthard (2014) argues, in settler colonial contexts like Canada, land-expropriation remains one of the primary fonts of capital accumulation into the present, while Indigenous peoples have been largely (although not exclusively) pushed to the margins and not proletarianized. Moreover, in recent years the dispossession of Indigenous peoples is often achieved less overtly through coercive and violent means and more through "asymmetrical exchange of mediated forms of state recognition and accommodation" (Coulthard, 2014, p. 15).

Silvia Federici (2004) meanwhile points to how in societies in which capitalism has supplanted the preceding mode of production, primitive accumulation also produced a profound transformation of the family. While in Feudal society, production often took place in domestic groups and reproduction had a more communal and collective structure, primitive accumulation produces an increased separation between the family and the site of production. In the process, the relation between production and reproduction (in the sense of biological, generational, and social reproduction) was also radically transformed. As she writes: "the family emerges in the period of primitive accumulation also as the most important institution for the appropriation and concealment of women's labour" (Federici, 2004, p. 97).

Marx's analysis of primitive accumulation extended not only to the expropriation of use-values embedded in the land, but also the appropriation of existing means of production, along with the forms of knowledge bound up with them. Capital therefore develops production on the basis of the "technical conditions" it inherits. The way these existing forces are harnessed and then converted and developed in the labour process as a means of producing vendible use-values (and following the separation of producers from the land), establishes the historically specific content and character of industrial capitalist people-nature relations. We turn to Marx's analysis of this historical development now.

3   Instruments of Labour and Primitive Accumulation

In his analysis of the capitalist labour process, in Chapter 7 of *Capital*, Marx reminds us that the appropriation of nature is characteristic of all of human history. The human body, including the hand and the head, are the most basic productive forces through which that purposive-appropriative relation occurs:

> Labour is, in the first place, a process in which both man and Nature participate, and in which man of his own accord starts, regulates, and controls the material re-actions between himself and Nature. He opposes himself to Nature as one of her own forces, setting in motion arms and legs, head and hands, the natural forces of his body, in order to appropriate Nature's productions in a form adapted to his own wants.
> MARX and ENGELS, 1976, 283

These elemental productive powers and capacities – the forces of the body, the head and the hand – can be transformed and augmented through various means such as through social organization, by the accumulation and transmission of knowledge, as well as through various "adjuncts" such as tools and physical infrastructures. As we will see, the development of instruments of labour or produced means of production[4] (together with the skills and forms of knowledge they embody) are critical in capital's effort to increase the productivity of labour. However, they first need to be produced:

> Nature builds no machines, no locomotives, railways, electric telegraphs, self-acting mules etc. These are products of human industry; natural material transformed into organs of the human will over nature, or of human

---

4   I refer to "produced" instruments of labour as a shorthand to designate technologies and built infrastructures. In his analysis of the capitalist labour process, in Chapter 7 of *Capital Volume I*, Marx considered means of production to consist in "instruments" and "objects" of labour, both of which originate in non-human nature and have a persisting non-human component. Objects of labour, or raw materials, may be given more or less directly by non-human nature or are natural objects modified by previous labour processes. The instruments category is very broad and includes tools and machines manufactured out of natural materials, and even the earth itself (which serves as an instrument in agriculture). At times Marx defined instruments of production in yet more expansive terms, to include various natural conditions (including physical, biological and climatic natural systems) that while not directly "conducting" human labour processes and practices, are necessary conditions for it (see Burkett, 2014, pp. 38–41). Based on the conceptualization offered here the latter are part of the total conditions of production, but not productive forces.

participation in nature. They are *organs of the human brain, created by the human hand*; the power of knowledge, objectified.

MARX, 1993, p. 706

In this well-known passage from the *Grundrisse,* Marx evokes the notion of instruments of labour as "organs", which also meant tools, regarded as "artificial organs" of human beings. Marx is here extending an insight that reaches back to the *Economic and Philosophical Manuscripts,* to indicate that our relation to nature is mediated not only through human labour, but through tools and infrastructures (bodily organs) – themselves products of the human transformation of nature and materializations of a distinctive mental capacity.

Through the process of primitive accumulation capitalists take control of the instruments of labour: "at first capital subordinates labour on the basis of the technical conditions within which labour has been carried up to that point in history" (Marx, 1976b, p. 425). However, as the drive for the production of surplus value becomes ever more powerful, capitalism must build technologies and infrastructures, as well as an evolving knowledge system and set of skills *adequate for its own purpose.* In this, the development of machinery is vital:

> The development of the means of labour into machinery is not an accidental moment of capital, but is rather the historical reshaping of the traditional, inherited means of labour into a form adequate to capital. The accumulation of knowledge and of skill, of the general productive forces of the social brain, is thus absorbed into capital, as opposed to labour, and hence appears as an attribute of capital, and more specifically of fixed capital, in so far as it enters into the production process as a means of production proper.
>
> MARX, 1993b, p. 694

Capital historically expropriates and then reshapes productive forces in a manner "adequate to its form" through the only way it knows: via commodity production. This occurs within a work process that is internally organized by capital. In *Capital* Marx analyzed the process through the categories of formal and real subsumption of labour to capital.

4   Formal and Real Subsumption of Labour to Capital

Under formal subsumption, which Marx analyzed in relation to what was called the "putting out system", we find relatively independent workers working for capital. Merchant capitalists would take materials to labourers in their cottages and collect the worked-up product at a later date. Capital here draws into itself an *existing* labour process, which continues much as before in terms of the techniques, skills and methods of labouring that are employed; however, by monopolizing the workers' means of subsistence, the merchant *compels* the worker through the latter's need, to submit to wage labour. The cottagers depended on merchants for a wage and did not own the products they produced.

Real subsumption, on the other hand, begins when workers are brought into the factory where capitalists direct and supervise their activities and intensify production by making every effort to ensure that as little socially necessary labour-time as possible goes into making a unit of the product. Making workers work longer, harder or more intensively is sufficient for the production of "absolute" surplus value. Real subsumption, however, entails not only the bringing of the labour process under the supervision of the capitalist, but more broadly, the subordination of the technical labour process to the process of value expansion (Van der Pijl, 1998). Put differently, it involves not only a social relationship of wage labour, but also an internal reorganization and a technical revolution in the labour process at the hands of the capitalist manager. Production has now been colonized by an alienated form – commodity production.

This reorganization and technical revolution raises the productivity of labour to an unprecedented degree and enables the acquisition of "relative surplus value". The raising of productivity in pursuit of relative surplus value was historically accomplished through 1) the organization of the factory system through scientific management (with separations of occupations, divisions of labour and specializations of work functions); 2) the introduction of machinery (whose development on a large-scale requires the motive power of fossil fuels and also implies the reorganization of work and divisions of labour); and 3) the conscious application of scientific knowledge to production.[5]

As discussed in the sections below, the effects of this drive for relative surplus value via increased productivity in the form of large-scale industry are rising matter and energy throughput and greater total waste output (including

---

5 While Marx appeared to predict a tendency from formal to real subsumption, the relationship is not strictly speaking historical (in the sense on one leading to the other), except that real subsumption presupposes formal subsumption (Boyd and Prudham, 2017). Formal subsumption may develop alongside and even displace real subsumption in particular historical situations (Swidler, 2018). It is also important to note that in numerous parts of the Global South, petty-commodity production and subsistence agricultural practices, which are neither formal nor real subsumption to capital, continue to meet the needs of large segments of the population (see Shiva, 2016).

carbon emissions). The immense collection of commodities that are produced also necessitate the expansion and opening of new markets and the creation of the spatial conditions that allow for their circulation through means of transportation and in fixed, heavy, secure, durable and often immobile physical infrastructures. Moreover, the real subsumption of labour to capital can be seen to entail a parallel "subsumption of nature" – or an "appropriation and technological development of the objects, forces, and life forms present in nature as a whole", through the application of science to production (Burkett, 2014, p. 66). This process simultaneously provokes steady developments in the means and methods of search, discovery, and extraction of natural resources over time, another form of "scientific progress".

The technological revolutions introduced through real subsumption further propel an increase in the centralization and concentration of capital. As production becomes more capital-intensive, based on fossil energy and machinery, it becomes dominated by a handful of large corporations. Paralleling this process is the partial socialization of the forces of production, hence "the conscious technical application of science, the *planned* exploitation of the earth" (Marx, 1976b, p. 929, my emphasis). On these terms, the emergence of capital industrial development implies nothing less than a radical transformation of the forces of production and therefore in the *societal relation to the rest of nature*.

In the following sections, I provide a closer analysis of these various interlinked processes and develop their implications via contemporary scholarship. I begin with the chapter on "Machinery and Large-Scale Industry" in *Capital Volume I* where we find the core of Marx's analysis of how large-scale 19th century industry came into being during the Industrial Revolution. I emphasize the importance placed on the transition from human and animal muscle power as a key physical force of production to fossil fuels, while gesturing to interlinked processes (divisions of labour and the application of science to the production process).

5   Capitalist Industrialization: What Technology Reveals

In the chapter on "Machinery and Large-Scale Industry" Marx began by interpreting Darwin's work as showing "the formation of the organs of plants and animals, which serve as the instruments of production for sustaining their life". Subsequently he asked, "Does not the history of the productive organs of man, of organs that are the material basis of every particular organization of society, deserve equal attention?" (Marx, 1976, p. 493). Technology, Marx then asserted, does not dictate or determine socio-ecological relations; instead, it "*reveals* the active character of man to nature, the direct process of production of his life and thereby it also lays bare the process of production of the social relations of his life, and the mental conceptions that flow from these relations" (Marx, 1976, p. 493, my emphasis).

Stemming from his suggestion that technologies help *reveal* or *disclose* the relations and practices linking us to nature, Marx started piecing together the transformations in machinery and large-scale industry with a discussion of the transition from tools to machines:

> The machine, which is the starting point of the industrial revolution, re-places the worker, who handles a single tool, by a mechanism operating with a number of similar tools and set in motion by a single motive pow-er, whatever the form of that power. Here we have the machine, but in its first role as a simple element in production by machinery.
>
> MARX, 1976, p. 497

Machinery performs the same operation as the worker formerly did with tools. It is the starting point of the Industrial Revolution, as it allows the capitalist to separate the tool from the worker and install it in the machine. Given this func-tion of machinery, it is given primacy over power supply and the mechanism that is used: it is set in motion "whatever the form of that power". Marx is here pointing to the primacy of social relations, as the power of the capitalist to separate the tool from the worker and the subsequent application of science for the improvement of machinery in search of profit, presumes that the work-er has been separated from the means of production.

On these terms, Marx was quite clear that the steam engine itself did not give rise to the Industrial Revolution. It was, "on the contrary, the invention of machines that made a revolution in the form of steam-engines necessary" (Marx, 1976, p. 497). While Marx asserted the pre-eminence of the machine as a point of departure, this did not prevent him from grasping the crucial en-abling role of fossil power in the development of large-scale capitalist industry. He noted that with the growing scale of machinery human sources of motive power were displaced and supplemented by "natural forces":

> Increase in the size of the machine, and in the number of its working tools, calls for a more massive mechanism to drive it; and this mechanism requires, in order to overcome its resistance, a mightier moving power than that of man, apart from the fact that man is a very imperfect instru-ment for producing uniform continued motion. But assuming that he is acting simply as a motor, that a machine has taken the place of his tool, it is evident that he can be replaced by natural forces.
>
> MARX, 1976, p. 497

The displacement of human labour power as a core force of production by natural forces started with a call for the application of animals (especially horses), water and wind. Marx noted that water power remained the principal motive source of energy well into the nineteenth century (dominating the initial stage of industrialization or "machinofacture"), before being replaced by the steam engine, which drew power from coal and water. As he suggested, the transition to coal allowed capital to separate industry from local and geographically embedded sources of power (water-wheels and biomass), and to concentrate industry in urban centres, as the material elements and means of production could effectively be shipped anywhere. Thus, Marx noted that the storability and transportability of coal was the principle advantage over water power for capital:

> Despite this, the use of water, as the main motive power brought with it various added difficulties. The flow of water could not be increased at will, it failed at certain seasons of the year, *and, above all, it was essentially local.* Not till the invention of Watt's second and so-called double-acting steam-engine, was a prime mover found which drew its own motive power from the consumption of coal and water, was entirely under man's control, was mobile and a means of locomotion, was urban and not – like the waterwheel – rural, permitted production to be concentrated in towns instead of – like the water-wheels – being scattered over the countryside, and finally, of universal technical application, and *little affected in its choice of residence by local circumstances.*
> MARX, 1976b, pp. 498–499, my emphasis

The shift to fossil powered large-scale machinery simultaneously led to the formation of a more complex division of labour, as skilled labour was expressed in machines and workplace design for maximum efficiency and manual labour was charged with machine minding. The process brings with it the conscious technical application of science to production. As machinery becomes a key instrument of labour, Marx suggested "it assumes a material mode of existence which necessitates the replacement of human force by natural forces and the replacement of the rule of thumb by the conscious application of natural science" (1976b, p. 508).

The result, moreover, was a dramatic reduction of worker power and control over the labour process, as capital was freed from its reliance on labour as a crucial *physical* force of production, which could be replaced by inanimate stored fossil energy (see Burkett and Foster, 2006). As Marx emphasized: "The steam engine was from the very first an antagonist of 'human power', an antagonist that enabled the capitalists to tread underfoot the growing demands of the workers, which threatened to drive the infant factory system into crisis" (1976, pp. 562–563).

Elsewhere Marx emphasized that energy is a key aspect of the means of production. Within the instruments category, he made a distinction between resources which form the "principal" substance of a product, from those that enter its formation as an "accessory", and allow for the conduct of work itself. As Marx wrote:

> An accessory may be consumed by the instruments of labour, as coal under a boiler, oil by a wheel, hay by draft horses, or it may be mixed with the raw material in order to produce some modification thereof, as chlorine into unbleached linen, coal with iron, dye stuff with wool, or again it may help to carry on the work itself, as in the case of the materials used for heating and lighting workshops.
>
> 1976, p. 181

Marx here distinguished between coal and other fuels as sources of energy, as opposed to materials that are transferred to the product itself in the course of the labour process.

6   Fossil Capitalism

These are foundational points for analyzing the role of fossil fuels as a key force of production. Indeed, a rich and bustling body of historical materialist scholarship under the rubric of "fossil capitalism" explores this role and the necessary role of extractive industries to that relationship (Altvater, 2007; Angus, 2016; Huber, 2009, 2013; Malm, 2016). Historically, it argues that the consolidation and diffusion of capitalist relations is closely bound up with the shift from energy "flows" (energy from rivers, the sun or wind) to mineralised energy "stock" (condensed inanimate energy contained in the crust of the earth).

For Elmar Altvater (2007), who is often credited with introducing the term fossil capitalism,[6] capital's attraction to fossil fuels is partially explained by the qualities of coal and oil themselves. Extending Marx, he argues that hydrocarbons fulfill the requirements of the capitalist process of accumulation in three ways: first, as fossil fuels become the key source of energy, the local availability

---

6   A similar term "carboniferous capitalism" was introduced by Lewis Mumford in *Technics and Civilization*, originally published in 1934 (Mumford, 2010).

of energy resources is no longer the main reason for the location of manufacturing and industries; instead energy resources can be transported anywhere in the world; second, in contrast to solar energy, fossil energy can be stored and then consumed without reference to natural time patterns (used 24hrs a day, 365 days per year); third, fossil energy allows for the speeding up of production by technical means and the annihilation of space by time. There is therefore a "tight fit" between the physical properties of fossil fuels and both the socio-economic logic and "spatiotemporality" of capitalist development.

Building from Altvater, Matthew Huber (2009) adds theoretical sophistication in accounting for the interplay between capitalist development and fossil fuels. Treating energy as a social relation, Huber avoids any semblance of "energy determinism" by arguing that fossilized production "hastened the *generalization* and *extension* of the wage labour relationship on a scale hitherto unseen" (2009, p. 110). Huber argues that while something like capitalist social forms pre-exist the Industrial Revolution, the development of a specifically capitalist mode of production involves not only the generalization of the wage, but requires large-scale industry. He explicitly argues that fossil fuels should be thought of as the core "productive force of production" or as "*internally powering* the forces and relations of capitalist production" (Huber, 2009, p. 108).

In his *Fossil Capital*, Andreas Malm (2016) contributes historical depth to this body of research. In a masterful rereading of the eclipse of water by steam power in the period 1825–1850, he argues that nineteenth-century mill owners switched from water power to coal power not because coal was cheaper, more reliable, or more abundant, as conventional views suggest. Instead, Malm argues that ultimately the transition to steam power offered capital the ability to discipline labour. The transition from energy flow to stock allowed for the relocation of production to settings with a high surplus population, enabling capital to seek out the most profitable pools of labour power and to level down wages. A crucial aspect of capital's mid-19th century response to labour militancy in this period was also to speed up and expand the use of machines, meaning that more and more fossil fuels are burned, an approach maintained throughout its history. For Malm, capital's response to labour insurgency, was therefore key in the emergence of fossil fuels as the "general lever for surplus value production" (2016, p. 353).

The shift towards coal in the early nineteenth century, not only transformed societies within Europe, but had far-reaching global consequences. As Bruce Podonik writes:

> This energy shift became intimately associated with a new process of conquest that forcibly incorporated new regions into an expanding

world-system. Coal powered ships and railroads allowed Britain and its continental rivals to seize control over territories in Asia, Africa, and the Middle East that had long resisted conquest.

> as cited in ANGUS, 2016, p. 130

Steam-powered gunboats were critical in shifting the balance of military power between Europe and Asian and African societies. Further, a key task of British naval expeditions was to locate and take control of coal deposits and establish coaling stations in order to fuel further colonial ventures (Angus, 2016).

While much of the literature is concerned with the emergence of fossilized modes of industrial production, the "making" of fossil capitalism of course did not end in the 19th century. Indeed, the symbiosis between capital and fossil fuels has only deepened subsequently. At the end of the 19th and into the 20th century, the transition to electric (rather than steam) powered production dramatically transformed the technical bases of the forces of production. Electrified industry enabled the transition from the heavy machinery of the coal age, to the Fordist mass production assembly lines (Smil, 2010).[7] Meanwhile, "automobilization", especially in the United States, before the First World War to 1929 exploded and transformed the carbon-extractive industry into a supplier of gasoline (Baran and Sweezy, 1966). In the decades following World War II, the production of synthetic substances – from plastics to fertilizer to napalm to pesticides – greatly accelerated our consumption of petroleum (Angus, 2016).

In *Lifeblood*, Huber (2013) extends this understanding and focuses on the sphere of reproduction more sharply, by analyzing how fossil energy has provided the ecological foundation for a "peculiarly privatized sociospatial existence" (p. xvi). He considers how beginning in the post-war period, oil has been fundamental to the growth of the "American way of life" for a specific stratum of workers, based on privatized social reproduction, single-family housing and automobility. The entire "electric-oil-auto complex" he argues, reconfigured the geographies of social reproduction for many workers, allowing for the postwar social construction of life as composed of "homes, cars, yards" (2013, p. xiv). In this material transformation of social and societal reproduction, he argues that the productive forces of capital (large-scale industry based on fossil fuels) have been extended "to the reproductive forces of everyday life" (2013, p. xv) or that there has been an "industrial revolution of the reproductive forces of everyday life" (2013, p. 16).

---

7 The electrification of industry also provides material conditions for an industrial transition to alternative forms of power, such as hydroelectric and solar (Smil, 2010).

As Altvater suggests (2007), the enhanced globalization of production and consumption that has accompanied the recent phase of neoliberal capitalism beginning in the 1970s, has only come about with the development of extremely energy-intensive systems of production and transport. Newly industrializing countries have added to the consumption of fossil fuels by already industrialized countries, with China and India now ranking as the second and third largest consumers of oil, respectively (International Energy Agency, 2018). While this industrialization produces commodities that serve domestic markets, as numerous authors demonstrate (Malm, 2012; Minx et al., 2011), in the case of both China and India much of this development has taken place through foreign direct investment by transnational corporations and has a strong export-orientation, such that most of the commodities produced in the host countries are exported.

The globalization of production includes the development of energy-intensive agro-exporting industries, which has given rise to a global livestock complex supplied by international chains of feedstuffs, alongside long-distance shipments of fruits, vegetables and seafood (McMichael, 2007). Thus, the "offshoring" of production from high income to low income countries (motivated by the search for cheap labour and nature), requires the establishment of new (carbon) infrastructure, and leads to more extended and dispersed supply chains, meaning that more oil will be burnt in trucks, trains and supertankers.

By the close of the 20th century the "tap" of easy to access, conventional fossil fuels had been depleted. While this raised concerns of "peak oil", the depletion of known reserves provoked the resort to unconventional fossil fuels – tar sands, fracked oil and gas and deep-water drilling (Pineault, 2018). The global growth of unconventional fossil fuels has led to the expansion of industry into countless new territories and requires vast new infrastructural complexes to support its development.

While capitalism existed before fossil fuels were introduced into the production process, since the 18th century the development of the productive forces based on capital has become heavily dependent on them. The fossil fuel regime is now embedded in virtually every productive and reproductive process within the system – not just to manufacturing industry, but to food production and distribution – and cannot be easily peeled away.

7   Matter and Energy Throughput

As we have seen, the development of fossil-powered machinery, along with the conscious application of science to production, leads to an unprecedented increase in the productivity of labour. Marx referred to profit making through asymmetry in such productivity advances as relative surplus value. In numerous passages he uses this to explain why individual capitalists are engaged in an unrelenting search for new technologies and constantly driven to introduce technical change. This extends to the competitive dynamics of an advanced market economy: under the "whip of competition", the firm that innovates gains an extra measure of profit over its competitors (better sales or lower unit costs), and one that fails to adopt newer and better methods will be driven out of business over time. Thus, the competitive position of capitalist society's industrial decision-makers compels them to increase the productivity of production processes. This perpetual tendency to redeploy the social surplus into technologies that increase the productivity of labour reveals capital's abiding drive and mission: "Accumulation for accumulation's sake. Production for production's sake" (Marx, 1976b, p. 742).

The rise in the productivity of labour means that modern industry generates an ever-greater mass of commodities, which requires an ever-larger quantity of inputs, whether of wood, iron, water or energy. As Marx suggested: "the increasing productivity of labour is expressed precisely in the proportion in which a greater quantity of raw materials absorbs a certain amount of labour, i.e. in the increasing mass of materials that is transformed into products, worked up into commodities, in an hour for example" (as cited in Foster and Burkett, 2016, p. 158). In addition to raw materials, Marx also reflected specifically on how rising productivity means an ever-greater consumption of energy sources: "after the capitalist has put a larger capital into machinery, he is compelled to spend a larger capital on the purchase of raw materials and the fuels required to drive the machines" (as cited in Foster and Burkett, 2016, p. 158).

Marx's analysis of rising matter and energy throughput under capitalism, which points to what is now often referred to in the environmental sociology literature as the "treadmill of production" (Gould et al., 2004; Schnaiberg, 1980), coloured his understanding of the relation between production and consumption, as he considered the latter to be mostly determined by the former. The goal of capital in the sphere of production is to produce more commodities containing surplus value. However, capitalists themselves, as Marx noted, do not want the commodities; instead, they aim to sell them. They must thereby enter the sphere of circulation, this time as sellers of commodities, to realize their potential profits. The capitalist producer, however, faces a barrier to such realization, based on the extent of the market. Just as capitalists seek ways to increase surplus value in the sphere of production (through productivity advances or driving down wages), they must also work to expand markets as the means of realizing capital, of selling commodities. The "sales effort", the production of new needs, is vital in this process (see Lebowitz, 2006).

Capital's problem in the sphere of circulation, in realizing the potential profits, is moreover, tied to its tendency towards the "overproduction" of capital. There is a recurring tendency, as Marx noted, for capital to expand productive capacity more than the existing market will justify. The propensity derives directly from capital's drive to increase the rate of exploitation and extract relative surplus value. The inclination towards overproduction correspondingly produces an immense drive towards the boundless pursuit of consumption goods. In effect, consumer demand becomes bloated because production does not have "consumption-values" as its controlling goal; that is, if the production process were oriented to the consumption of use-values rather than exchange-value, many fewer consumption goods (much less use-value) would be produced and consumed (Cohen, 2000). The capitalist, Marx therefore wrote, is "also a producer of overproduction, production for others. Over against this overproduction on one side must be placed overconsumption on the other, production for the sake of production must be confronted by consumption for the sake of consumption" (as cited in Lebowitz, 2006, p. 32).

Both rising matter and energy throughput and the problem of realizing capital drives Marx's analysis of infrastructural formation. We turn to this below, while emphasizing its ecological dimensions.

8   Spaces of Circulation and Fixed Capital

A key component of forces of production is what Marx considered fixed capital of a "large-scale and great durability". This category refers to a broad array of items such as ships, docks, canals, ports, dams, factory buildings, blast furnaces, pipelines, highways, electrical power transmission lines, power stations, railways and so on. Such infrastructures structure, process, mediate and enable the flow of resources appropriated from the rest of nature, while supporting social reproduction more broadly.

Marx's analyses of fixed capital are primarily found in *Capital Volume II* and *The Grundrisse*. He reflects on how early industrialists in England acquired much of their fixed capital by putting old infrastructures (mills, barns, transport systems) to new productive uses. Through appropriation, conversion and primitive accumulation, a vast reservoir of assets could be put to new productive uses. Yet if capital is going to produce on an extended scale, it must be able to carry out such projects on a capitalist basis (while it will continue to appeal to and seek to involve the state where possible).

While emphasizing the role of the credit system and other mechanisms as conditions enabling the development of fixed capital of "large-scale and great durability" (Marx, 1967, pp. 220–221), Marx pays close attention to the formation of physical infrastructures of transport, circulation, exchange and consumption, conceiving of them as instruments through which we are purposefully linked to the rest of nature. He analysed two interrelated dimensions surrounding their formation. The first aspect concerns fixed capital for processing "raw materials" and the movement of those materials from sites of extraction through to sites of production and manufacturing. As we saw, Marx remarked on the geographical separation of extraction from production in the case of coal, and reflected on the long-distance transport of fibre into the cities, for textiles and other manufacturing purposes. As stated in the *Grundrisse*, infrastructural networks enabling the transport of both raw materials and more finished commodities belong to capital's development of productive forces: "Whether I extract metals from mines, or take commodities to the site of their consumption, both movements are increasingly spatial. The growth of the means of transport falls into the category of the development of the productive forces generally" (1993b, p. 523).

Capital is driven to produce a massive growth in infrastructural networks in order for a mass of extracted raw materials to reach (often distant) points of production and manufacturing. This development goes hand in hand with increasing matter and energy throughput. Indeed, intensified and accelerated metabolic transformations of raw materials in commodity production, requires more extensive fixed capital networks to facilitate this an ever-larger quantity of inputs. In relation to agriculture, Ekers and Prudham nicely capture this dialectic of intensive and extensive processes that are internal to fixed capital formation:

> The adoption of *intensified* forms of agriculture requires inputs, including for instance, improved (and more recently genetically modified) seed, water for irrigation, energy, fertilizer and pesticide inputs, and so on. These flows in turn are supported by *extensive* socioecological geographies that might include massive watershed transformations and extensive networks of energy supply.
>
> 2017, p. 6, my emphasis

The second, closely related feature concerning capital's revolution in this dimension of productive forces concerns investment in infrastructure for commodity consumption and the so-called "production-consumption disconnect". Here the dynamic productivity of large-scale fossilized industry (its vast panoply of commodities) comes up against concrete physical and geographical barriers, which capital "cannot abide". While capital produces an immense collection of commodities, this in no way guarantees their sale; the realization of this productivity requires expanded markets for exchange, as well as the creation of extensive and long-term investments in the form of fixed, often immobile infrastructural networks that connect points of production to points of consumption.

As Marx asserted, "Economically considered, the spatial condition, the bringing of the product to the market, belongs to the production process itself. The product is really finished only when it is on the market...The reduction of the costs of this real circulation (in space) belongs to the development of the productive forces by capital" (Marx, 1993b, pp. 533–534). By reducing circulation costs individual firms increase profits and gain a competitive edge over other firms. In a well-known passage in the *Grundrisse*, this drive to overcome space by revolutionizing the means of transport is described as follows:

> Capital by its nature drives beyond every spatial barrier. Thus the creation of the physical conditions of exchange – of the means of communication and transport – the annihilation of space by time – becomes an extraordinary necessity for it.
>
> 1993b, p. 524

As Huber suggests (2009), prior to the emergence of fossil-powered large-scale industry, commodities were transported by horse-drawn vehicles, by waterways (rivers, lakes, sail boats) and by walking. However, the sheer magnitude of commodities produced by large-scale industry could not find markets through transportation systems based on these sources of power. Fossil powered production was therefore simultaneously hastened by the emergence of "fossilized" transportation and infrastructural networks, which radically reduced the amount of time required for transporting commodities and allowed for the geographical expansion of markets.

Malm, drawing on Henri Lefebvre's distinction between absolute and abstract space, further reflects on how fossil fuels have been vital to the construction of space "steeped in exchange-value"(2016, p. 300). "Absolute space", as he explains, is made up of components of nature located at sites chosen for their intrinsic qualities (such as caves, springs, rivers, mountain-tops, valleys). It involves building, dwelling and producing around the inherent properties of these sites, such as building a sanctuary around a well, or constructing an industrial watermill. However, these natural features and qualities are "smashed" by capitalism and replaced by the abstract space of accumulation. In "abstract space",

> Capital tears material components from their natural beds and heaps them up in places of its own choosing. Instead of going reverently to mountain tops and rivers and establishing businesses there, as some temples on holy ground, capital carries away what it needs and pours it out in places where the production of more exchange-value can best proceed.
>
> MALM, 2016, p. 301

Capital strives to emancipate itself from "natural space" (and its qualities) and produce space in its own image. Malm argues that only the stock of energy resources, with its key quality of abstractness (its storability and transportability), could have permitted this "breakout into spatial abstraction" (2016, p. 302). However, this results in a paradoxical situation: a great immobile strata of concentrated energy, along with techno-industrial complexes fixed to the ground are required to extract and process fossil energy.

Capital therefore "produces" and organizes space (Lefebvre, 1992) via infrastructures (often fossil powered), to try and annihilate space. The transformations to the physical landscape wrought by capital in its drive to overcome every spatial barrier and produce space in its own image are nothing short of staggering. While already staggering in Marx's time, today's continent-spanning "mega-corridors" (Hildyard, 2017) and the associated re-engineering of ecologies and geographies they entail, dwarf those he could have possibly imagined. While Marx glimpsed the beginnings of this process, particularly in the nineteenth-century development of railway networks, with fully-fledged globalization in the last decades of the 20th century, the geographies of raw material extraction, production and consumption, have been reconfigured to an unprecedented degree.[8]

So far we have considered how capital's efforts to increase the productivity of labour and nature produce (1) the transition to large-scale industry and machine-based production and with it the replacement of labour power with fossil fuels, as the key motive source of energy, and (2) the spatial conditions that allow for the circulation of an "immense collection of commodities", through

---

8   As Reynolds and Szerszynski (2012) point out, innovations that facilitate the global flows of matter and commodities, such as advances in shipping containerization, diesel engines and gas turbines that propel container ships and air traffic, are key components of capital's contemporary development of productive forces.

means of fossilized transportation and in fixed, heavy, secure, durable and often immobile physical infrastructures. Closely intertwined with and enabling these developments is the emergence of the modern corporation. The "socialization" of productive forces – their concentration and centralization in large firms, as well as their control and planning both within and across firms – provides a critical foundation and platform for their development based on capital. In the next section we outline this development.

9   Corporate Capitalism and the Concentration of Productive Forces

As intimated above, competition between different capitalists in the pursuit of increased profits and enlarged markets, leads capitalists to reinvest profits into the development of new machinery, technologies, and productive techniques. Those who cannot keep up with the application of the latest technology and technique produced at a higher cost are undercut by their competitors. In this manner, competition between different capitalists leads not only to intensive growth but also over time to a concentration and centralization of capital.

For Marx, capital concentrates in few hands, firstly through the process of compound growth, as in each round of accumulation the capitalist acquires an increasing mass of capital in the form of money power. While this is a slower and more gradual process, concentration also occurs through a process of centralization of capital. This is achieved as larger-scale capitalists gobble up smaller ones through ruthless competition (and via means such as takeovers and mergers). Competition between different capitalists leads to a concentration and centralization of capital in the form of large firms or the corporation. While corporations were not fully consolidated until the 20th century, Marx points to some of the earliest corporate forms, which emerged from growing accumulation and the need to have a structure that reflects that accumulation and its unending expansion. The corporation allows for the aggregation and socialization of key aspects of forces of production: it concentrates labour power, while appropriating, organizing and monopolizing science and technology. It also provides a structure for raising and pooling capital.

Marx reflected on the latter development in the third volume of *Capital,* through his notes on the emergence in the nineteenth century of the modern joint stock company (JSC). With the JSC and its accompanying form of shareholder ownership, barriers to raising capital for large-scale capital-intensive projects (such as infrastructures and machinery) were overcome by shares issued on the stock exchange. In the JSC, available money capital becomes less of a barrier to expansion, as firms gain access to a larger pool of capital and are no longer dependent on concentrations of individual property. With this aggregation of capital, there was also a growing need to separate ownership from management, since ownership took the form of shares and no share or group of shares carried the sole right to manage.[9]

The second major path to the concentration and centralization of capital occurs through credit and the credit system. As Marx noted, the source of money capital in the productive circuit may come in the form of a loan to a "productive capitalist". Marx referred to this form of money capital as "interest bearing capital", that is, money lent out for a price in the form of interest for which the lender relinquishes control of the sum lent. The process of financing constitutes a relationship between financial and industrial capitalists, with the former earning interest by lending to the latter. Credit therefore emerges from exchange relations between different "fractions" of capital.

Yet the supply of interest-bearing capital requires *recurrent* access to idle (hoarded) savings of all capitalists. In a developed credit system, financial institutions pool idle savings and turn them into concentrated money capital resources available to a few industrial producers (Marois, 2013). Credit therefore relieves individual capitalists of the burden of hoarding massive amounts of capital in advance of the purchase of fixed capital and converts the payment for that fixed capital into an annual one. This enables capital-intensive development and more aggressive accumulation, while leading to further centralization of capital. As Marx writes of the credit system:

> In its first stages, this system furtively creeps in as the humble assistant of accumulation, drawing into the hands of individual or associated capitalists by invisible threads the money resources, which lie scattered in larger or smaller amounts over the surface of society; but it soon becomes a new and terrible weapon in the battle of competition and is finally transformed into an enormous social mechanism for the centralization of capitals.
>
> MARX, 1976b, pp. 777–778

Possession and control over socialized means of production (and the social surpluses that ensue) and capital endow corporations with an enormous

---

9 As Marx intimated, the corporate form assumes the expansion of a managerial class that becomes relatively autonomous from the owners of capital. Conceptualized sociologically and in terms of power, this separation of management and ownership means that at the apex of the corporate hierarchy and endowed with final authority over the affairs of the corporation, is the board or directors. Thus, directorates are key *sites* of authority within corporate power structures, while individual directors are *agents* of corporate power (Carroll, 2010).

amount of power. Given huge concentrations of economic resources, workers, communities and states are "unilaterally dependent" on large corporations that may (or may not) choose to invest in a given time or place (Carroll, 2010). This power enables corporations to frame agendas, make decisions and secure compliance.

Several interlinked processes accompany this concentration and centralization of forces of production and capital. As Marx writes,

> Hand in hand with this centralization, or this expropriation of many capitalists by few, other developments take place on an ever-increasing scale, such as the growth of the co-operative form of the labour process, the conscious technical application of science, the planned exploitation of the soil, the transformation of the means of labour into forms in which they can only be used in common, the economising of all means of production by their use as the means of production of combined, socialized labour, the entanglement of all people in the net of the world market, and with this, the growth of the international character of the capitalist regime.
>
> 1976b, p. 929

Historically, capitalism concentrates previously scattered means of production into giant monopolistic firms and develops them to the point of establishing an interconnected capitalist world market. The expanded scale of production leads to the growth of the cooperative form of the labour process, the conscious technical application of science and the introduction of elements of planning and control, both in the plant and in the wider economy. I turn to these in more detail below.

10   Cooperation, Divisions of Labour, Planning

As suggested in Chapter 2, Marx consistently treated cooperation as one of the most basic productive forces. As Marx and Engels asserted in *The German Ideology*: "a certain mode of production or industrial stage is always combined with a certain mode of cooperation, or social stage, and this mode of cooperation is itself a "productive force"" (1976, p. 76). Further along in the same work, they state that the "social power" which arises through the "cooperation of different individuals as it is determined by the division of labour" is a productive force (1976, p. 77). This understanding is carried through the *Grundrisse* where Marx speaks of the "productive force arising from social combination" (1993b,

p. 700) and where he also refers to how the "association of the workers – cooperation and division of labour" is a "unification of their forces" and an "increase in their productive force" (1993b, p. 585).

In *Capital* Marx analyzed how socially combined production in the form of large-scale firms brought together and augmented previously scattered means of production, skills, techniques and knowledge. In the process, wealth-creating powers of fragmented workers become developed as collective social powers in a way that was not possible with production organized around personal, family or only local ties. In the chapters from "Cooperation" through "Machinery and Large-Scale Industry" he reflected also on the enhanced and growing scale and increasingly complex forms of cooperation found not only within the workplace or firm, but also beginning to extend beyond it, through wider divisions of labour. Machine technology for example, presupposes complex levels of cooperation between firms, as well as between knowledge workers or scientists and between firms and states. Similarly, the infrastructures and communication networks that support globalizing production networks both enable and pre-suppose an increasingly complex, variegated and universal form of cooperation. Reflecting on these developments Marx wrote, "not only have we an increase in the productive power of an individual, by means of cooperation, but the creation of a new power, namely the collective power of the masses" (1976b, p. 443).

Marx's reflections on the "mode of cooperation" created by capitalism are complex. In general, he was laudatory towards the complex networks of human production created by capitalism. He continually stressed the *potentiality* of cooperation and socialized labour, in contrast to the alienated and often negative form it takes under capitalism. Despite his often-scathing reflections on capitalist work relations, Marx saw capitalism enabling and potentiating ever larger, more varied and cosmopolitan communities of cooperation. Based on both the centralization of capital in large-scale firms and capital's need expressed in the *Manifesto* to "nestle everywhere, establish connections everywhere"(Marx and Engels, 2004, p. 65), capital provided a foundation for more universal-communal people-nature relations and for networks collaboration and mutual aid. Cooperation and well-organized divisions of labour are from this perspective, considered as positive human capacities that add to our collective powers.

Marx therefore recognized that cooperation within the firm, as he described, took place under the despotism of capitalists who organized and directed a supervisory authority. Broader networks of socialized production also fragment the working class into distinctive hierarchical groupings (especially along gendered and racialized lines), materializing imperialist economic interdependencies. However, what drives Marx's analysis is his insistence again and again in *Capital* that the productive force of cooperation is a common property belonging to the "associated producers" and that capital is merely appropriating it, distorting it and putting it to its own particular advantage. He maintained that, "the special productive power of the combined working day, is under all circumstances, the social power of labour, or the productive power of social labour. This power arises from cooperation itself" (Marx, 1976b, p. 447). It is, however, seized upon by capital through real subsumption and developed for its capacity to augment the productivity of labour in search of relative surplus value. He wrote:

> The socially productive power of labour develops as a free gift to capital whenever the workers are placed under certain conditions, and it is capital which places them under these conditions. Because this power costs capital nothing, while on the other hand it is not developed by the worker until his labour belongs to capital, it *appears* as a power which capital possessed by its nature – a power inherent in capital.
>
> MARX, 1976b, p. 451, my emphasis

Capital appropriates, "mystifies" and turns into a private power the fruits of a vast and collaborative process of socialized labour.

Moreover, he argued that while capitalists love planned organization of production in the factory, they continually resist conscious social planning of production in wider society (Harvey, 2010). There is a deep contradiction, in Marx's view, between socialized production and private appropriation, leading him to suggest that under socialism society-wide planning would eliminate capitalist "anarchy of production", ensuring a more rational allocation of economic resources, eliminating economic crises and developing productive forces to augment the material well-being of everyone.

11   Knowledge and Science as a Force in the Production Process

I have argued at various points that knowledge and science are part of the forces of production. Marx suggested that historically, while capitalism does not invent science, the system is unique in so far as it "is the capitalist mode of production which first [systematically and routinely] puts natural sciences to the service of the direct production process" (1992, p. 32). In its productive application, he suggested that scientific knowledge is appropriated by capital as a "free gift". This is the case in so far as knowledge and its conceptual and methodological underpinnings are typically not the products of wage labour: "Apart from the natural substances, it is possible to incorporate in the productive process natural forces, which do not cost anything, to act as agents with more or less heightened effect. The degree of their effectiveness depends on methods and scientific developments which cost the capitalist nothing" (as cited in Burkett, 2014, p. 71).

While its is privately appropriated by capital, Marx understood scientific knowledge to be a collective capacity, an accumulated effect of networks of social cooperation. Bob Jessop, echoing Marx, asserts: "knowledge is a collectively generated resource and, even where specific forms and types of intellectual property are produced in capitalist conditions for profit, this depends on a far wider intellectual commons" (2002b, p. 129). Thus, even where scientific research is made central to the process of technological change in the economy, it is not totally subsumed under the commodity form. However, under capitalism, the collective nature of the productive force of knowledge, is mystified: "The accumulation of knowledge and of skill, the general productive forces of the social brain, is thus absorbed into capital, as opposed to labour, and hence *appears* as an attribute of capital" (Marx, 1993b, p. 694, my emphasis).

While science is relatively autonomous from capital and is not totally subsumed to the dictates of the accumulation process, Marx saw capitalism propelling and profoundly shaping its development. As with other aspects of forces of production, the growth of science occurs in part by socially separating knowledge from the control of the direct producers. After being separated from the producer vis-à-vis proletarianization and placed in the hands of management (as analyzed in detail by Braverman), the application of science to the production process takes numerous forms. The creation of the physical hardware for production, exchange and communication itself requires scientific knowledge. Marx also emphasized the importance of science for pressing "natural agencies" (such as coal and water) into the service of capital. This function of science is vital in capital's effort to increase the productivity of labour: "Large scale industry raises the productivity of labour to an extraordinary degree by incorporating into the production process both the immense forces of nature, and the results arrived at by natural sciences" (Marx, 1976b, p. 509).

The heightened productivity that capital achieves (which "frees" social labour-time for new productive uses), combined with its need to expand constantly the circle of production and consumption, leads to the development of new branches of production, based on discovering, appropriating and developing the objects and forces in the rest of nature:

Hence exploration of all of nature in order to discover new, useful qualities in things; universal exchange of the products of all alien climates
and lands; new (artificial) preparation of natural objects, by which they
are given new use-values. The exploration of the earth in all directions,
to discover new things of use as well as new useful qualities of the old;
such as new qualities of them as raw materials etc.; the development,
hence, of the natural sciences to their highest point; likewise the discovery, creation and satisfaction of new needs arising from society
itself.

MARX, 1993b, p. 409

Capital works ceaselessly to discover, develop and subject to itself all aspects of
nature that are conducive to accumulation. This process can be described as
the "subsumption of nature by capital" (Boyd et al., 2001; Burkett, 2014). Burkett
(2014, pp. 64–68) follows Marx in connecting the real subsumption of labour to
the subsumption of nature; as he suggests, Marx's views surrounding the "new
(artificial) preparation of natural objects" and the "subjugation of the forces of
nature" (1993b, p. 700) on a large-scale coincide with or parallel the techno-
scientific and managerial transformation of the labour process. As we have
seen, fossil capital theorists similarly focus on the harnessing of "buried sunshine" as internal to the transition to industrial capitalism, based on the real
subsumption of labour to capital.

While they do not directly connect the issue to the real subsumption of labour, Boyd et al. (2001) analyze "nature-based industries" – those that confront
the rest of nature directly in the process of commodity production, such as
industries based on raw material extraction, as well as those based on
cultivation – through the lens of the subsumption of nature to capital. Additionally, they introduce a distinction between the formal and real subsumption of nature. In the formal subsumption of nature, which applies mainly to
extractive industries, there is an appropriation and technological development
of "objects" in nature, but for the most part, the natural processes upon which
they are based remain unchanged. The oil and gas sector, for example, can enhance drilling and recovery techniques, as well as develop new uses for hydrocarbons, but firms cannot increase the absolute quantity of oil or gas. The real
subsumption of nature, by contrast, applies mainly to "biologically-based" industries that depend upon "cultivation", and wherein there are manipulations
or intensifications of biological processes. As witnessed in cultivation-based
industries such as aquaculture, forestry, and agriculture, real subsumption entails efforts to target and enhance the productivity of biophysical process,
through means such as selective breeding and genetic modification (Boyd et

al., 2001; Boyd and Prudham, 2017). Large fields of applied science are devoted to such processes (Boyd, 2001; Prudham, 2003).[10]

As suggested above, Marx's gestures towards the subsumption of nature emphasized the subordination of new scientific understandings into the dynamics of capitalism. While this encourages the growth of science to an unprecedented degree, Marx pointed to its less progressive aspects. Like Braverman, he recognized that the unification of science within the production process entailed the progressive alienation of the process of production from the worker, including the separation of the intellectual potentialities of the process from the individual labourer, which became concentrated in the hands of management.[11]

---

10   The real subsumption of nature framework can also potentially be extended beyond its original context to consider attempts to mitigate environmental problems and degradation. Geo-engineering processes, for example, aim to consciously change and re-work atmospheric conditions, evoking the logic of real subsumption at the planetary level (Carton et al., 2017). While these are productive lines of inquiry, Boyd and Prudham (2017) point out that their framework of formal versus real subsumption of nature was not intended as the basis of any broad theory of socio-ecological transformation. It has been taken in this direction by scholars who strongly emphasize the real subsumption of nature as an ever-deepening process. Thus, Neil Smith suggests that in the 21st century, capitalism's real subsumption of nature goes "all the way down" (2007, p. 29). This position tends towards seeing nature as completely internalized by society and appears to leave little space for considering how non-human nature has its own dynamic, turbulent and contingent processes, which are outside of human production (Foster and Clark, 2016).

11   Marx again glimmered possibilities on the side of labour, stemming from capital's use of divisions of labour. Marx wrote: "Large Scale industry, through its very catastrophes" means that "the partially developed individual who is the bearer of one specialized function, must be replaced by the totally developed individual, for whom the different social functions are different modes of activity he takes up in turn" (Marx, 1976b, p. 618). Marx thereby suggested that the mass of workers may be paradoxically freed from being the possessors of a narrow specialization that previously characterized craft production and instead may increasingly be able to perform a variety of social tasks, as perpetual innovation and development demands the prevalence of "all around skill" and flexibility in adapting to differing modes of activity. Elsewhere, Marx argued that public education arose (and continues to adapt in part) out of the need to produce the literate, flexible and well trained labour force required for constantly changing conditions of production, and he was an enthusiast for the potential future development of an education that would emphasize the multifaceted potentiality of human beings and schools that would provide basic training in a variety of technical, agricultural and vocational matters, as opposed to specialized and private teachings, often required for past forms of production. For Marx, the goal of finding a form of production that would allow for the cultivation and realization of all the qualities of the human social being, was continually thwarted by the social relations and class power that configure our forms of labour and that employ people to perform narrow, monotonous and repetitive tasks.

As Burkett shows (2014, pp. 158–161), Marx also saw capital placing an "anti-ecological" character on the development of science, which is rooted in capital's treatment of nature as a vehicle for the production of saleable use-values. This delimited both the development and application of ecological knowledge to production in several important ways. As he suggests, the concern among competing capitalists for immediate useful effects and commercial purposes of new discoveries promotes a narrow emphasis on monopolizable knowledge, or knowledge that can earn rents (Marx, 1993b). This inhibits the development of science generally, but leads particularly to the *underdevelopment* and *under prioritization* of ecological insights that are needed for a sustainable co-evolution of society and the rest of nature (Burkett, 2014).

At the same time, as we have seen, Marx recognized that based on its increasingly intensive appropriation of nature and environmental dysfunctions, capitalism cannot help producing new and also more universal forms of ecological consciousness, knowledge and science. With Engels, he showed enthusiasm for emerging forms of ecological understanding, which took account of the ecological interdependencies between different locations and of the unintended consequences of our metabolic interaction with nature. As Engels wrote: "...with every day that passes we are learning to understand these laws [of nature] more correctly, and getting to know both the more immediate and the more remote consequences of our interference with the traditional course of nature" (as cited in Burkett, 2014, p. 162).

In *Capital Volume III*, Marx expressed enthusiasm for the development of soil chemistry that was required to manage the environmental impacts of capitalist agricultural techniques. This produced the "material conditions for a new and higher synthesis" between agriculture and industry (Marx, 1993a, p. 673). He argued that transformation of agriculture into a "conscious application of agronomy" was "one of the great results of the capitalist mode of production" (1993a, p. 754).

12   Socialization, Cadre, and Knowledge Workers

Key strategic implications of the socialization of productive forces are elucidated by Kees Van der Pijl (1998, 2004). While Marx largely neglected them, Van der Pijl notes that paralleling the expropriation of skills and knowledge from worker is the rise of a techno-scientific and managerial "cadre". For Van der Pijl, the cadre class (managers, engineers, and various of knowledge workers) represents a middle stratum of workers between capital and labour. This group emerges with changes to the labour process, reflecting the increased incorporation of science within production and the need to organize produc-tion within large-scale factories. Indeed, to the extent that corporations have "internalized" science and technology, scientific-technocratic workers, while subordinate to capitalists themselves, often hold prominent positions within corporations and provide expertise that is vital to corporate business.

Cadres are often employed by large-scale corporations and entrusted with conception and direction in production. Moreover, as Van der Pijl argues, the expanded scale of production requires organization in combining different ac-tivities, planning the availability of goods and control of the production pro-cess not only in the firm, but across wider society. Thus, cadre are employed by the state and quasi-state bodies and engage in limited forms of planned coop-eration, use of science, collective use of means of production, across the social. Meanwhile, business journalists, academics and other professionals, which Gramsci (1971) referred to as organic intellectuals, occupy important positions in civil society that align them closely with the needs and interests of corpo-rate capital.

Importantly, Van der Pijl argues that capital pays a major price as it increas-es the number of functionaries and intermediaries that are required for pro-duction and reproduction. The ruling class, he writes, "cedes aspects of its rule to the cadre stratum with every advance in the complexity of production and social organization generally" (1998, p. 139). The result is a major fault line in capitalist re-production, as Van der Pijl portrays the managerial-technical cad-re as fluid in perspective and potentially open to left initiatives (2004).

While Van der Pijl considers cadre broadly, earlier left thinkers, such as Thorstein Veblen (2012) and later John Galbraith (2007), had put a great deal of emphasis on scientists and engineers developing anti-capitalist orientations and interests as science became more integral to capital accumulation. Veblen pointed out that scientists and engineers were thrust into key new positions within corporations, as experts in the technology they were employing, and were integral to functioning of industrial capitalism more broadly. However, he argued that knowledge workers and experts were guided by different impera-tives than those of businessmen and business organization. The latter were driven by "pecuniary values" – driven to increase the value of their monetary capital. This often ran against the vision and aim of various knowledge workers and experts, who were driven towards the "effective use and development of technology" (understood by Veblen, mostly in terms of a drive to increase in efficiency).

Both Veblen and Galbraith's believed that scientists in various positions across the industrial system would be a key group to move society towards so-cialism. While their commitment to this group as key agents of change appears overstated, like Van der Pijl, they pointed to a major strategic fault line in capitalist re-production, and to the possibility of scientists and knowledge workers developing (and being "won over" to) anti-capitalist orientations.

13   Marx and Metabolic Rift

So far this chapter has advanced a broad and ecologically grounded concept of the productive forces. I have considered how the basis for such an interpretation is found in Marx's own work and implied in more contemporary eco-Marxist scholarship. This provides a foundation for analyzing how capital's appropriation of the forces of production produces epochal developments in them, torqueing them in a quantitative direction bound up with the compulsion to increase labour productivity and output. While analyzing such development is vital to understanding capitalism as an "ecological regime"(Moore, 2011) up to this point in the chapter I have scarcely remarked on the negative ecological consequences of this distinctive social metabolism.

While Marx expressed optimism surrounding certain aspects of the growth of productive forces based on capital, he also recognized the ecological destructiveness of this development. Indeed, Marx developed a materialist critique of industrial capitalism and of agriculture in particular, employing the concept of a metabolic rift to understand how capitalist operations were undermining the regenerative capacities of ecosystems, particularly the soil nutrient cycle. As Foster (2000, 2010) shows, Marx's analysis of metabolic rifts was strongly influenced by the work of 19th century natural scientists, in particular by the German chemist Justus von Liebig. The latter had discovered that natural systems, like the nutrient cycle, have their own metabolism which operates independently from the social and allows for longevity and re-generation.[12] While the interchange between human beings and the rest of nature can be ecologically sound and sustainable, it can also be disrupted and generate distinct rifts or ruptures in natural cycles and processes.

---

12   As Magdoff (2011) explains, metabolism refers to the work done inside an organism or a cell as it goes about its normal operations. It involves the building up of new organic chemicals and the breaking down of others, the recovering of energy from some compounds, and the use of energy to do the work. However, a critical part of the metabolism of a cell or large organism is constituted by the exchange of materials with its environment and with other organisms: obtaining energy-rich organic molecules and individual elements necessary to make all the stuff of life, including oxygen, carbon dioxide, nutrients (such as nitrogen, phosphorus, potassium, and calcium), and water.

Marx's understanding of how industrial capitalism created an ecological rift in the soil nutrient cycle is expressed most powerfully in the last section of Chapter 15 of *Capital Volume I*. Marx wrote there that industrialized capitalist agriculture "disrupts the metabolic interaction between man and the earth, i.e., it prevents the return to the soil of its constituent elements consumed by man in the form of food and clothing; hence it hinders the operation of the eternal natural condition for the lasting fertility of the soil" (Marx, 1976b, p. 637).

Marx subsequently refers to capitalist production as a "robbery system", taking from human labourers more than it returns in wages, *and* taking from non-human nature more than it replenishes in usable energy and biological life:

> All progress in capitalist agriculture is a progress in the art, not only of robbing the worker, but of robbing the soil; all progress in increasing the fertility of the soil for a given time is the progress towards ruining the more long-lasting sources of that fertility. ... Capitalist production, therefore, only develops the techniques and the degree of combination of the social process of production by simultaneously undermining the sources of all wealth – the soil and the worker.
>
> MARX, 1976b, p. 638

The problem is exacerbated and becomes "irreparable" due to long-distance trade. Capitalist production "collects the population together in great urban centres" (Marx, 1976b, p. 637), producing an antagonistic separation of town and country, through which minerals and nutrients in food, fibres and agro-industrial raw material were transported long distances to cities, while the waste resources and animal waste were not returned to the soil. While Marx primarily analyzed the dynamics of soil exhaustion within nations, he became increasingly aware of how capital's disturbance of the social and natural metabolism is extended globally through international trade (Saito, 2017, pp. 202–212). In a manuscript prepared for *Capital Volume III* Marx wrote:

> Large-scale ownership, on the other hand, reduces the agricultural population to a constantly decreasing minimum and confronts it with a constantly growing industrial population conglomerated together in large towns; in this way it produces conditions that provoke an irreparable rift in the interdependent process between social metabolism and natural metabolism prescribed by the natural laws of the soil. The result is a squandering of the soil and *trade carries this devastation far beyond the bounds of a single country* (Liebig).
>
> as cited in SAITO, 2017, pp. 205–206

Ecological problems, including the desertification of soils, manifest (and often mostly sharply) at the periphery of capitalism, which are transformed into sources of ever-growing exports of agriculture and raw materials to the capitalist centre. In *Capital Volume I* Marx also remarked of this process of "ecological imperialism" in relation to Ireland, writing that "It must not be forgotten that for a century and a half England has indirectly exported the soil of Ireland, without even allowing its cultivators the means for replacing the constituents of the exhausted soil" (Marx, 1976b, p. 860).

The depletion of the soil was in no way undone by the development of scientific agricultural techniques, and Marx recognized that soil sciences were incapable of being developed and applied in a manner than would ensure the longevity of the natural basis of life, subservient as those techniques were to the capitalist development and the prerogatives of capital accumulation. The application of agronomy to agriculture occurred only narrowly and "in so far as this is at all possible within the conditions of private property" (Marx, 1993a, p. 754). He subsequently concluded that "the entire spirit of capitalist production, which is oriented towards the most immediate monetary profit – stands in contradiction to agriculture, which has to concern itself with the whole gamut of permanent conditions of life required by the chain of human generations" (Marx, 1993a, p. 754).

Marx's theory of rift was not merely an incidental observation or limited to the sphere of agriculture, but rather a logical extension of his analysis of the outward expansion of capitalist industry up to that point. It was used to analyze the problems in capitalist production of accelerated tempo, scale of production and spatial disjuncture (especially the antagonistic separation of town and country). By the time of *Capital,* Marx clearly regarded the rehabilitation of the metabolism between humanity and nature as a central project of socialism. The productive forces, given their entanglement in capitalism's (ecological) contradictions, would need to be significantly and conscious transformed (and not simply accelerated) to achieve this.

14   Treadmill of Production and the Carbon Rift

While Marx was primarily on soil erosion, a chief concern of environmental degradation in his time, he extended the analysis of metabolic rifts to issues such as deforestation and livestock farming (Saito, 2017, pp. 217–255). Researchers have subsequently extended Marx's model of the metabolic rift to understand the interruption of the cycling of material elements that support various ecosystems, including ocean metabolisms, hydrological cycles, and up to the "level" of the biosphere in general, and the carbon cycle in particular. Focus on the latter seeks to understand how capitalism has created an expanded rift in the carbon cycle, which leads to global climate change (see especially, Clark and York, 2005; Foster et al., 2011a).

The carbon cycle describes the movement of carbon as it is recycled and reused throughout the biosphere. It involves a constant interchange of carbon dioxide (CO_2) between the land, atmosphere, and ocean. This cycle keeps the earth from becoming too hot or too cold. Over millions of years geological processes buried plant matter in the earth and turned their content in fossil fuels. For most of human history, the deposits were left untouched, locked out from the active carbon cycle. The current rise in temperature on Earth follows from the increasing concentration of CO_2, which had disrupted the carbon cycle. This disruption in turn is a function of cumulative carbon emissions that have been released back into the atmosphere, following the commencement of large-scale consumption of those fuels in the late 18th and early 19th century.

While Marx himself did not (and could not) have fully registered the ecological implications of the transition to fossil-powered industry (specifically the "by-product" of rising carbon emissions), his analysis of rising matter and energy throughput under capitalism is foundational for this understanding. As Malm (2016) asserts, in a competitive market, the compulsion to accumulate capital (particularly to speed up machines through high-pressure steam and thereby extract relative surplus value) is translated to "grow by burning or die" (p. 353). As a result, the correlation between capitalist industrial growth and increasing emissions since the 1800s has been so close that it amounts to a general law: "where capital goes, *emissions will immediately follow*" (2016, p. 353). While this is true at a general level, successive historical periods of capitalism have deepened the fossil economy, advancing and solidifying the developments Marx had observed, while accelerating the disruption of the carbon cycle. Indeed, the post-war period of "organized capitalism" which consolidated the developments of an earlier period of monopoly capitalism, including the rise of large corporations and accompanying transformations in the relation between science and industry, greatly expanded the consumption of fossil fuels through the production of vast petrochemical and oil-auto complexes and new forms of privatized suburban consumerism (Angus, 2016; Huber, 2013). Neoliberal globalization has also deepened fossil capitalism, through the expansion and relocation of industry to countries with low-wages, while greatly expanding long-distance (fossil powered) trade. Scientific studies of atmospheric concentrations of CO_2 have registered the associated acceleration of CO_2 emissions both in the post-war era, especially beginning in 1950 (Ribes et al., 2017) and in the closing decades of the 20th century, particularly in early

2000s (Anderson and Bows, 2008). Meanwhile the exhaustion of conventional fossil fuels has recently provoked resort to "extreme oil" – tar sands, fracked oil and gas, deep-water drilling – carrying yet greater emissions and ecological risk (Pineault, 2018).

With the expansion of fossil powered and compounding economic growth, the rift in the Earth's carbon metabolism has steadily widened and has now spun out of control. While the metabolic processes and problems that Marx and Engels knew of were local and regional, the carbon rift is truly planetary in nature.

15   Decarbonization and De-growth

Mending the climate rift will require yet more profound transformations in the productive forces. In some instances this may include a retreat in their development, in others it implies the growth of alternative green forces of production. Deep decarbonization and simultaneous renewable energy transition is an urgent priority. As Daniel Tanuro (2014) and David Schwartzman (2012, 2016) assert, the construction of an industrial energy systems based on cleaner and renewable fuels is part of development of the production forces. While a rapid shift from fossil fuels is an urgent necessity within the next two decades,[13] to date its development has been slow and there is little evidence that current growth in renewable energy is displacing the consumption of fossil fuels (York, 2012; York and McGee, 2017).

Increasing environmental efficiencies – shrinking the carbon and environmental footprint of exiting productive processes – are also advancements in the productive forces and have an important role to play in mending the carbon rift. As Marx recognized, investments in productivity gains do include improved environmental efficiency (individual firms in a competitive system work to reduce the costs of waste and inefficient use of materials). Efficiency, moreover, extends to carbon emissions: more efficient use of resources leads to lower emissions intensity per unit of production. However, as critics of ecological modernization approaches suggest, this does not reverse the rising *absolute* flow and consumption of materials and energy and the accompanying rise in *total* volumes of emissions, which more than offset intensity gains. Indeed, re-

---

13   Estimating our current "carbon budget", Oil Change International finds that between 68 and 85 percent of extractable fossil fuel reserves must remain in the ground if we are to have a realistic chance of limiting global warming to 1.5 to 2 degrees Celsius (Muttitt, 2016).

search on the "Jevon's paradox" shows that decline in carbon intensity in developed nations has been accompanied by a rise in total emissions (Foster et al., 2011a, pp. 169–181; Lohmann, 2013, pp. 32–36). This is because in industrial capitalist societies, efficiency makes more funds available not only for consumption but also for new rounds of capital investment, leading to an expansion of the overall scale of production. The Jevon's paradox points therefore to a fettering of the ecological potential or use-value of advancing eco-efficiencies, within a system devoted to endless compounding economic growth.

While energy transition and enhanced environmental efficiency are central components of green transformation, such measures will not be enough to mend the climate rift. What Enerst Mandel had glimpsed by reference to "overdevelopment" has become increasingly clear: capitalism, particularly in the Global North, has gone too far in the way it develops quantitative dimensions of productive forces. In the circumstances, the socialist alternative no longer implies growth in the processing of natural resources and the production of things requiring matter and energy throughput, but instead implies a retreat in this aspect of their development. Along with the construction of a new energy system, highly polluting industries and entire branches of production beyond the fossil fuel sector, will likely need to be shut down.

Today's global and highly dispersed supply chains also produce a huge font of emissions. While Marx often shows enthusiasm for the potentiality of enhanced forms of human cooperation enabled by globalizing productive networks and associated infrastructures, already in the 19th century he recognized that production chains were overstretched and wasting resources. Although not explicit in *Capital*, contemporary calls for partial de-globalization, including the shortening of commodity chains, the re-municipalization of infrastructure, the re-localization of much production and food sovereignty, yet without entirely abandoning the global, are necessary and quite compatible with Marx's critique of capitalism (Candeias, 2013b; N. Klein, 2011; Tanuro, 2012).

16   The Growth of Ecology and Cooperation

Marx considered ecological knowledge and cooperation to be positive productive powers. These are collective capacities, common properties that can be mobilized in the service of (re)making the world. With Engels he showed enthusiasm for emerging forms of ecological understanding that took account of the ecological interdependencies and of the unintended consequences of our metabolic interaction with nature. In his late notebooks, reflecting on crises of capitalism, Marx wrote:

Today it finds that system, both in Western Europe and the United States, in conflict with the working masses, with science, and with the very productive forces it generates – in short in a crisis that will end in its own elimination, through the return of modern societies to a higher form of an 'archaic' type of collective ownership and production.

as cited in SAITO, 2017, p. 265

The crisis of capital emerges out of a conflict with the working class masses who are driven to exhaustion and also through a "conflict" with science. There a contradiction between science and capital in so far as the latter demonstrates the metabolic rifts generated by capitalist development, and points to the need to realize an alternative sustainable form of production.

While the science of ecology and the knowledge of the unintended consequences of our actions was relatively limited in Marx's time, such understandings have since developed and deepened. By virtue of the sheer scale, complexity, scope, and consequences of contemporary socio-ecological transformations, ecologists and climate scientists have learned more about how ecosystems, including the global climate system function and the pressures that our actions exert on them. Ecology is itself an important historical development, emerging as it does within the explosive development of capitalism and its global impact. It aims at a dialectical unification of social and natural phenomena and breaks down dualistic understandings by explaining the complex interdependencies of organisms in the environment and bringing forth knowledge concerning the protection and well-being of humans and other species (see Foster et al., 2011b, pp. 289–343).

Contemporary eco-Marxist analyses such as those of Foster, Burkett and Ian Angus, show a clear enthusiasm for the development of ecological science and ecological thinking, seen as representing a movement towards more relational, complex, historical, and materialist forms of analyses. As these thinkers have asserted, various branches of earth science producing high-quality, complex descriptions and understandings of ecological problems such as anthropogenic climate change should be one of the key sources of information contributing to the eventual resolution of environmental degradation under socialistic conditions. This knowledge is not in opposition to the productive forces, but a part of them.

Marx, as discussed above, pointed to a deep contradiction between socialized production and private appropriation. This led him to suggest that under socialism, society-wide planning would eliminate capitalist "anarchy of production" ensuring a more rational allocation of economic resources, eliminating economic crises and developing productive forces to augment the material well-being of everyone. How we think of cooperation and divisions of labour is of vital importance in addressing large-scale planetary problems, such as climate change. Capitalism's increasingly large-scale and intensive system of biospheric appropriation generates problems that are collective in nature and global in scope. Planning is required to augment material well-being in the sense of satisfying basic consumptive needs, while managing the human metabolism with nature in a rational and sustainable way. While capitalism develops limited (predominantly market-based) forms of eco-regulation and a modicum of planning and coordination of divisions of productive labour across society, these are highly limited. The ability across the system to "plan for tomorrow", to learn from past experience, is highly circumscribed.

In the current context, this could suggest that a 21st century socialist alternative would develop new forms of (planetary) productive associations and enhanced modes of cooperation (new productive forces). It could also develop new institutions and means for coordinating and planning those associations (new relations of production), in terms not only of "resource management", but also in the regulation, management and mitigation of global eco-metabolic problems. The re-affirmation of collective design and conscious planning (in a way that is non-homogenizing and avoids the disastrous legacy of the command state in favour of more democratic and participatory processes) has been a theme in contemporary eco-Marxist theorizing. David Harvey (2000) has interestingly set his arguments in the context of 'species being' capacities and powers raised by the young Marx. Against the romanticism of spontaneous rhizomatic connections, he highlights the role of collective deliberation and foresight in projects of social emancipation. The view is nicely anchored in Marx, who in one of his few references to species being in *Capital* wrote: "When the worker co-operates in a planned way with others, he strips off the fetters of his individuality, and develops the capabilities of his species" (Marx, 1976b, p. 447).

17   Conclusion

In contrast to narrow interpretations of the concept of forces of production that reduce them to technological hardware, Marx's concept was much more ecologically embedded. It can be taken to refer to the dimension of human existence through which we are purposefully linked to the rest of nature. This broad usage provided him with a means of examining how capital's appropriation and development of such forces torques them in a quantitative direction and activates epochal transformations and developments in them. From this vantage, he did not blindly endorse the "total development" of the productive forces, as critics (and some supporters) aver. Instead, he considered how such development took place at the expense of disrupting the sustainable metabolic interaction between humans and the rest of nature, eroding the material conditions for sustainable and friendly human life. His work provides a vital foundation for understanding how under capitalism, forces of production substantially take the commodity form and are embroiled within its (ecological) contradictions. At the same time the potentials Marx gleaned in the productive forces included qualitative capacities, which allow us to appropriate aspects of non-human nature in ways that preserve and enhance rather than degrade ecosystem health. The growth of cooperation and ecological knowledge are part of the material conditions that can help enable a sustainable and rational regulation of the social metabolism in our times.

CHAPTER 4

Ecological Marxism(s) and the Productive Forces

This chapter puts an ecological re-conceptualization of forces of production in dialogue with contemporary eco-Marxist frameworks, beyond those previously discussed. I begin with the quasi-Marxist variant of the de-growth perspective advanced by Serge Latouche, as well as contemporary frameworks offered by James O'Connor and Jason Moore. A full review of their works is beyond the chapter's scope. Instead, I point to differences (sometimes implicit) surrounding the concept of productive forces and consider how this informs our understanding and approach to the current climate crisis. Engaging them helps to distinguish and sharpen the vantage point offered here.

1   Latouche and Radical De-growth

Serge Latouche is one of the leading figures of today's de-growth perspective. His *Farewell to Growth* (2010) articulates a radical version of the de-growth perspective, while positioning this against strains of contemporary thought, including that of "productivist socialism". Latouche argues that Marx's critique of capitalism is essential as it captures the internal logic of the system, including "production for production's sake". However, because the critique remains wedded to the project of realizing the abundance generated by capitalism, it continues to express an ideology of progress, achieved through the ever-advancing domination of nature. For this reason, it fails to provide, and is incapable of providing, a critique of the "growth society". Therefore, an alternative perspective needs to be developed. The basic principle for Latouche is that we need to "de-grow" in order to get human production and consumption in line with the biosphere's capacity for regeneration. While this unites various strands of de-growth politics, Latouche belongs to the radical wing of this movement, such that de-growth is understood to entail a broad contraction of the economy (or an "exit" from it, whatever that might mean), which is impossible to harmonise with the capitalist system.

Latouche's project is aimed at achieving "sustainable de-growth", encompassing a vision for a transition that is just and equitable. Many of Latouche's proposals for such transition (such as those for reducing working hours, local

food and energy co-operatives) are helpful. Problems arise, however, in identifying the drivers of the growth society. While Latouche provides some analysis
of the economic activities that propel energy throughput, he strongly emphasizes the sphere of consumption. In this sphere, Latouche mentions a host of
under-specified sources of growth: "turbo- and hyperconsumers" (20), "worka-
holic managers" (20), "the capitalist and techno-economic marketing mega-
machine" (3), "Western states" (30), and "dominant ideologies". Since Latouche
informs us that he has assumed Marx, we might anticipate that consumerism
will be understood as reinforcing production for production's sake, but we find
little explicit and focused analysis of their interaction. The cultural criticism of
consumerism is important, but without an analysis of the deep complemen-
tarity of production-consumption (or as I would argue, the overdetermination
of consumption by production), Latouche's analysis becomes focused on "consumption for consumption's sake", while lacking material anchorage.

Bound up with this arguably shallow analysis of consumerism is a vague
and problematic critique of "development". Latouche boasts a radical anti-
capitalist position, asserting that the critique of "consumption and development" is "ipso facto a critique of capitalism" (2010, p. 75). However, in place of
a sociological or historical analysis of the specific character of capitalism, including its logic and the nature of its historical development, we find a perspective that criticizes over-consumption, while at the same time roundly con-
demning all development. Capitalism and productivist socialism are in his
view "both variants on the same project for a growth society based upon the
development of the productive forces" (2010, p. 90), variants the de-growth
perspective opposes. His is an effort to overcome both these modes of production, "the fantasy of an alternative economy, an alternative growth and an alternative development" (2010, p. 89). In a recent article in *Capitalism Nature
Socialism*, Latouche re-affirms this view, arguing that de-growth is not about
"substituting... *good* growth or *good* development for a bad one and repainting
it green, or social, or equitable...It is about *exiting* the economy" (2012, p. 77).

The perspective fails (in fact appears to refuse) to come to terms with the
distinction between qualitative and quantitative aspects of growth and development (see Schwartzman, 2012; Tanuro, 2014). It side-steps the debate around
what kinds of development are needed, in what regions and levels of the world
system and advanced by whom. Latouche misses the likelihood that various
developments, including in the productive forces, will be critical to avoiding
catastrophic climate change. As I have argued, the development of industrial
energy systems based on renewable energy (including the expansion of non-
fossil fuel transportation infrastructure) are advancements in the productive
forces that are necessary to mend the climate rift.

Ecological knowledge is also an aspect of the productive forces that is presently underutilized. In addition to the "misuse" of this existing productive capacity, we can consider how alternative economic arrangements would encourage the further *growth* of ecological knowledge, through increased funding and support for various forms of sustainable earth science, pursued on the basis of their ecological or metabolic use, rather than exchange, value.[1] Development of these forces implies precisely "alternative growth", "alternative development".

Like many environmental perspectives (and other radical left ones, including anarchist), Latouche places strong emphasis on the need to "re-localize", and the "local" is positioned as the exclusive scale where solutions to environmental problems should be found. In an existing world of globalised flows and evolved political and economic interdependencies, practical barriers limit the effectiveness of potential local solutions. The return to "the local" also seems explicitly to rule out cooperation in climate and atmospheric mitigation and adaptation, which would require coordinated redistributions to respond to issues such as pandemics of water-supply failures and reduced agricultural yields, as well as new governance mechanisms and institutions to accompany them. Latouche implies that grand changes and global redistributions will occur, yet it is hard to see how this could take place without some sort of a planned large-scale economy (including some empowerment of organizations that enable complex forms of coordination across multiple sites and scales). As suggested in Chapter 3, a re-thinking of one of the most basic productive forces – cooperation – with a view towards an alternative mode of its development is called for.

2   James O'Connor and Ecological Conditions of Production

One of the earliest and most powerful attempts to understand contemporary ecological crises through a Marxian framework and vocabulary came from sociologist James O'Connor (1988). In an effort to reframe the terms of the debate in the late 1980s, O'Connor argued that there were two central contradictions of capitalism. The "first contradiction" of capitalism revolves around the forces and relations of production. The capitalist drive to increase productivity by advancing forces of production (especially machine technology) reduces the

---

1   Saed (2011) for example, points out that there is a current dearth of knowledge on large-scale organic crop yield potentials for local consumption and of mechanical harvesting methods not based on fossil fuels.

need for labour. This limits the capacity of worker-consumers to buy back the products they produced, generating a trend towards under-consumption. At the same time and as production becomes more capital-intensive the basis of profit – labour – shrinks in relation to investment in technology and this diminishes the overall rate of profit.

In addition to this first contradiction, O'Connor argued that a largely ignored "second contradiction" emerges in Marx's analysis of capitalist reproduction, revolving around the underproduction and undermining of the natural bases or "external physical conditions" of production (1988, p. 17). These conditions are in many cases non-renewable (such as water, ore and oil), and their degradation and underproduction was leading to a specific and new form of crisis in capitalism. O'Connor argued that capitalism's tendency to both degrade and underproduce these conditions of production would drive up the costs of production and depress profit, for both individual private firms and capital as a whole.[2] It would produce a whole series of unanticipated costs for individual companies that limit accumulation in the interim (such as replenishing trees, restoring soil-eroded land, cleaning up hazardous waste sites, fishing well off-shore as stocks run thin and inlets become more polluted, and having to drill for oil in evermore remote and precarious places), while erecting a barrier to continued capitalist growth in the long run. Thus, by re-framing Marx's explicit ecological reflections in *Capital* (which O'Connor viewed as unsystematic and incomplete), he argued that the second contradiction, is contributing to and re-enforcing a wider crisis in accumulation.

Moreover, corporations along with capital as a whole, would attempt to off-load the social and environmental costs of this process on to a broader public. In this way, underproduction problems and crises bleed into society at large, often obliging the state or other quasi-governmental bodies to regulate problems of scarcity and environmental degradation. Attempts by capital and state to cope with rising ecological costs would create further fault lines, creating an opening for social movements to push the system in a green direction. Environmental movement successes would generate even more costs by pressing for the imposition of various environmental regulations.

O'Connor's work was path-breaking and powerful. It drew fruitful connections with social reproductive feminism and work on new social movements

---

2   In addition to costs of reproducing external physical conditions, rising costs of reproducing social conditions of production at the system level include items such as the health care costs necessitated by capitalist work and family relations; drug rehabilitation costs; the vast sums expended as a result of the deterioration of the social environment (e.g., police costs) (O'Connor, 1997).

(such as urban movements) in theorizing the environmental movement as one focused on a (re)valorization of conditions of production. While O'Connor himself envisioned more acute and economic crisis-induced forms of planning, this perspective can speak to the vast panoply of technocractic and elite-engineered forms of regulation (developing eco-efficiencies and technologies such as carbon capture and storage), designed to manage and mitigate the damage inflicted upon the rest of nature. This points to a system that strives towards "sustainable degradation" (Luke, 2006).

As powerful as O'Connor's framework was, it had crucial limitations. Chief among these was the tendency to subsume environmental contradictions within economic crises, failing to consider how ecological crises are problems in their own right (Foster and Burkett, 2016). Thirty years after O'Connor's initial thesis, we find little evidence of feedback mechanisms that are translating ecological degradation into economic crises, demanding an immediate response from capital. More broadly, it may well be vital to recognize how the contradiction leads to dynamism within the system and that capitalism can continue to advance and prosper indefinitely even when threatening the planet as a place of human habitation.[3]

Furthermore, while O'Connor provided helpful tools for registering the destruction of nature, his framework is simultaneously hobbled by an under-theorization of the category of non-human nature and an uncritical acceptance of nature's externality to production (Huber, 2009). Working from the category of conditions of production, he does not register the way objects and aspects of nature, such as fossil fuels, are "put to work" in the production process and are part of the productive forces. As Huber puts it (2017), O'Connor's framework only pays attention to the nature that capital does not value, while ignoring the nature that its does value, namely "natural materials that are mediated by human labour and also easily quantifiable and divisible into clear units"(p. 48). By seeing "nature" as an external condition that imposes a set of barriers, obstacles and conditions (rather than being internal to the social relations, forces and cultural politics of capitalism), his work is limited in its ability

---

3 It is possible that the costs have been deferred into the future, a position that accords to some degree with Jason Moore's (discussed next). Firms have indeed shifted production to regions with less environmental regulation and where other elements of compensation (e.g., health insurance) are lower, such as from Detroit and other American centres of the mid-West and East to the American South, China, and Southeast Asia. The thesis may therefore be defensible, but I maintain that there is no current compelling evidence that capital cannot continue to accumulate in conditions of ecological devastation. Indeed, as Naomi Klein demonstrates through the notion of a "disaster capitalism complex" (2008), corporations have learnt how enhance profits through natural disasters.

to register socio-ecological transformation and development. We need a more robust assessment of the ways that extra-human nature and resources are constituted by historically distinct processes, relations and material practices, without denying that nature has its own dynamic, turbulent and contingent processes, which are outside of human production and which come to bear on the social. In short, we need a fuller analysis of how capitalism develops *in and through* the rest of nature. Jason Moore's work (2015, 2016) which we consider next, attempts to give full expression to the latter.

3   Jason Moore and World Ecology

Moore has offered an ambitious outline of an ecological history of capitalism in an approach he calls *world-ecology* (2014, 2015, 2016). The approach draws on the historical sociology of World-System Theory (WST) and also shares much with O'Connor. Moore's framework centres on a reinterpretation of capitalist processes of appropriation in the production of surplus value, arguing that the exploitation of labour and capitalist increases in labour productivity depend on a tight relation to the "zone of appropriation". In making this argument, Moore takes on a standard reading of Marx's "law of value" considering how capital strives to boost labour productivity in the sphere of production. He argues that these efforts (which require an ever-greater quantity of inputs), are united with another imperative: capital must ceaselessly search for, and find ways to produce, "Cheap Natures" as inputs to commodity production. Advances in productivity, and every act of producing surplus value, he argues, is bound up with the appropriation of "Four Cheaps": labour-power, food, energy and raw materials (2015, p. 17).

Continually cheapening staple food is key to keeping the costs of labour power low as household expenditure accounts for much of the base of hiring workers. Foisting the reproduction of labour onto unpaid workers, especially women, is also vital. The easiest way to obtain Cheap nature and labour, however, is to look outside of the capitalist economy in search of new "commodity frontiers". Capitalist firms seek out new sources of cheap inputs such as displaced farmers, unploughed soils or minerals drawn from the commodity frontiers of uncapitalized natures.[4] On Moore's view, frontiers lie outside the commodity system, but within the reach of capitalist power.

---

4 Commandeered assets such as land and dependent agricultural labour also generate low-cost means of subsistence for waged-workers in the form of food and clothing. Appropriated

Arguing for the centrality of "appropriation" alongside exploitation in capital's overall expansion (with exploitation now appearing somewhat subordinate to appropriation), Moore maintains that the law of value is accompanied by and dependent upon a "law of cheap nature", a zone of appropriation that manifests as a series of growing commodity frontiers. At the core of this law, which is operative from the inception of capitalism in the "first sixteenth century" (1450–1550), "is the ongoing, rapidly expansive, and relentlessly innovative quest to turn the work/energy of the biosphere into capital (value-in-motion)" (2015, pp. 13–14). In terms of the processes by which the products of people and nature working outside the capitalist system enter commodity circulation, Moore highlights accumulation by dispossession, whereby not only natural use-values but the labour of millions of dispossessed peasants enter as cheap inputs. He also discusses "capitalization", wherein a capitalist sets up a mine or mill and hires wage workers, but the land, resources and workers come cheap as land has been seized from Indigenous people, where little has been paid in rent for the land lease, or the displaced people have been coerced into the workforce. Although not explicitly discussed by Moore, as has been explored by ecofeminists, we could also point to the way that the products of subsistence farmers and small commodity producers become drawn into capitalist markets (Federici, 2004; Salleh, 2010).

On the basis of the importance of Four Cheaps to maintaining rising labour productivity since the "long sixteenth century" (1450–1640), one of Moore's aims is to challenge the importance placed on the industrial and fossil revolution in the second half of the 18th century (Moore, 2016). This narrative, prominent in eco-Marxist and non-Marxist green thought, is seen to ignore the massive increases in labour productivity and epochal revolution in landscape change (in terms of speed, scale, scope) that occurred between 1450 and 1750. These changes are again premised on a fundamentally new law of "environment making": capitalism's law of Cheap Nature. And this law is premised on new imperialisms, new sciences and new forms of state power.[5] Such processes, for Moore, historically include a revolution in "technics" – including new strategies of global appropriation, new administrative technologies and new knowledge regimes in surveying, navigation, road building – suited

---

(cheap) nature therefore lowers the cost of reproducing labour power, reducing wages and raising the rate of exploitation.

5 For Moore, fundamental to this surveying and coding of the web of life for what it can do for capital accumulation has been the construction of a binary of Humanity/Nature, with most humans – Indigenous peoples, Africans, nearly all women, and even many white skinned men (Slavs, Jews, the Irish) – regarded as belonging to the latter and being treated accordingly.

to identifying, coding, rationalizing and delivering the work of Nature on the cheap (2016). However, these fundamental transformations in early capitalism's way of "organizing nature", are missed in approaches that treat the Industrial Revolution as the lodestar of the transformation (and destruction) of nature on a planetary scale.

In Moore's reconceptualization, so long as there are frontiers of Cheap Nature and so long as the costs of reproducing labour power, food, energy and raw materials are kept off the books, periodic productivity and accumulation crises can be overcome. However, he identifies barriers or counter-tendencies to capitalism's ability to appropriate Cheap Nature indefinitely (barriers which in fact worsen over historical time). From this follows Moore's view of current systemic crises, which are "crises of what nature does for capitalism, rather more than what capitalism does to nature" (2015, p. 17). Since the 1970s, he asserts, the possibilities of appropriating Cheap Natures have narrowed and we have begun to see an exhaustion of the centuries-long model of appropriating unpaid work/energy outside the cash nexus (2016). There has been no revolution in agricultural productivity (in fact, its rate of growth has slowed since the mid-1980s) and no major sources of cheap energy have appeared (rather only unconventional sources based on high cost frontiers have expanded).

There are different reasons why capitalism's Cheap Nature strategy is currently being exhausted and why it must eventually lead to system-wide and terminal accumulation crisis. Chief among them, and echoing O'Connor, is that the capitalization of the Four Cheaps outstrips their contribution to labour productivity. Increasingly, we find that capitalism must "capitalize rather than appropriate" – hence the importance of factory farmed animals, tree plantations and aquaculture (2015, pp. 92–93). Similarly, many oil companies now spend more on exploration and production than they earn for every barrel of crude that they extract. While capitalization can have middle run benefits of increasing labour productivity, it also leads to rising costs of production (due to rising costs of labour and nature as inputs) generating an "underproduction crisis". Another barrier that Moore discusses is the degradation of the biosphere through carbon emissions, soil erosion, biodiversity loss, acidification, and so on. The degradation of natural conditions themselves threatens to raise the cost of the Four Cheaps (especially food and in turn labour) in ways that will make the valorisation of capital impossible.

Moore's world-ecology approach has contributed numerous conceptual innovations and captured many components of historical and contemporary capitalism. The framework is laudable in its attempt to intersect with (eco)feminist and post and anti-colonial analyses, pointing to the vital importance of expropriation and "unpaid work" to capitalist development and accumulation.

The basic insight that commodity production will cost least where *both* workers and materials cost least is helpful. The point may seem obvious, but the importance of cheapening "circulating capital" has often eluded Marxian value analysis. The focus on technological innovations aimed appropriating work/energy from the rest of nature – in the "means of discovery and extraction" – is also highly pertinent to our discussion of forces of production, while the notion of declining cheap nature provides a broad framework for understanding the resort to tar-sands and other forms of "extreme energy" that are increasingly costly (both economically and ecologically). Much of this can be taken on without adopting Moore's proposed methodological framework or following him to his specific conclusions. I raise here a few points of disagreement, for our purposes.[6]

Firstly, Moore, like O'Connor, wants to read ecological and economic crises together. He writes:

> The crises of capitalism-in-nature are crises of what nature does for capitalism, rather more than what capitalism does to nature. This point of entry offers not only a fresh perspective – one that includes, centrally, the work of human natures – but also provides an opportunity for synthesizing two great streams of radical thought since the 1970s: the theory of accumulation crisis and the study of environmental crisis.
>
> 2015, p. 17

He is yet more forceful in his claim, suggesting that approaches that treat crises separately are again a form of dualism and that prominent analysts of the 2008 crash are guilty of "nature blindness".

As suggested above, ecological and economic crises interact, but they do not determine each other. While Moore's focus on crises of what nature does for capitalism is in some ways illuminating, in other ways it narrows our understanding of the current ecological crisis and its human effects. A focus on resource crises for capital (or how the raising costs of the Four Cheaps undermines

---

6   Moore has argued that the theory of metabolic rift is "dualist" and based on a nature-society binary. His critique of dualism within Marxist ecology and virtually all quarters of contemporary green thought has produced strong criticisms and led to quite polarized debate surrounding his work. While I do not enter far into this debate here, as my embrace of the theory of metabolic rift suggests, I find Moore's criticism of dualism in regards to the concepts of social metabolism and metabolic rift to be incoherent. As Foster argues in response, dialectics which are decisively non-dualistic, are fundamentally about the *mediation* of totality, the process that both *separates and unites* individuals and society, humanity and nature, parts and wholes (Foster, 2016).

capital valorization), can speak to some of the human effects of climate change (e.g., rising food costs and lower agricultural productivity can have devastating human consequences), however, the erosion and degradation of the conditions that support and sustain human life exceeds this dynamic. Climate change and other ecological crises compromise the material conditions of the world's inhabitants, especially the planet's "third-class passengers" (Davis, 2010), in ways that have little to do with the (potential) rising costs of the Four Cheaps.

A further point of disagreement concerns Moore's view of a fundamental transformation in capitalism's way of "organizing nature" during the long sixteenth century. While his perspective is presented in some degree in opposition to the Marxist view, much of what Moore writes of the historical processes of "accumulation by appropriation", is consistent with Marx. While there are differences in periodization, Marx recognizes the origins of capitalism in the mercantilist age from the mid-fifteenth to the mid-eighteenth century and the importance of expropriating what Moore calls Four Cheaps in this period (see Altvater, 2016). His analysis of primitive accumulation and the "free appropriation" of natural conditions focuses on land enclosures in England, yet this is understood as part of an even greater age of global expropriation, in which land and labour were seized through colonization, enslavement, and the plundering of resources (see Foster and Brett, 2018; Harvey 2010, pp. 299–313). In this analysis of "early capitalism", he registers profound transformations and accelerations in production, circulation, reproduction, communication and consumption.

Yet, as Altvater suggests (2016), the onset of fossil-fuel driven production and transportation in the late eighteenth and early nineteenth century amplified, accelerated and generalized these trends. Modern machinery, concentrated in large factories, allowed for new technical divisions of labour and produced a decisive increase in labour productivity. With it came the first great transition of agricultural labour into urban factories. Therefore, while Braudel and others from the WST tradition may be right to see the origins of capitalism in the long sixteenth century and in the quest to appropriate Cheap Nature, the Industrial Revolution also produced a decisive shift, marking the end of a "protoindustrial capitalism" and signalled the rise of modern industrial capitalism. From the totality of historical capitalism, Altvater considers both positions (what he calls the "Braudel and Polanyi hypotheses") to be correct (2016).

The view of the Industrial Revolution as a decisive shift, producing new forms of work and new ways of life is contained in Marx's notion of the transition from the formal to the real subsumption of labour (and nature) to capital. Marx writes that the formal subsumption of labour "stands in striking contrast to the development of a *specifically capitalist mode of production* (large-scale industry, etc.); the latter transforms not only the situations of various agents of production, it also *revolutionizes* the actual mode of their labour and the real nature of the labour process as a whole" (Marx, 1976b, p. 1021). Real subsumption activates the potential for relative surplus value, or the competitive struggle to increase labour productivity and reduce the worktime necessary to produce commodities through the technical reorganization of the labour process. As we have seen, this is one of the central dynamics of capitalism, and it completely transforms the competitive dynamics of the economy, leading to the socialization of forces of production via the modern corporation, as well as new dynamics of dependency and imperialism. Moreover, the real subsumption of labour under capital implies a parallel subsumption of nature through the scientific and technological development of objects, forces and life forms of nature (Burkett, 2014). On these terms, the transition to large-scale industry and machinery is a watershed not only in terms of crystalizing social relations, but also in terms of transforming the *societal relation to the rest of nature*.

One of Moore's objectives in challenging the historical view that equates capitalism with the Industrial Revolution and the exploitation of fossil fuels, is to argue that since the problem goes deeper than fossil capitalism, so must our solutions. Moore, presumably responding to theories of people like Elmar Altvater, Matthew Huber and Andreas Malm, writes, "To locate modernity's origins through the steam engine and the coal pit is to prioritize shutting down the steam engines and coal pits, and their twenty-first century incarnations. ... Shut down a coal plant, and you can slow down global warming for a day; shut down the relations that made the coal plant, and you can stop it for good" (2016, p. 94).

While Moore is exaggerating here, it is worth re-emphasizing the enormity of the challenge of decarbonization and energy transition. Energy transition is not only an enormous challenge and an urgent priority; a comprehensive political economic and ecological perspective on decarbonization opens to deeper structural critiques, not only of Big Carbon, but of capitalism itself. Accomplishing a transition within the current "carbon budget" will *require* incursions into capitalist property, shifting us away from the logic of private capitalist accumulation. It will require new forms of democratic planning, different forms of social property and likely aspects of socialization and democratization of investment. As Naomi Klein (2014) has so effectively argued, a transition to a future based on cleaner and renewable fuels is also an opportunity to enhance social justice.

While Moore criticizes a focus on *fossil* capitalism in terms of the political strategy it implies, it is unclear how his renewed historical interpretation produces an alternative strategy, beyond a call to shut down a 500 years old civilizational project of power, wealth and value. While we can appreciate conviction in the need for fundamental and revolutionary change, it is entirely unclear from his work how or where to begin a reversal in the relations of production.

The absence of a clear strategic dimension in Moore's work extends to the way he approaches the natural sciences. As McKenzie Wark (2015) points out in a review of *Capitalism in the Web of Life,* there is a variant of social reductionism in relation to science in Moore and this is tactically unhelpful in the context of the climate crisis. For Moore, ideas about and ways of understanding nature are densely bound up with waves of primitive accumulation. As Moore writes: "Crucially, science, power, and culture operate within value's gravitational field, and are co-constitutive of it" (2015, p. 54). While the notion of a "gravitational field" implies caution against determinism, in Moore's account, the various scientific ways of knowing nature appear to be entirely internal to capital. The physical and life scientific are not socially and politically neutral, but it is important to assert, as Wark does that science is "only partially contaminated in its aims and metaphors by historically determinate social relations" (2015, third to last para.) Moreover, as she suggests, the best accounts of this contamination, such of those found in the work of Donna Haraway, base their critiques on other kinds of science.

As Wark argues (2016), in so far as vital sources of information about present ecological circumstances and future effects of human activity are coming from ecological studies, including climate science (and as these form part of the radical critique of capitalism), a more collaborative and comradery approach to knowledge production is called for. Indeed, as Wark suggests, exiting today's climate crisis requires an unprecedented collaboration of workers of all kinds, including knowledge workers.

In the context of the deepening crisis, the "class affiliations" of environmental and other scientists remain very much in question, as does the issue of whether they might actively participate in anti-capitalist or anti-neoliberal struggle. As Chaktabarty suggests, despite their often limited social analysis, scientists pointing to the nature and extend of the crisis "are not necessarily anticapitalist scholars, and yet clearly they are not for business-as-usual capitalism either" (2009, p. 219). At the level of strategy, the implication is that winning over these workers and intellectuals is an important component of today's counter-hegemonic politics, as is a non-dismissive engagement and dialogue between social, historical and natural sciences.

Perhaps at some point in the not- too-distant future, we will encounter ecological limits that make sustained capital accumulation impossible. But then there would still remain the problem of how to continue to feed, clothe and house eight billion people without destroying their conditions of existence. Capitalist relations of production have produced the climate crisis, but the challenge of climate stabilization also exceeds those relations. Based on these considerations, I find it vital to contemplate alternatives and possibilities that emerge both within and outside the conditions set by the current mode of production.

4   Conclusion

This chapter placed an ecological reinterpretation of the concept of forces of production developed so far in dialogue with some contemporary eco-Marxist frameworks. While the latter offer valuable insights into the ecological costs and consequences of capitalist development, I pointed to important differences of methodology and understanding, and suggested that the green-dialectical understanding of productive forces developed here offers some distinctive advantages, particularly in understanding and coming to terms with the contemporary climate crisis.

The analysis provided in the book so far has been abstract-simple. It has focused on reconceptualizing productive forces, while examining their development and fettering through reference to the broad dynamics of capital accumulation. Drawing from Marx, as well as contemporary scholarship, I have examined capital's appropriation of and "discipline" over the various powers and capacities through which we are linked to the rest of nature. Understood dialectically, this leads us to consider how under capitalism, forces of production substantially take the commodity form and are embroiled within its (ecological) contradictions. In the context of today's deepening climate rift, gaining social control over the mediations and means through which the social metabolism takes place is an urgent matter. In decommodifying the forces of production, a 21st century alternative must detach these mediations from capital's growth imperative and begin a process of their democratic creative-destructive transformation.

Moreover, I have argued that a generous conception of productive forces, read in light of recent Marxist scholarship, helps not only reveal the wastefulness and destructiveness that accompanies capital's development of productive forces, but also discloses nascent and unfulfilled productive capacities vital for developing a less antagonistic coevolution with the rest of nature. While they were already glimpsed by Marx, today, in our era of global ecological crisis, we can more clearly see ecological thinking and knowledge as such an advancement in the productive forces. Yet such knowledge is clearly underutilized, operating at the margins of an anti-ecological system. It has provoked only minor adjustments to the system that do not halt, but instead narrowly mitigate ecological degradation. Associated contemporary technologies, such as systems for harnessing and transmitting renewable energy flow, are also part of the development of productive forces and vital for restoring the carbon cycle. Indeed, the scientific consensus on global warming and on the imperative of timely climate action is clear. A rapid shift away from fossil fuels and a transition to renewable energy sources is an urgent necessity within the next two decades.

Part 2 of this book moves from an abstract-simple account to a concrete-complex analysis of fossil capitalism in action. Through case studies in the Canadian context, I analyze the deepening of fossil-powered productive forces – pointing to the infrastructures, technologies and knowledge networks bound up with unconventional fossil fuel extraction, processing, transport – and the simultaneous fettering of renewable energy and ecological knowledge itself. In the movement from abstract-simple to concrete-complex, a greater number of agencies, processes and actors, both economic (circuits and fractions of capital, corporations and accumulation strategies), and "extra-economic" (state bodies, as well as civil society organizations) are brought into view, as is the role of current political struggle.

Within relations of production, I emphasize modalities of corporate power, particularly the power of "carbon capital", including the science and technology infrastructures that support the sector, without losing sight of how this power is rooted in the structural features of capitalism. On this analytic plane, the examination of fettering includes an investigation into carbon capital's strategic efforts to fashion such green productive forces in a manner that is consonant with the accumulation strategies and power relations permeating fossil capitalism. This situation requires a more nuanced view of fettering; hence I examine aspects of *relative*-developmental and use fettering of green productive forces, analyzing this process not only theoretically, but through empirical study into current tendencies.

The concrete-complex account calls for some methodological eclecticism. While continuing to work from Marx's general theory of capital accumulation (complemented by contemporary elaborations), I draw from the tradition of power structure research to examine networked relations between fractions of capital, as well as corporate power's (particularly the fossil-fuel sector's) "reach" into the state and civil-society. Neo-Gramscian scholarship provides additional insights into the interweaving of the economic, political and cultural in the establishment and diffusion of corporate power and hegemony and into the broad tactics of counter-movement and counter-hegemony.

The focus on fossil capitalism in motion necessarily limits a green-dialectical take on productive forces to the most pressing of contemporary interlinked ecological crises and to the urgent present impasse of fossil capitalism, as it is posed in a specific national context. The movement from abstract-simple to concrete-complex, As Jessop maintains (2002a), is both analytically and strategically necessary. Case studies are required to provide a complex assessment of the barriers to advancing green productive forces. This in turn informs concrete and immediate courses of strategic intervention and transformation. These are vitally needed, especially in the context of the climate emergency. At the same time, the abstract dialectical treatment is necessary in understanding the root causes of ecological and climactic destruction and in outlining more long-term programmatic and efforts aimed at metabolic restoration.

I begin by "mapping" key oil and gas infrastructure networks in Canada and analyzing several pipeline and infrastructural proposals being contemplated to facilitate the expansion of these industries. This provides context and background on fossil fuel development in Canada, while pointing to the inertia posed by fixed fossil capital.

PART 2

Canadian Fossil Capitalism, Climate Change and Productive Forces

∵

CHAPTER 5

Climate Change and the Networked Infrastructures of Canadian Fossil Capitalism

In Chapter 3, I pointed to fixed capital as a key component of the productive forces. While relatively few society-nature researchers examine large-scale infrastructure formation, Marx considered them to be a vital component of that relation. They are constructed from natural materials, often involve the reorganization of ecologies, and subsequently process, structure and mediate the flow of resources to sites of production and consumption, while supporting social reproduction more broadly. In and of themselves, infrastructures are not negative; they do not necessarily imply the conquering of or even control over extra-human nature. Infrastructures like other aspects of the productive forces do, however, express certain political and economic priorities, interests and power relations, and have important social and ecological consequences.

In the context of the deepening climate crisis, recent research has focused on the ecological (especially carbon) footprint of fixed capital, particularly energy production and transport networks and energy intensive infrastructure, such as transportation and buildings (Huber, 2013, 2015; Sayre, 2010; D.N. Scott, 2013). Other work has extensively discussed social resistance to and contestation surrounding fixed capital (such as pipelines) (Awasis, 2014; Estes, 2019; N. Klein, 2014) and pointed to infrastructural transformation as a key facet of green transition (Castree and Christophers, 2015; Ekers and Prudham, 2017; Holgersen and Warlenius, 2016).

Building from this work, this chapter provides a networked and metabolic analysis of the infrastructures that surround, process and move mined carbon in Canada, and highlights pipelines and other fixed capital proposals designed to facilitate the expansion of the fossil fuel industry. First, I trace the flow of oil and gas through a system of pipelines, processing plants, petrochemical complexes, refineries, tankers, and gas distribution infrastructures, and highlight the patterns of production, consumption and waste (especially emissions) that surround them. Second, building from Marx's analysis of the circuit of capital, I elucidate the networks of corporate interest and power expressed and embedded in them. I reveal connections between fossil fuel and other industrial firms along the commodity chain, as well as structured relations between carbon capital and financial fractions, via shareholding and lending arrangements. Together, these two "networked lenses" provide insights on the deep path dependencies of existing and proposed fossil capital infrastructure, while also identifying prominent firms whose interests are bound up with them. A focus on these key "architects" of our economic and ecological future informs a discussion of the barriers to energy transition, while an analysis of energy infrastructures invites reflections on the spatial dimensions of alternative energy futures.

As a point of departure, I revisit Marx's insights on the political economic and ecological dynamics of infrastructural formation. His perspective provides a foundation for contemporary interdisciplinary research on the urban or industrial metabolism via networked infrastructures, which we review following Marx. This literature sets the context for the analysis of fossil fuel infrastructures in the Canadian context.

1   Social Metabolism and the Role of Infrastructure

As we have seen Marx introduced the concept of 'social metabolism' to understand the complex material interchange between human beings and natural systems. He analyzed the metabolic interchange with the rest of nature primarily through production and commodity circulation (both of which belong to the process of production broadly defined), as well as in terms of the wastes this produces. Constructed instruments of labour – tools, machines, infrastructures and means of transport, together with the knowledge and skill they embody – facilitate commodity production and circulation. As Marx suggested, "Nature builds no machines, no locomotives, railways, electric telegraphs, self-acting mules etc. These are products of human industry; natural material transformed into organs of the human will over nature, or of human participation in nature" (Marx, 1993, p. 706). While Marx pointed here to the importance of both machinery and means of circulation in "mediating" our relation to the rest of nature, in *Capital* he focused on infrastructures that facilitate commodity production and circulation more sharply, defined as fixed capital of "large-scale and great durability". The category refers to a range of items such as ships, docs, canals, ports, dams, factory buildings, pipelines, highways, electrical power transmission lines, power stations, railways and so on.

As we saw in Chapter 3, Marx analysed two interrelated dimensions surrounding the formation of physical infrastructures of transport, circulation and consumption, under the dynamics of "generalized commodity production". The first aspect concerns the movement of "raw materials" from sites of extraction to sites of production. Capital is driven to develop infrastructural networks for the processing and transport of a mass of extracted raw materials to reach (often distant) points of production and manufacturing. The growth of this aspect of fixed capital goes hand in hand with increasing matter and energy throughput, which is a key feature of large-scale industrial capitalism. As Marx remarks "after the capitalist has put a larger capital into machinery, he is compelled to spend a larger capital on the purchase of raw materials and the fuels required to drive the machines" (as cited in Foster and Burkett, 2016, p. 158). Intensified metabolic transformations of raw materials in commodity production and manufacturing across the system as a whole, requires more extensive fixed capital networks to facilitate this flow.

Marx also noted that the commercial viability and value of raw materials depend in part on transport costs, writing that "an individual product might be made so much more expensive, owing to the transport costs, that it could not be sold" (1993b, p. 523). The commercial viability and value of raw materials, he intimated, depends in part on transport costs, and therefore capital is driven to produce innovations in transport infrastructure (including growing "economies of scale" in transport). In this connection, innovations in one part of the commodity chain, such as new techniques for extracting gas from shale formations via hydraulic fracking, demand and often stimulate innovations at further points in the chain, such as in the production of LNG tankers, designed to move liquefied natural gas over long distances to reach de-liquefaction plants.

The second, closely related feature concerning capital's revolution in this dimension of productive forces, concerns the separation-in-unity of production and consumption. By virtue of the dynamic productivity of large-scale fossilized industry, capital produces an immense collection of commodities, yet, as Marx suggested, this in no way guarantees their sale. The *realization* of this productivity requires expanded markets for exchange and the creation of extensive and long-term investments in the form transport networks (typically powered by fossil fuels) and fixed, often immobile infrastructures that connect points of production to points of consumption. Capital will continually seek to overcome spatial barriers in an effort to reduce the time between the production and exchange of commodities: "Capital by its nature drives beyond every spatial barrier. Thus, the creation of the physical conditions of exchange – of the means of communication and transport – the annihilation of space by time – becomes an extraordinary necessity for it" (Marx, 1993b, p. 524).

2 Concentration of Capital and Credit

As with other forms of fixed capital (i.e., machines), Marx emphasized the tendency of infrastructures to return their value piecemeal, rather than all at once. They require a considerable initial outlay of resources, resources that do not immediately generate a complete return on the initial investment. Fixed capital's lack of flexibility also means that once it is installed, it can only be used in a single way, and subject to particular spatio-temporal parameters. It is frozen into a given functionality. Because fixed capital can return the value invested in it only piece by piece, it can also do so only so long as the conditions for its functionality are maintained.

In the early stages of English industrial capitalism, Marx noted that large infrastructural projects were rarely carried out on a capitalist basis, but instead at communal or state expense. Given the massive outlays of capital required for large-scale fixed capital projects and the risks associated with them, this dynamic is ongoing and individual capitalists, as Marx already noted, continually seek to shift the burden onto the shoulders of the state (1967, p. 233). Yet for accumulation to function smoothly and consistently, capital must be able to produce large-scale infrastructures within its own production process. Marx highlights the concentration and centralization of capital in the form of the corporation and the credit system as necessary enabling conditions. Without these developments, large-scale capitalist infrastructural projects would be virtually impossible.

While the corporate form was not fully consolidated until the 20th century, in the third volume of *Capital* Marx reflected on its early emergence in the nineteenth century in the form of the modern "joint stock company" (JSC). The JSC represents the aggregation and pooling of socialized forces of production. Moreover, with the JSC and its accompanying form of shareholder ownership (ownership taking the form of shares issued on the stock exchange), barriers to raising capital for large-scale and infrastructural projects could be overcome. Therefore, in the JSC, available money capital becomes less of a barrier to expansion, as firms gain access to a larger pool of capital and are no longer dependent on vast concentrations of individual property.

The second major path to the concentration and centralization of capital occurs through credit and the credit system. As Marx noted, the source of money capital in the productive circuit may come in the form of a loan to a "productive" capitalist. Marx referred to this form of money capital as "interest bearing capital", that is, money lent out for a price in the form of interest for which the lender relinquishes control of the sum that is lent. The process of financing constitutes a relationship between money capitalists who earn interest by lending to productive capitalists. Credit therefore emerges from exchange relations between different "fractions" of capital.[1] Yet the supply of

---

1   Capital never exists as a unified entity but as many units, of which corporations are the most important. Just as the expanded scale of capital requires an extensive financial apparatus for

interest-bearing capital requires *recurrent* access to idle (hoarded) savings of all capitalists. In a developed credit system, financial institutions pool idle savings and turn them into concentrated money capital resources available to a few industrial producers (Marois, 2013).[2] Credit therefore relieves individual capitalists of some of the burden of hoarding massive amounts of capital in advance of the purchase of fixed capital and coverts the payment for that fixed capital into an annual one.

Because money capitalists can decide whether to finance a firm (or a governmental or non-governmental organization), they are a particularly powerful fraction of capital. By virtue of control over credit financial fractions exert "allocative power" (Carroll, 2010; Scott, 1997). And while this raises the potential for intra-class conflict (the particular interests of money capitalists may not correspond to the general interests of capital), both investment and credit in industrial operations often pull financial firms and industry together into a tight association, expressed in the concept of "finance capital" (Hilferding, 2006; Marois, 2013).

3   Spatial Fix and Built Environment

David Harvey has illuminated the dynamics of large-scale infrastructural development, including through his notion of "spatial fix" (Harvey, 2001, 2007). Broadly, he argues that fixed capital can function as a sink for over accumulated capital and idle labour power, while securing anew an expanding scale and scope of capital accumulation. Spatial fixes for Harvey extend beyond fixed capital for commodity circulation and consumption, to that of the spatial infrastructure of the "consumption fund" (Harvey, 1978). The latter includes a wider built environment, involving social infrastructures, such as public roads and shopping malls, which facilitate consumption and social reproduction more broadly.[3]

---

the circulation and consumption of commodities, surplus value is competitively subdivided among not just among industrial, resource and financial capitalists and corporations, but along all lines of investment, including in areas such as real estate and retail commerce (Carroll, 2010; Van der Pijl, 1998). These functional divisions within total capital are part of what Marx refers to as fractions of capital. As in the relation between industrial and finance capital, there is both competition and repulsion between these various fractions, as well as *attraction*.

2   Harvey (2007) updates this by examining how capitalists gain access to idle savings of not only other capitalists, but also individuals and collectives who are drawn into the financial system through interest on savings, mortgages, pensions and so on.

3   Harvey provides a fruitful analysis of the imbrication of capital and the state in the construction of the built environment, pointing to the contemporary predominance of private-public

As Harvey points out, numerous forms of infrastructure function as both fixed capital and consumption fund. For example, roads and railways are used for both commodity transport and public mobility. The electricity grid also powers both homes and production, while gasoline stations fuel trucks that move commodities to sites of further production or consumption, as well as enabling privatized automobility. Here fixed capital belonging to the productive forces strictly speaking is necessarily blended and conflated with infrastructures that belong to the "reproductive forces of everyday life" (Huber, 2013). Thus, as Harvey writes the built environment "functions as a vast, humanly created resource system, comprising use-values embedded in the physical landscape, which can be utilized for production, exchange and consumption. From the standpoint of production, these use-values can be considered as both general precondition for and direct forces of production" (2007, p. 233).

In analyzing fixed capital and built environment formation, Harvey emphasizes a recurrent contradiction, noted by Marx, surrounding the fixity and mobility of capital. The more capital circulates in fixed form the more the system of production and consumption is locked into activities that support and realize fixed capital:

> In order to overcome spatial barriers and to annihilate space with time, spatial structures are created that themselves act as barriers to further accumulation. These spatial structures are expressed in the form of immobile transport facilities and ancillary facilities implanted in the landscape. We can in fact extended this conception to encompass the formation of the built environment as a whole. Capital represents itself in the form of a physical landscape created in its own image, created as use values to enhance the progressive accumulation of capital. The geographical landscape which results is the crowning glory of past capitalist development. But at the same time it expresses the power of dead labour over living labour and as such it imprisons and inhibits the accumulation process within a set of specific physical constraints. And these can be removed only slowly unless there is a substantial devaluation of the exchange-value locked up in the creation of these physical assets.
>
> HARVEY, 1978, p. 210

---

partnerships and how the coordination and management of monetary flows required for large-scale infrastructural projects draw the state and capital together in what he calls the "state-finance nexus" (2011, p. 48).

Sunk infrastructures produce inertia, locking-in particular productive forces, forms of accumulation and conditions of production. Firms invested in them have a strong interest in their valorization over time and in maintaining the conditions of their functionality.

In the next section, I turn to recent research on the "industrial" and "urban metabolism". This research extends Marx's perspective on the ecological dimension of infrastructure, including their role in sustaining and exacerbating ecological rifts.

4   Industrial Metabolism and Networked Infrastructures

Work in environmental sociology, and urban political ecology on the industrial and urban metabolism, draws heavily from Marx's concept of social metabolism and his analysis of fixed capital formation. Such approaches frame and analyze this metabolism, broadly, as a dialectical process by which the raw materials of nature are transformed into commodities, services and finally wastes. There are two distinct but closely related approaches advancing this view.[4] "Industrial ecology" is concerned especially with quantifying material and energy flows in "socioeconomic systems", be they the global economy, a nation state or national economy, a regional unit such as a city, or an economic sector (Fischer-Kowalski, 1998; Fischer-Kowalski and Haberl, 1993; Girardet, 1996; Pauliuk et al., 2015). It follows the circulation of materials and energy in industrial society through the chain of extraction, production, consumption and disposal and has introduced a suite of metrics to measure these flows. These include techniques such as Material Flow Analysis (MFA) (a systematic assessment of the flows and stocks of materials within a system defined in space and time) and Lifecycle Assessment Analysis (LFA) (which evaluates multiple environmental impacts of a product from "cradle to grave") (Pauliuk et al., 2015).

Most commonly, the approach is used to map the ecological footprint of nation states, cities, economic sectors or industrial processes and to develop strategies for reducing throughput and optimizing resource use (J.P. Newell and Cousins, 2015). It has also been used to address broad historical materialist questions concerning transitions in modes of production (such as from agrarian to industrial societies) (Fischer-Kowalski and Haberl, 1993; Haberl, 2007), and has been fruitfully combined with world-systems approaches to analyze unequal patterns of development and ecological exchange (Hornborg, 2010).

---

4 For historical and comparative reviews of "industrial ecological" and "urban political ecology" approaches see (J.P. Newell and Cousins, 2015) and (Wachsmuth, 2012).

Girardet's (1996) influential work draws heavily from Marx's analysis of metabolic rifts in framing the flow of raw materials from an ecological "hinterland" into the metropolis, as entailing "linear metabolisms". To recall, a key part of Marx's analysis of a rift in the soil nutrient cycle concerned the spatial disjuncture in production, and the separation of town and country. He considered specifically how minerals and nutrients in food, fibers and agro-industrial raw material were transported long distances to cities, while the waste resources and animal waste were not returned to the soil. While Marx mostly analyzed the dynamics of soil exhaustion within nations, he became increasingly aware of how capital's disturbance of the social and natural metabolism is extended globally through international trade. Indeed, Marx likened 19th century industrialized agriculture to a robbery system, pointing to a one-way movement by which the transportation of food and fibre over long distances meant that the soil was depleted of essential and regenerative nutrients. Echoing Marx, Giradet argues that while nonhuman nature is sustained by a series of "circular metabolisms" (the waste of one organism is the sustenance of another), with growing urbanization and the long distance transport of agricultural goods, energy and raw materials from the "extractive periphery" into the "metropolitan core", there are a proliferation of one-way flows – resources in, wastes out (see also Wachsmuth 2012; Sassen, 2009).

The closely related literature in urban political ecology (UPE), a hybrid field at the intersection of political ecology and urban geography, focuses on the socio-natural metabolism of cities, mapping the flows of goods, materials, water, nutrients and waste into and out of the metropolis (Kaika and Swyngedouw, 2000; Monstadt, 2009; D.N. Scott, 2013; Swyngedouw, 2006). Such flows, the literature emphasizes, enter and exit the city and communities via networked infrastructures, such as energy, water, wastewater and transport systems (Kaika and Swyngedouw, 2000; Monstadt, 2009; D.N. Scott, 2013). These infrastructures are understood to act as a critical "interface" between society and nonhuman nature (Kaika and Swyngedouw, 2000).

In a metabolic analysis, infrastructures, such as the "end" of a pipeline, are thereby conceived of as systems in which labour processes convert raw materials (crude oil, gas or bitumen), energy and labour, into commodities (gasoline, liquefied gas, petrochemicals) and into waste (especially water and atmospheric pollution) (D.N. Scott, 2013). While emphasis is often placed on the complex networks of circulatory systems within urban environments or "socio-natures", the urbanization process extends beyond the city's (indeed also the nation state's) political borders (Ghosn, 2010; Swyngedouw, 2006). Infrastructures in this view are understood to extend and accelerate the ecological metabolism of the city, connecting the metropolis to often distant sites of resource extraction and production that sustain them and which in turn act as a sink for its emissions (Monstadt, 2009).

While a number of commodity flows are analyzed in these literatures, corresponding to growing environmental concerns with climate change, the role of energy flows and energy networks (and in turn their contribution to rising emissions) is increasingly theorized (Castree and Christophers, 2015; Granoff et al., 2016; Huber, 2015; Monstadt, 2009; Sayre, 2010). Carbon arteries, like other infrastructures of commodity transport, fix capital in place to move fossil fuels from sites of resource extraction to industrial sites and urban environments. Carbon powered electricity networks energize production and built environments, while oil and gas pipelines connect to refineries and a further network of tanks, trucks, ships, roads, rails, as well as gas distribution infrastructures, further fuelling industry, transport, buildings and homes.

As Huber (2015) suggests, echoing Mitchell (2011), "following the carbon" through infrastructural networks reveals the extent to which production and reproduction have been constructed around fossil fuels and how these networks work to lock-in the fossil economy and therefore to ensure rising emissions. As Sayre (2010) submits, the infrastructures of fossil capitalism steer and regulate energy related behaviour in ways that are often beyond the "user's" control. Transportation infrastructure, for example, shapes the flow of materials and people, while electricity generation and energy infrastructure largely determines the emissions intensity of buildings, homes and factories. Given its fossil fuel dependence, the built environment, Sayre writes, "mediates economic production, exchange, and consumption in ways that both presuppose and reinforce high rates of GHG emissions" (2010, p. 85).

Recent research has pointed to the cultural and ideological dimension of fossil fuel-intensive infrastructure, including the way in which they form a foundation of capitalist hegemony (Ekers and Prudham, 2018; Huber, 2013). For example, in *Lifeblood*, Huber (2013) brilliantly analyses the cultural practices attached to (or which can be seen as spatial expressions of) carbon-based energy systems. He considers how in fossil capitalism's epicentre, the United States, oil has been fundamental to the growth of suburbanized consumerism and lifestyles. As oil became capital's "lifeblood", and as petroleum products come to saturate everyday life, parts of the working class have been "energized", gaining a form of privatized power (2013, p. 151). All this gives the suburban consumer a stake in the endless growth of carbon-driven consumer capitalism, creating the geographies and material structures of a "petro-culture" that are a critical barrier to movements for a just transition.

In the current landscape, fixed fossil capital projects are often highly contested and recent literature has focused on growing resistance and opposition to new developments. Indeed, Naomi Klein (2014) popularized the term "Blockadia" to describes recent global, but somewhat disparate efforts to halt and disrupt the expansion of fossil capital infrastructure and other forms of extractivism. Blockadia signals a spread of this activism in response to the expansion of unconventional fossil fuel development in particular, which carries new and increased environmental risks (e.g., ground water contamination, oil spills and high levels of water use), including climate risks.

5   Canadian Carbon Corridors and Landscapes of Power

In the Canadian context, Danya Nadine Scott (2013) has provided an overview of key networked infrastructures of unconventional carbon extraction, centring the environmental justice implications of new oil pipelines and their associated infrastructural complexes. With the shift to unconventional carbon extraction (fracked gas and oil, the tar sands, deep offshore oil and gas) or "extreme energy", she notes that these corridors of transport have become increasingly diffuse and the fixed capital sunk in extractive chains to process and refine carbon has become more costly, both economically and in terms of ecological impacts. Moreover, by mapping these infrastructural arteries, she reveals that the immediate environmental costs of this connectivity are typically born not in urban centres, but upstream at sites of extraction, midstream in rural and First Nation communities, as well as downstream at "end of the pipes" often located at the outskirts of cities where the inputs of labour, capital and technology (in the form of refineries and shipping depots) required to transform energy into usable form are located. As she argues, the routes of a chosen pipeline reflect existing (and geographically embedded) power relations and further cement the spatial organization of environmental inequalities in Canada (see also Flanagan and Grant, 2013; Grant et al., 2013; Hansen et al., 2013).

While Scott points to the skewed distribution of costs locally, a sizeable body of literature in Canada draws from Harold Innis and the notion of a "staples trap" or "resource curse" to analyze carbon-extractive chains and transport corridors in relation to Canada's economic development more broadly (Clarke et al., 2013; Haley, 2014; Pineault, 2014; Watkins, 2006). As this literature suggests, with the current oil development model in Canada, features of a "staples economy" are evident. This is reflected in enormous investments in production and transportation infrastructure for the export of oil to more powerful industrial centres in the global economy (especially the United States (US)), relatively high levels of reliance on foreign capital and enhanced political

influence of carbon corporations, which together help constitute the formation of a "first world petro-state" (Adkin, 2016b; Clarke et al., 2013).

Laxer (2015) provides a concise history of pipeline development in Canada,
emphasizing the export orientation of fossil capitalism in Canada, while pointing to the role of neoliberal deregulation and free trade agreements in cement-
ing that orientation. He notes that the building of gas and oil pipelines heading
south to the US and the eclipse of Canadian east-to-west routes began in the
1970s and that the 1989 Canada–US free trade agreement and the 1994 North
American Free Trade Agreement (NAFTA) bolstered these patterns.[5]

Perspectives pointing to features of staples trap that accompany carbon-
extractive development, suggest an old "dependentist" interpretation of Canadian economic development. Indeed, Mel Watkins (2006) influentially combined sociological elite theory and dependency theory in analyzing what he
saw as the underdevelopment of Canada's industrial sector and overdevelopment of resource and commercial sectors. In this view, Canada's technological
underdevelopment and resource-based export structure had rendered it a
"rich dependency" or "the worlds richest underdeveloped country" (2006,
p. 116). As McNally (1981) and Klassen (2009) argue, this perspective ignores the
capital-intensive nature of Canada's mining and energy sectors and the way
they operate as sophisticated forms of industrial capital. Subsequently, it presents a false image of the Canadian power bloc (Klassen, 2009). Carroll (1986),
developed this point through his study of the national network of finance capital in Canada.

In the analysis that follows, I trace the flow of Canadian oil and gas through
a network of pipelines, processing plants, petrochemical complexes, refineries,
tankers, and gas distribution infrastructures. I concentrate on the networks operated by the three largest transporters in Canada – Enbridge, TransCanada
and Kinder Morgan – and detail a relentless push by them to expand and deep-
en these and the flow of oil they represent. Next, I reveal relations between

---

5 As he explains, the proportionality clause in NAFTA, drafted under input from carbon corporations, formerly mandated that three-quarters of Canadian oil production and just over half
   of its natural gas are made available for export to the US. Under proportionality, Canadian
   exports of oil and natural gas could rise or fall through "market" changes (essentially, the decisions taken by carbon corporations) – but the federal government could not legally reduce
   carbon energy exports to cut emissions, nor redirect oil currently exported to the US to eastern
   Canadians. These investor rights provisions, which empower foreign investors, would thwart
   efforts at reducing emissions, including the development of a national decarbonization plan.
   However, a new trade agreement that builds on and modifies the trade policies of NAFTA,
   called the "United States-Mexico-Canada Agreement" (USMCA) was created on October 1,
   2018. While USMCA has not yet been ratified, it removes NAFTA's "energy proportionality
   clause", eliminating this barrier to a managed wind-down of the oil and gas industry.

carbon capital and financial fractions along these commodity chains, via shareholding and lending.

To provide context for the analysis (and the analyses in subsequent chapters), I begin with a broad overview of oil and gas development in Canada, before highlighting the extensive infrastructure operated by the "big three" transporters.

6   Canadian Oil and Gas Boom

Canada has long been a producer and exporter of fossil fuels. However, beginning in the early 2000s, the boom in unconventional fossil fuels (especially bitumen from tar sands located in the province of Alberta, along with fracked shale gas), has precipitated changes to the structure and composition of the Canadian economy, steadily elevating the importance of hydrocarbon resource extraction as a core industry (MacNeil, 2014). By 2014, at the peak of the oil boom, the fossil fuel sector accounted for nearly 25 percent of private investment, up from less than 5 percent in the early 1990s (Pineault, 2018). At this time, Canada also experienced a version of the "Dutch Disease", whereby the effects of the unconventional oil and gas boom caused an inflated dollar, leading to a decline in manufacturing and other export sectors, thereby further torqueing the economy towards carbon extraction (Laxer, 2015).

Former Prime Minister Stephen Harper was forthright in linking Canada's prosperity to its emergence as an "energy superpower" (Fekete, 2012). Under his administration we subsequently witnessed a spate of new federal regulatory rollbacks and the formation of policy frameworks aimed at facilitating oil and gas development and other resource extraction (Carter, 2014; Gibson, 2012; MacNeil, 2014). Most notably, amendments in 2012 to the Canadian Environmental Assessment Act eliminated much of the core of federal environmental assessment in Canada (Gibson, 2012). In practice, the changes have meant that approximately 90 percent of major industrial projects that would previously have undergone federal environmental review no longer do (Johnston, 2015). In the case of large pipelines and energy infrastructure projects, which cross provincial and international borders, the 2012 changes transferred responsibility for environmental assessments from the Canadian Environmental Assessment Agency to the National Energy Board (NEB), which must also conduct its own "national interest" assessment.

This growth occurred during the same period that the climate crisis has become an urgent threat and Canada now has the dubious honour of having one of the highest per capita levels of carbon emissions in the world (Schaaf et al.,

2018). Moreover, Canada's carbon-extractive development occurs in a context of settler colonialism, structured towards an ongoing process of accumulation by dispossession (Coulthard, 2014). The expansion of the carbon-extractive industry produces frequent clashes with First Nation's rights, title and sovereignty (Manno et al., 2014; Stendie and Adkin, 2016; Thomas-Muller, 2014), while First Nations and other communities in the regions where industry is located and downstream, continue to suffer numerous and disproportionate negative environmental effects from fossil fuel development.

The election of the Trudeau Liberals in 2015 appeared to portend a more circumspect approach to carbon-extractive development, including the likelihood of tougher environmental regulations on industry and a serious commitment to achieving climate targets. Along with changes to environmental reviews, Trudeau actively campaigned on a shift away from the previous government's derisible model of consultation with First Nations on resource development. After years of federal Conservative inaction on the file, the Liberals pledged to adhere to the United Nations Declaration on the Rights of Indigenous Peoples (UNDRIP), which requires free, prior, and informed consent for large-scale industrial projects.

Following his assumption of office in 2015 and in advance of COP 21, Prime Minister Trudeau further announced that:

> Canada looks forward to playing a constructive role at COP 21...We have an opportunity to make history in Paris – an agreement that supports a transition to a low-carbon economy that is necessary for our collective health, security, and prosperity. Canada is back, my good friends.[6]

The later ratification of the Paris Agreement in 2016 appeared to confirm this change of direction on climate policy. In Paris, Trudeau's Minister of Environment Catherine McKenna promoted a target of 1.5 degrees Celsius while most of the talks were about not exceeding two degrees of warming.

Yet federal policy continues to move away from the commitments made in Paris (D. Hughes, 2016; Lee, 2017), while Indigenous rights, title and sovereignty are disregarded in favour of fossil development.[7] Trudeau's 2016 Pan-Canadian

---

6   Prime Minister Justin Trudeau, speaking at the UN Paris climate talks on November 30, 2015.

7   That this was a target that Canada had no intention of meeting became more apparent in the following year (see Gutstein, 2018, pp. 154–171). Indeed, the Liberals merely carried over Harper's previous goal of reducing greenhouse gas emissions by 30 percent below 2005 levels by 2030. Interestingly, as Gutstein suggests (2018), McKenna was among those insisting at Paris that there be a clause in the agreement authorizing carbon trading to assist governments in achieving their nationally determined contributions. The clause, which now appears in

Framework on Clean Growth offers a policy program of slow domestic and market-based energy transition, to be funded by expanding capacity for bitumen production and transport in the medium term, alongside the taxation of those same resources when used domestically. Within this framework, the government has approved and actively championed new pipelines, despite affected Indigenous communities lack of consent, and despite clear evidence that the pipeline is at odds with Canada's commitment to lower its greenhouse gas emissions. Indeed, by 2017, Trudeau was singing a different tune on fossil fuel development, asserting that "No country would find 173 billion barrels of oil in the ground and just leave them there. The resource will be developed".[8]

7   Canadian Oil Expansion

Canada is currently the fourth largest producer and third largest exporter of oil in the world, and the fourth largest producer and exporter of natural gas (Natural Resources Canada, 2017). Most oil production in Canada (nearly 80 percent) occurs in the province of Alberta, with the remaining 13.5 percent occurring in Saskatchewan, 4.5 percent in the province of Newfoundland and Labrador and 1 percent in both British Columbia and Manitoba. Most of the oil produced in Alberta comes from its tar sands – an enormous unconventional petroleum deposit containing a tar-like mixture of sand, clay and water saturated with a dense and extremely viscous form of petroleum – bitumen – found under Alberta's boreal forest and wetlands, in a region that is larger than Florida. The tar sands are estimated to contain 1.7 trillion barrels of crude oil (the world's third largest reserves) or 98 percent of Canada's established reserves (Natural Resources Canada, 2017), though a significant fraction of that total is non-recoverable at current levels of technology and market conditions. Tar sands development is possibly the largest industrial project in the world (Berman, 2017).

The first decade of the 21st century was a period of unprecedented expansion for Canadian bitumen development, the bulk of which has flowed south to the US. Indeed, approximately 70 percent of oil produced in Canada is exported, 98 percent of which goes to the US, especially the Mid-West (Natural Resources Canada, 2017). Oil and gas pipelines continue to be built for

---

Article 6 of the agreement, means that high emitters like Canada can putatively reduce their emissions by buying credits from other nations. The arrangement keeps the door to tar sands expansion open.

8   Prime Minister Justin Trudeau, speaking at the CERAWeek Global Energy and Environment Leadership Award Dinner in Houston, Texas on Thursday March 9, 2017.

American consumption and we have recently witnessed a growth of pipelines that connect Canadian crude to refineries in the US Gulf. The latter is home to the world's largest concentration of complex refineries that have coking units to break down heavy crude into lighter refined products.

Increasingly, however, the expansion of infrastructure for tar sands is justified as a means of getting bitumen from inland regions to new markets (especially China) via pipelines to "tidewater", where it would be loaded onto tankers for export. As Laxer (2015b) suggests, two key factors produced changes leading to the "search" for tidewater access. First, the discovery of major unconventional gas and shale oil reserves throughout North America has led to a North American oil and gas glut and depressed prices. Second, in 2011 President Obama halted the Keystone XL pipeline, prompting the need to find other markets for new additional volumes coming from Alberta's tar sands. While expanding the infrastructure to transport bitumen is publicly justified as a means of reaching East Asian and other developing global markets, many analysts suggests that there is little to no demand for tar sands oil in Asia (McKay, 2018; Mikulka, 2018). They therefore understand the push for tidewater access as a highly speculative move by an oil industry with few other options to increase production and suggest that any new coastal pipeline terminals are likely to ship their product overwhelmingly to the United States.

8   Tar Sands Growth and Infrastructural Networks

Until the mid-1990s the tar sands were deemed to be too risky and not commercially viable in the immediate future. However, with the combined effects of rising oil prices, the peaking of conventional production, and the creation of an investment friendly royalty regime and low tax rates, production from Alberta's tar sands increased by 260 percent between 1990 and 2010 (Huot and Grant, 2012). It has taken huge capital investments to get the industry off the ground, not only in extraction but also for processing, refining and transport. By 2014, McCormack and Workman (2015) find that nearly 35 percent of business engineering structures in Canada (e.g., buildings, roads and dams, machinery and equipment) were owned by firms that operate in Alberta. In fact, Alberta's oil and gas industry alone holds 26 percent of the country's entire business engineering capital stock, representing an enormous commitment to the production of fossil fuels (McCormack and Workman, 2015).

Most bitumen production takes place in open-pit mines, some as large as three miles wide and 200 feet deep. Only a fraction of the reserves are close enough to the surface to be mined in this way, while bulk of the established reserves (over 80 percent) are deeper and must be extracted by an energy intensive process of "steam assisted gravity drainage" (SAGD). The latter entails injecting high pressure steam into the ground to soften the bitumen so that it can be pumped to the surface. The tar sands and its appetite for energy have simultaneously spurred the development of natural gas pipelines and other infrastructure, while opening up new areas of natural gas drilling, especially in Northeast British Columbia (BC). At the tar sands, natural gas is used both as an energy source to fuel the mining of bitumen via SAGD, and natural gas condensate is used to dilute bitumen (create dilbit) so that it can flow through pipelines. Ben Parfitt (2018) reports that from 2007–2017 Alberta-bound shipments of natural gas from northeast BC increased by more than 230 percent. In fact, he finds that virtually all the sizeable increase in BC's overall gas production in this period went to Alberta, where the largest consumer is the heavy oil industry (2018). Demand for condensate has also led to the construction of pipelines carrying diluting liquids from the US to Canada, such as Enbridge's Southern Lights, which runs from Chicago-area refineries to Edmonton. The Vantage pipeline, owned and operated by Pembina Pipelines and commissioned in June 2014, also delivers ethane from North Dakota to Alberta.

The massive expansion of tar sands development requires an extensive network of pipelines heading south, as well as construction of new refineries and upgrading of existing ones designed to handle tar sands bitumen. About 40 percent of Alberta's bitumen is upgraded into a lighter, higher-value crude oil (bitumen is transformed into an intermediate crude oil product by fractionation and chemical treatment) before being piped downstream to refineries for further processing. There are four upgraders at the tar sands, one each at Suncor Energy's base site, Syncrude's Mildred Lake, CNRL's Horizon, and Nexen's Long Lake operation. Whether upgraded or piped as dilbit, bitumen reaches a series of oil way stations, storage tanks, railheads and pipeline terminals on the outskirts of Edmonton, as well as in the small town of Harsity just south of Fort McMurray. The region northeast of Edmonton, often referred to as "Alberta's Industrial Heartland", is home to more than forty industrial facilities, mostly hydrocarbon related, including numerous petrochemical plants – the largest operated by Dow Chemical and MEGlobal (Turner, 2017). In all, there are eight upgraders across Alberta, seventeen tank farms at six terminal sites and fourteen oil-by-rail terminals (Turner, 2017).

Only a specialized refinery with a coker unit can process bitumen and turn it into refined products such as fuel and only four refineries in Alberta and one in Ontario have them. Tar sands production has prompted coker builds and expansions in the US (especially between 2008–2013), the construction of which has huge capital costs of US$2 billion (Stockman, 2013). After being refined, the tar sands oil that remains in the US is primarily used to produce fuels (gasoline, diesel, jet fuel, heating oil) and petrochemicals. In 2016, transportation accounted for nearly 70 percent of total US fuel consumption, with 24 percent consumed by industrial production (US Energy Information Administration, 2016).

Given the energy intensive extraction process and extensive processing, upgrading and refining required to transform bitumen into commodified energy, recent studies have found that the lifecycle emissions (from extraction, upgrading, pipeline or tanker transport, refining and use) of bitumen from the tar sands range from eighteen to twenty-five percent higher than conventional crude (Cai et al., 2015). As a result, tar sands products are the fastest growing source of greenhouse gas emissions in Canada.

Below I provide a closer view of the flow of oil through existing and proposed fossil capital infrastructure. Alberta's tar sands feed four major export lines that provide the bulk of export capacity leaving the province: Enbridge's Mainline System, Kinder Morgan's Express and Trans Mountain Pipelines, and TransCanada's Keystone.

8.1   Enbridge's Oil Pipeline Network

Enbridge operates the world's longest crude oil and liquids pipeline system, with 30,040 kilometres of active pipe. It delivers approximately 2.8 million barrels of oil per day (bpd), primarily through its Mainline pipeline network (consisting of interconnected numbered lines), and transports roughly 64 percent of Canadian crude oil destined to the United States. One of Enbridge's main export pipelines in the Mainline system, Line 3, carries crude from Hardisty, Alberta, to Superior, Wisconsin. There it feeds into a network that carries oil to refineries in the US Midwest and, increasingly, to the Gulf Coast, via Exxon Mobile's Pegasus pipeline. The latter carries diluted bitumen for 858 miles from Patoka, Illinois to refineries in Nederland, Texas. Enbridge has also recently completed construction of the 800 km Seaway pipeline from Cushing to Freeport, Texas, with its joint partner Enterprise Products. The Seaway system has 400,000 bpd capacity and reaches a terminal and distribution oil network originating in Texas City, Texas that serves all of the refineries in the Greater Houston area.

Enbridge is currently seeking to expand and replace Line 3, the largest project in Enbridge's history (Enbridge Inc., 2019). The $8.1 billion project is positioned by Enbridge principally as a replacement and upgrading of existing pipes, yet Line 3 will also boost the capacity of its main export pipeline by 375,000 bpd, with the ability to expand it further in the future. The expansion is also being used to justify a second new pipeline, Line 66, from Superior onward across Wisconsin. The new larger pipeline would subsequently carry 760,000 bpd and would have the capacity to do so for the next 50–60 years. Considering only the upstream GHG emissions in Canada[9] (emissions from the extraction and processing of crude oils prior to their injection in the Line) Environment and Climate Change Canada estimates that the Line 3 project would contribute between 19 and 26 megatonnes of carbon dioxide equivalent per year (Natural Resources Canada, 2016).

Line 3 expansion faces active on-the-ground resistance. An Indigenous led camp near the Canada–US border south of Winnipeg is protesting construction already underway in Canada, and direct-action protests have been held at the Wisconsin–Minnesota state line to protest the Minnesota regulator's decision in July 2018 to approve a certificate of need for the project.[10]

8.2   *TransCanada's Main Oil Lines*

TransCanada operates an approximately 4,300-kilometre oil transport network. Its Keystone pipeline runs from Hardisty, Alberta, east into the province of Manitoba where it turns south and crosses the US border into North Dakota. From there, it runs south through South Dakota to Steele City, Nebraska, where it splits: one arm runs east through Missouri for US refineries in Wood River and Patoka, Illinois, and the other runs south through Oklahoma to Cushing. From Cushing, crude is pumped to US Gulf Coast refineries and distribution networks via TransCanada's 700,000 bpd Marketlink Pipeline System, completed in 2015.

Keystone XL is a proposed extension of the Keystone pipeline, involving a 2,785 kilometre route that would carry roughly 800,000 bpd from Alberta to refineries along the Texas Gulf Coast, passing through Indigenous territories

---

9   Environment and Climate Change Canada considers only upstream emissions associated with new pipelines based on the assumption of a "presumed substitution effect" (that is, if we do not extract, other regions will).

10   Enbridge also headed up the Northern Gateway Pipeline, a project that would have piped diluted bitumen and condensate between Kitimat in Northern BC and the tar sands region in Alberta. If constructed, Northern Gateway would expand the Kitimat Marine Terminal to include two ship berths and 19 storage tanks for diluted bitumen, while also increasing tanker traffic on the coast – bringing to up to 220 oil tankers per year that would navigate the waters of the Great Bear Rainforest. The project provoked widespread opposition from First Nations whose territories would be impacted, and in 2015 eight First Nations, four environmental groups and the private sector union launched a joint case claiming that the federal environmental assessment had failed to consider the threats to wildlife, oceans and Indigenous rights which the project posed. In 2016, the Federal Government rejected the Northern Gateway application.

in Montana, South Dakota, Nebraska, Kansas and Oklahoma. The Obama administration repeatedly delayed the pipeline and ultimately rejected it in November 2015, yet President Trump has since reversed Obama's rejection of Keystone XL and signed executive orders aimed at facilitating its construction. TransCanada has recently won approval for the pipeline, and despite enormous resistance from environmentalists, landowners, Indigenous groups and municipalities, is championing its development.

Canada already exports about 3.76 million barrels of oil a day to the United States. Line 3 and Keystone XL would add 1.2 million bpd to that total, much of it destined for the US Gulf Coast. It is unclear whether any Canadian crude reaching this coast will be exported. Currently, shipping the fuel from the US Gulf Coast to Asia involves a 25-day trip through the Panama Canal, or a 50-day trip around South America. Reaching BC tidewater would cut travel time to twelve days, however, as suggested above there appears to be little to no current demand for tar sands oil in Asia.

8.3   *Kinder Morgan Canada*

Kinder Morgan Canada is a fossil fuel pipeline and terminal company operating in British Columbia, Alberta, and Saskatchewan. It is majority-owned by Texas-based Kinder Morgan Inc., one of the largest energy infrastructure companies in North America. Kinder Morgan Canada holds a series of pipeline and storage assets and formerly owned the Trans Mountain pipeline (TPL). In a move that expresses the Government of Canada's deep commitment to sustain the oil industry, in 2018 the Government bought the TPL and its expansion project (discussed below) from Kinder Morgan for $4.5 billion.

The TPL transports both crude oil and refined products from Edmonton, Alberta to the west coast, with a capacity of approximately 300,000 bpd. In the Greater Vancouver area, transportation fuel (such as gasoline, jet fuel, and diesel) and lubricants reach the Burrard Terminals (three separate facility locations in both Port Moody and Burnaby) operated by Suncor Energy. Suncor distributes the products on land (by train and truck) and on water via barges to distribution stations held by Petro-Canada (a subsidiary of Suncor).

Conventional crude from the TPL is processed at several marketing terminals and refineries in the central British Columbia region and the Greater Vancouver area. Of the oil that remains in British Columbia, Chevron's Burrard Inlet area refinery and distribution terminals receive the most. Crude arriving from the TPL is transformed here into approximately 55,000 barrels of jet fuel, diesel, gasoline, asphalts, heating fuels, heavy fuel oils, butanes and propane each day (Chevron Canada, n.d.; Moreau, 2012). An additional 30 percent of crude transported by the TPL arrives at the Westridge Marine Export Terminal, in Burnaby. For every ten tankers that leave Westridge, eight go to California, one goes to the Gulf Coast and one goes to China.

The Trans Mountain Expansion Project (TMX) proposes to expand the existing TPL system by twinning the existing pipeline through Alberta and British Columbia. The project would increase pipeline capacity from 300,000 to 890,000 bpd. Thirteen oil producers have signed 15- and 20-year commitments of on the Trans Mountain Expansion, that represent 80 percent of its capacity (Transmountain, 2017). In addition to the construction of the new pipeline, the project includes new pump stations and storage tanks, and a new dock at the Westridge Marine Terminal in Burnaby, British Columbia. Considering the GHG emissions associated with extraction, upgrading, and refining within Canada, Environment Canada estimates that the expansion to the Trans Mountain pipeline system would contribute approximately 13 to 15 megatonnes of carbon dioxide equivalent per year to Canada's total emissions, bringing the total emissions of a 890,000 barrels per day pipeline to 21 to 26 megatonnes of carbon dioxide equivalent per year (Canadian Environmental Assessment Agency, 2016).

At the time of writing, growing protests and legal challenges organized by Indigenous, environmental, and local citizen-driven groups are underway against the Trans Mountain Pipeline Expansion (Zeidler, 2018), and the provincial government in British Columbia has made some moves to hinder the pipeline's construction (Nikiforuk, 2019). Mounting anger and counter-protests have also been developing in Alberta and to some extent Saskatchewan (Patterson, 2019).

9   Growing Natural Gas

Currently, nearly two-thirds of Canada's gas production take place in Alberta with a further 30 percent occurring in British Columbia and just 6 percent in the rest of Canada (D. Hughes, 2015). With declining conventional reserves, the potential for Canada's gas future lies primarily in developing fracked shale and tight gas which are found in substantial plays in Northeast British Columbia and Northwest Alberta (National Energy Board, 2013, 2015). As intimated above, Alberta's oil sands operations currently account for more than 25 percent of Canadian natural gas demand (National Energy Board, 2017), while an addition fifty percent of Canada's remaining gas production goes to the US Here the industrial sector is the largest consumer of gas, accounting for nearly 40 percent of consumption (US Energy Information Administration, 2016). Major natural gas consumers in the US include the petrochemical industry (where natural gas is used as a feedstock in the production of methanol, ammonia, and fertilizer) and other energy-intensive industries that use natural gas for heat and power.

Facing a North American gas glut, and in order to benefit from what appeared a few years ago to be a substantial mark-up between North American natural gas prices and those in Asia, the natural gas industry also began aggressively pursuing the development of a number of liquefied natural gas (LNG) facilities on British Columbia's west coast aimed at reaching Asian markets. Developing LNG export would require a massive expansion of natural gas production and entail large-scale infrastructural development throughout the northeast of the province, a region covered by territories of First Nations.

Corporations and industry associations along with intergovernmental organizations (such as the International Energy Agency (IEA) and the Intergovernmental Panel on Climate Change (IPCC)) have characterized natural gas as a "bridge fuel", capable in aiding in the transition to renewable sources of energy.[11] The bridge fuel argument is that natural gas burns cleaner and more efficiently than coal (in particular) and that, by coupling renewable energy with "low carbon" natural gas, renewable power's intermittency problem can be overcome by "firm" power available for the electricity grid. In BC, because Asian markets are the intended target, industry proponents argue that exporting LNG will enable reductions in coal use in particular (which is commonly used for electricity generation in South Korea and China), contributing to the construction of a "global green economy". However, the climatic merits of natural gas are often based solely on emissions from its combustion, while the lifecycle GHG emissions of natural gas (which include extracting, processing and transporting the gas; liquefying and regasifying in the case of LNG; and then combusting the gas to supply heat, generate electricity, or move vehicles) are significantly greater (Howarth, 2014; D. Hughes, 2015; Stephenson et al., 2012). In the case of BC LNG, geoscientist David Hughes estimates that the liquefaction, transport, and regasification process would consume close to 20 percent of the total extracted gas (2015). In considering the lifecycle emissions of LNG extracted from shale and tight gas plays, recent studies suggest that if methane emissions are minimized and the energy intensity of transport is reduced, the lifecycle GHG emissions of LNG are marginally lower than those of

---

11   For their part, organizations like the IEA and IPCC have included caveats about both landscape level risks and climate impacts surrounding the development of unconventional sources, and indicate that further research is needed (Intergovernmental Panel on Climate Change, 2007; International Energy Agency, 2011).

coal (Council of Canadian Academies, 2014). Nevertheless, marginal emissions benefits over coal are no grounds for the "transition fuel" claim.

Licences and permits for exports fall to the National Energy Board, which has to date approved eighteen LNG export terminals in the province. As with other extreme energy projects, LNG development requires massive amounts of capital outlay: terminals often involve investments of $10 billion or more, in addition to large expenditures on pipeline and upstream infrastructure. As a result, British Columbia has seen some foreign investment and the announcement of a number of joint ventures between some of the largest global oil and gas companies.[12] Below I provide a closer view of key existing and proposed natural gas infrastructure networks, focusing on major lines operated by Enbridge and TransCanada who are also Canada's largest natural gas transporters and own substantial midstream operations.

In addition to its extensive oil transport network, Enbridge is Canada's largest natural gas distribution company with 330,598 kilometers of natural gas pipelines across North America and the Gulf of Mexico. It also has a large, growing interest in natural gas storage and midstream operations. A large proportion of its natural gas infrastructure takes place through subsidiaries. Enbridge is 50 percent owner of Alliance Pipeline, which transports fracked gas from northeastern BC and northwestern Alberta, underground through Saskatchewan, North Dakota, Minnesota, Iowa, to Chicago. Gas from the Alliance Pipeline connects to natural-gas processing venture, Aux Sable (which is jointly owned by Enbridge and Veresen and one of the largest natural gas processing plants in North America). Aux Sable's Channahon facility near Chicago supplies natural gas for home and industrial heating, and the natural gas liquids (NGLs) produced by Aux Sable are used in crude oil refining and gasoline blending, crop drying, as feedstock for the petrochemical industry and in the production of products such as polyethylene, rubber, plastics, solvents and foam materials.

In 2016, Enbridge began the process of a takeover of Houston-based Spectra Energy, which operated natural-gas pipelines (including the Westcoast Energy pipeline), local distribution companies and processing plants throughout North America, creating a $127 billion energy infrastructure company (Pulsinelli, 2016). Enbridge's Westcoast Energy pipeline transports fracked gas produced in the Western Canadian Sedimentary Basin throughout British Columbia and through interconnecting pipelines to other Canadian provinces and

---

12   Aside from initial site preparation, to date there has been little actual sunk capital in these proposed projects. Companies have, however, purchased stakes in properties in the region (held mainly by Canadian gas and oil companies).

the United States. The system in British Columbia accounts for 55 percent of gas produced in the province, while the gathering, processing and transmission of gas along Enbridge's Westcoast pipeline contributed a staggering 4,115,429 tonnes of carbon dioxide equivalent in 2016, approximately 35 percent of all emissions from large industrial processing facilities in BC (Government of Canada, 2016).

Within the province, the Westcoast connects to TransCanada's Nova Gas Transmission system (described below) and Fortis BC's extensive local distribution system in British Columbia's Lower Mainland. At the Canada–US border near Huntingdon, British Columbia, it connects to Williams Northwest Pipeline, which is a nearly 7,000-kilometer bi-directional pipeline system crossing the states of Washington, Oregon, Idaho, Wyoming, Utah and Colorado.

TransCanada for its part operates over 91,000 kilometres of gas distribution, connecting with virtually all major gas supply basins in North America. It is also the continent's largest provider of gas storage and related services. Its longest pipeline system, the Nova Gas Transmission Ltd (NGTL), is an extensive gathering and transport system for gas produced in the Western Canadian basin, especially the Montney and Duvernay shale gas plays, which are located in northeast BC and central Alberta, respectively. The NGTL system continues to expand at a rapid pace, and TransCanada has added more than $2 billion in facilities between 2010 and 2015. New supply has entered the system, particularly from the Montney shale formation in the northwest portion of the system. The NGTL interconnects with TransCanada's Mainline at Empress near the Alberta–Saskatchewan border. The Mainline serves as a long-haul delivery system transporting natural gas from the Western Canadian Sedimentary Basin across Canada to Ontario and Québec to deliver gas to downstream Canadian and US markets.

TransCanada is currently moving ahead with an additional $2 billion expansion to its NGTL system. The upstream (pre-transmission) GHG emissions in Canada associated with the production, gathering and processing of the additional volume of natural gas to be transported by the NGTL System alone are estimated to be 1.2 and 1.4 megatonnes of carbon dioxide equivalent per year (Canadian Environmental Assessment Agency, 2016).

The company is also actively pushing for LNG export development in BC. It has proposed major gas pipelines aimed at facilitating the growth of the industry. The most advanced proposal is the Coastal GasLink, a 670 km pipeline to deliver fracked gas from the Montney region to a proposed LNG facility near Kitimat, BC. Here the gas would be liquefied for export by LNG Canada (a consortium including Shell Canada, PetroChina, Korea Gas Corporation, and

Mitsubishi) and shipped to Asia by tanker. The LNG export terminal in Kitimat, British Columbia, has an estimated cost of approximately $40 billion, and would produce 8.6 megatonnes of emissions per year beginning in 2030 and rising to 9.6 megatonnes in 2050 (Heerema and Kniewasser, 2017). This would account for 3 to 11 percent of Canada's total carbon budget, designed to limit warming to 2 degrees Celsius.

10   Infrastructure and Path-Dependency

As Kaika and Swyngedouw (2000) write, once fixed capital is completed it is often "buried underground, invisible, rendered banal and relegated to an apparently marginal, subterranean underworld" (p. 121). Enormous networks of physical infrastructures are required to process, move and subsequently suffuse the economy (and everyday life) as a whole with fossil fuels and petroleum products. Yet they are mostly a part of our "energy and ecological unconscious" – a component of a series of interconnections that are often out of sight and out of mind (Shannon et al., 2011). By "following the carbon" through infrastructures and examining them in terms of webs, configurations or systems, these networks and the waste flows attached to them (especially emissions) are brought into view.

Enbridge, Kinder Morgan and TransCanada account for the vast majority of Canadian oil and gas transport, and as we find, they continue to concentrate capital within the carbon transport sector, through mergers and acquisitions. Just like extractive corporations, their reproduction is bound to the production and consumption of oil and gas. Fixed capital, moreover is subject to a long cycle of return; it can return the value invested in it only piece by piece. The lifespan of infrastructures, as we have seen, is planned in decades and their development (and financing) proceeds according to the projection of revenues to be generated by the long-term flow of fossil fuels.

Furthermore, we witnessed a massive push by the "big three" transporters develop new large-scale pipeline proposals across North America that would significantly expand unconventional oil and gas development in an era of deepening climate crisis. As Pineault (2018) points out, new fixed capital projects are planned relative to the projected long-term *growth* in the flow of oil:

> Investment in the extractive chain does not answer the current needs of crude transport: the relation between transport capacity and productive capacity is more dialectical than linear. ... investments in the extractive

chain increase the capacity of flow in an incremental, rather than continuous, manner, always overstepping actual production levels.

> p. 141

The realization of the value of fixed capital depends not only on maintaining,
but expanding the flow of fossil fuels.

New pipelines and ongoing investments in fixed capital that surrounds
mined carbon produce path-dependencies. They work to cement commitments to fossil capitalism, constraining the ability to choose a different energy
path. There are technical issues at play in the path-dependency of physical infrastructures, but there are also plain issues of political economic power.
A rapid energy transition implies a vast stranding of sunk assets, which will be
actively resisted by carbon capital. Moreover, a "networked" lens on fossil capital development encourages us to look a degree beyond carbon capital *per se*
by pointing to the financial sector's intimate relationship with it. Indeed, while
Canada's big three carbon transporters connect to extractive corporations and
various other producers along the commodity chain (midstream operators and
other fossil fuel-related industrial firms), they are also densely connected to
financial fractions.

11   The Structured Symbiosis between Carbon Capital and Finance

Drawing from the broader tradition of power structure research (Brownlee,
2005; Clement, 1975; Domhoff, 1980), sociologists have mapped the social relations that link across large corporations – in particular, the practice of sharing
directors or top managers, i.e., interlocking. Interlocks demonstrate the institutionalized relations between large firms, and thereby between the different
forms or fractions of capital – industrial, commercial, financial and so on (Carroll, 1986, 2010). As corporate directors serve on the boards of multiple large
companies, they form an integrated corporate elite, or an "organized minority"
(Brownlee, 2005, p. 19).

Recent research from William Carroll (2017) provides a wide-angle view on
the organization and architecture of the carbon sector in Canada, mapping its
internal structure as a network of interlocking directorates. Carroll's mapping
includes directorate ties to the financial sector and other segments of corporate capital – national and transnational. The research finds the architecture of
corporate power in and around the carbon-capital sector in Canada to be
densely integrated "to the point of resembling an entrenched oligarchy" (2017,
p. 254). Importantly, it reveals that carbon corporations are a central component

of a wider power structure, demonstrating also the financial industry's extensive directorate links to the oil and gas sector. These directorate linkages, as Carroll points out are to be expected given the "extensive financing needs of the [carbon] majors as they pursue megaprojects requiring massive fixed capital investment" (2017, p. 248). Indeed, interlocking directorates serve in part as *"vehicles* in the accumulation of capital often reflecting particular creditor-debtor or ownership relations" (Carroll and Alexander, 1999, p. 332).

Financial relations between banks and fossil fuel firms include the ownership of shares and financing of carbon-extractive development. Shareholding, which takes place as major financial firms purchase blocks of shares in large corporations (and through which they in turn gain a portion of a company's profits in the form of dividends), is part of the crucial "enabling" role of financial capital in carbon-extractive development. Table 2 displays the top ten shareholders in TransCanada, Enbridge and Kinder Morgan Canada,[13] as of 2017.

Given its large ownership stakes in Enbridge, US-based Capital Group has the highest percentage of total shares. Also among the top ten are Canada's "big five" banks: Toronto Dominion, Royal Bank of Canada, Canadian Imperial Bank of Commerce, Bank of Nova Scotia, and the Bank of Montreal.

In addition to ownership of shares, financial firms supply credit and loans to carbon capital. This financing is vital given the highly capital-intensive nature of carbon-extractive development, especially in the initial construction of pipelines and other large-scale infrastructure. TransCanada receives nearly $6 billion of financing via a number of term loans and revolving credit facilities for general corporate finance. This includes $1.5 billion revolving credit from JPMorgan Chase and $4.22 billion revolving credit from the Bank of Montreal (Donaghy, 2017). Enbridge also receives over $12 billion of financing via a number of term loans and revolving credit facilities for general corporate finance. These loans in include $4.39 billion in revolving credit from Toronto Dominion Bank, $2.22 billion revolving credit from Bank of Nova Scotia and $1.11 billion

---

13   The 2018 purchase of TPL and its expansion by the Canadian Government means that ownership shares in Kinder Morgan Canada (were they updated beyond 2017) would now refer to storage terminals and other pipeline assets held by the company (such as the Cochin pipeline system, which travels from Alberta to Windsor, Ontario). However, in addition to Canadian banks purchasing stocks in Kinder Morgan Canada in a mid-2017 Initial Public Offering, which displays their commitment to pipeline expansion (discussed below), Royal Bank Canada and Toronto Dominion Bank have made a more recent financing arrangement with Export Development Canada to support the TMX project (Meyer, 2018).

TABLE 2   Ownership shares in Canada's big 3 carbon transporters

Investor	Location	TransCanada	Enbridge	Kinder Morgan Canada	Total Shares
Capital Group	US	1.96%	12.34%	0.00%	14.30%
Royal Bank of Canada	CA	7.21%	5.44%	1.01%	13.66%
Toronto-Dominion Bank	CA	3.66%	3.10%	1.11%	7.87%
Power Corporation of Canada	CA	3.38%	2.76%	0.39%	6.53%
Bank of Montreal	CA	3.53%	2.18%	0.00%	5.71%
Canadian Imperial Bank of Commerce	CA	2.22%	2.32%	0.71%	5.25%
Vanguard group	US	2.55%	2.40%	0.00%	4.95%
Deutsche Bank	DE	3.18%	1.58%	0.00%	4.76%
Province of Quebec	CA	1.70%	2.65%	0.00%	4.35%
Bank of Nova Scotia	CA	2.71%	0.77%	0.00%	3.48%

SOURCE: COMPILED USING OWNERSHIP DATA FROM ORBIS – BUREAU VAN DIJK, A GLOBAL CORPORATE INFORMATION DATABASE. DATA IS CURRENT TO 2017.

revolving credit from Bank of Montreal (Donaghy, 2017). Kinder Morgan Canada has gained over $10 billion in credit, including $6 billion revolving credit from Barclays and $4.07 billion revolving credit from Canada's "leading energy bank" – Royal Bank of Canada. Additionally, a mid-2017 Initial Public Offering (IPO) of investment shares in KMC, valued at $7.25 billion, saw Canada's 5 largest banks holding 73.6 percent of the IPO, valued at $1.28 billion (McLachlan and Hatch, 2017).

Both network analysis and an examination of shareholding and lending, provide glimpses into the close relationship the fossil fuel industry and Canada's finance sector. Shareholding and lending relations produce a strong vested interest in pipeline expansion and the increased flow of oil they represent. The quest to valorize massive fixed capital investments runs against the requirement to decarbonize energy in a rapid and socially just manner.

12   Conclusion

Drawing from Marx, recent political ecology research analyzes the vital role of infrastructures in mediating the metabolic interchange between humanity and the rest of nature. Fixed capital of "large-scale and great durability" is part of the productive forces, enabling and structuring the flow of extracted resources to sites of production and consumption. The context of the current climate crisis has increased attention towards fossil fuels and the infrastructural complexes that support them. As this literature suggests, hydrocarbons are but one bundle of commodities, albeit a central one, whose production, transport and refining has vital social and ecological consequences.

Building on this literature, I provided an overview of the expansive networked infrastructures of Canadian fossil capitalism, focusing on the systems operated and proposed by the "big three" transporters – Enbridge, TransCanada and Kinder Morgan – firms which have the support of leading financial institutions. In addition to the massive scale of this infrastructure I pointed to the inertia and path dependency it poses. Moreover, despite the ecological imperative to launch an energy transition and increased public commitment on the part of some states and corporations to shift from fossil-based energy sources to non-fossil ones, carbon infrastructural networks are being relentlessly advanced in Canada, as in many other capitalist states. This further locks in a carbon economy, ensuring rising emissions and other negative impacts on the biosphere, while producing in Canada continued clashes with First Nation's rights and title and with many local communities' enjoyment and economic use of adjacent lands and waters.

While industry's push to expand extractive development is often legitimated by governments at the federal and provincial levels, no credible policies currently detail how such massive developments can take place in accordance with the need to rapidly decarbonize energy globally within the next two decades to avoid catastrophic climate change. Instead, new oil pipelines and burgeoning LNG exports, with their associated sunk costs and networked infrastructures, will only further lock-in carbon-intensive development in a period of deepening climate crisis and cement the economic interests driving the carbon-extractive sector.

Recognition of this explains the intensity and strategic value of blocking new pipelines. Political opposition from a combination of First Nations, environmental groups and some segments of labour, has proven quite effective in halting new development. Still, prohibitions on new fossil fuel infrastructure, let alone the enforced wind-down of production and stranding of capital assets, continues to be a titanic political challenge.

While recognizing the inertia that accompanies fixed capital, David Harvey points out that the forms that capital assumes, including its infrastructural "hardware", are historically contingent. Capital, he writes, must "build a fixed space (or "landscape") necessary for its own functioning at a certain point in its history only to have to destroy that space (and devalue much of the capital invested therein) at a later point in order to make way for a new "spatial fix" (openings for fresh accumulation in new spaces and territories) at a later point in its history" (Harvey, 2001a, p. 25). Following Marx and Joseph Schumpeter, he speaks to the "creative-destructive" tendencies inherent in capitalism. For him, the process of fixed capital (creative) destruction is part of overcoming capitalist crises historically. It is a response to an immediate crisis of profitability (specifically a crisis of overaccumulation), which acts as a temporary solution to the perennial "surplus capital absorption problem" (Harvey, 2011).

Today, a comprehensive decarbonization and a rebuilding of the entire energy system, is urgently needed. Holgersen and Warlenius (2016) point to the value of strategically supporting Green New Deal programs and proposals that have emerged since the economic crisis of 2008, and which have gained in profile more recently. These promise to catalyze the growth of green productive forces via a massive program of publicly directed investment in renewable electricity grids and infrastructure networks, along with major investments in public transportation, and retrofitting of houses and buildings for energy efficiency. At the same time, the authors encourage a recognition of the "darker side" of such a process of creative-destruction, arguing that averting climate change will simultaneously require policies trained at the active and planned dismantling and demolition of large parts of existing fossil infrastructure.[14] As Holgersen and Warlenius recognize, a planned wind-down of fossil fuel production, along with the dismantling of existing fossil infrastructure before the

---

14   Presumable due to political constraints, the Green New Deal resolution as introduced by Alexandria-Ocasio-Cortez in the United States in 2019 has so far avoided this "dark side". It emphasizes demand-side resolutions over active supply-side wind-down of the fossil fuel industry.

end of its useful life, is something carbon capital (and other closely linked industrial producers) will fiercely resist.

Moreover, as we have seen financial capital is a crucial enabler of carbon-extractive development, and major intuitional investors in Canada continue to be resolutely "dirty and brown" (Zadek, 2013). While left leaning analysts have pointed, from a "pragmatic" perspective, to moderate measures and incentives that might promote a "capital switch" towards more ecological ends (see Castree and Christophers, 2015), such a re-routing private capital is most immediately inhibited by the strong vested interest of financial fractions in valorizing investments in fixed fossil capital and in the flow of hydrocarbons they represent. Challenging and eroding the power of both carbon capital and financial fractions is pressing.

In this context, divestment, which seeks to withdraw capital from further investments in the production of fossil fuel, is an important social movement tactic. It can work together with "blockades" along carbon commodity chains that disrupt the smooth flow of carbon and the functioning of those chains. The combination can serve to prevent the expansion of the industry, while also opening space for alternatives. Rowe et al. (2016) argue that the power and "secret" of divestment lie in its ability to withdraw legitimacy from the fossil fuel industry, by exposing the destructiveness of their activities. Viewed as a movement capacity-building action, they see it as a potential "gateway campaign" that opens participants to deeper structural critiques not only of Big Carbon, but also of capitalism itself.

As divestment campaigns develop, activist learn that financial enablers of carbon capital are just as complicit as the producers and transporters, promoting a recognition of short-sighted and speculative investments that support ecological destructivity and relations of colonial domination. Divestment can thereby open to a critique of the allocative power of financial capital – that is, of the fact that although the world is awash in capital, control over it and the choice of where it flows (and thereby control over our economic, ecological and social futures) continues to belong to a group of financiers that are largely insulated from democratic control and accountability. It can encourage a more direct challenge to the corporate control over capital, exposing that the "directed destruction" of existing fossil infrastructure and heavy and re-directed investments towards green energy systems, will require bringing the financial sector itself under increased democratic control (see Candeias, 2013b; Carroll, 2017).

In addition to a greater focus on democratization, green-Marxist transition theories might yet go a (creative) step beyond the vision of energy transformation implied by Holgersen and Warlenius. This perspective, as well as that of other eco-socialists such as David Schwartzman (2011, 2016), who also advocates strategic support of a Green New Deal, implies a massive program for directly substituting an industrial energy system built on fossil fuels for one based on cleaner and renewable sources, grid for grid, pipe for pipe.

There is no blank slate upon which an alternative energy system can be constructed. And as Huber writes, "the way out of today's carbon society is to revolutionize the forces of production on which it is built" (2018, p. 518). Nevertheless, it is worth imagining, within this revolutionizing of the productive forces, a transformation in the energy system that goes beyond a change of fuels. The current fossil energy system, as we have seen, is highly centralized and wasteful; it is built around "extreme energy" frontiers and reliant on long infrastructural networks that connect fuels from distant points of extraction to sites of production and consumption. It has been broadly constructed to support the "abstract space of accumulation" and is geared to the underlying over-production of goods. An alternative energy system, organized in the long-term to mend and restore our metabolic relation with the rest of nature, would need to look quite different. It would need to be constructed around sustainable production for use and would be much more decentralized, working towards lessening the spatial antagonism in contemporary production, helping to make "town and country" whole again.

CHAPTER 6

Fossil Capitalism, Corporate Strategy and Post-carbon Futures

Earlier writing on fossil capitalism tended to imply that a social formation based on renewable energy would *necessarily* be post-capitalist. Elmar Altvater (2007), for example, asserted that "today, and possibly for ever, it is impossible to power the machine of capitalist accumulation and growth with "thin" solar radiation-energy. It simply lacks the potential of time and space compression, which "thick" fossil energy offers" (p. 45). The profile and tendency of renewables – their decentralized character, as well as their intermittent nature – appeared profoundly incompatible with the spatio-temporal dynamics of capitalist property relations. A "solar revolution", he asserted, will require not only new technologies, but must also involve "a radical transformation of the patterns of production and consumption, life and work, gender relations and the spatial and temporal organization of social life" (2007, p. 54).

Recent work avoids this close identity, however. This reflects technological developments in storage and long-distance transmission, and technical assessments suggesting that alternative forms of energy can meet all existing energy needs today without a radical transformation of capitalism (Jacobson et al., 2018). Indeed, research has pointed to the possibility of a "green capitalist" or "climate capitalist" project of energy transition (Adkin, 2017; Carroll, 2020a; P. Newell and Paterson, 2010, 2011; Sapinski, 2015, 2016). Newell and Paterson describe the project of climate capitalism as "a model which squares capitalism's need for continued economic growth with substantial shifts away from carbon-based industrial development" (2010, p. 1). It is a post-carbon but pro-capitalist project, proposing the ecological modernization of capitalism, including its energy base. It centres the agency of corporations and employs market-mechanisms aimed at reducing carbon emissions and redirecting flows of capital away from fossil fuels and toward renewable sources of energy (Sapinski, 2015). In this vision, large private energy companies (including fossil fuel firms) and the finance industry, gain control over an emerging energy system, slowly subsuming renewables under their centralized control (Candeias, 2013b; Lohmann, 2011, 2013; Muller, 2013). A climate capitalist project points to how renewable energy may develop slowly, unevenly and in a manner that imbues the technologies with relations of class power.

Such a project, as Adkin notes (2017), runs counter to the vision shared by many on the green-left, for whom, like Altvater, energy transition is seen to provide the foundation for a wider process of social and ecological transformation. Muller (2013) therefore considers there to be two broad paths in the expansion of renewable energy.[1] One (green or climate capitalism) leads to large-scale installations under the control of big energy companies, especially fossil fuel corporations. The other (energy democracy or green socialism) leads to an increasingly democratic energy sector, based on diversity of sources, owned publicly and developed substantially at the community level (Muller, 2013).

This chapter provides an empirical examination of the strategies adopted by Canadian fossil fuel corporations in relation to renewable energy development. It considers whether we are witnessing signs of "transition capture" as some oil and gas producers invest in a transition towards climate capitalism. Clearly, the idea that the fossil fuel industry would voluntarily shut down its operations and replace it with a renewable energy system overnight, stranding vast sunk assets (glimpsed in Chapter 5), is ludicrous. However, while oil and gas companies are driven by short-term profit seeking, we should not discount their ability to also develop long-term strategies that are geared toward both protecting current investments and ensuring future profit streams. To this end, I examine the extent to which Canadian carbon corporations are developing accumulation strategies that are consonant with climate capitalism (i.e., engaging in a longer-term business strategy to slowly move "beyond carbon", while simultaneously protecting current investments and sunk assets). This transition would be in some tension with the notion of fettering of green productive forces.

First, using recent financial reports, I investigate the extent to which the top ten Canadian carbon corporations (based on 2016 revenues) are diverting capital into renewable energy, in anticipation of declining future demand for fossil fuels. Second, I analyze intersectoral relations via a social network analysis of interlocking directorate relations between the fossil fuel sector and the renewables industry, including Crown corporations, renewable industry associations and climate-capitalist civil society organizations.

---

1   The suggestion of "two paths" skirts over the Green New Deal (GND) project, mentioned above. Mario Candeias (2013b) delineates "ideal-typical" features the GND, positioning it between green capitalism and green socialism. As he suggests, the GND could forge a path for energy democracy and green socialism. However, it may also become a version of climate capitalism with specified reforms to address labour and social-reproductive issues.

To provide further context for the analysis, the chapter begins with a brief review of research on the political economy and ecology of fossil capitalism. This work builds from fossil capital scholarship reviewed earlier, while highlighting additional social and political obstacles to the decarbonisation of the energy system. I review insights from the literature on political transformations that reinforce an oil dependent economy, as well as research on the organization and power of carbon capital.

1   Petro-politics and Petro-states

Building from the literature on fossil capitalism, recent political ecology approaches under the rubric of "first-world petro-politics", examine the long-run political implications and path-dependencies associated with fossil fuel development (Adkin, 2016b; Carter, 2014; Carter and Zalik, 2016; Nikiforuk, 2010). Drawing from work on "rentierism" and staples theory, heavy reliance on hydrocarbon exports is argued to pose a series of political economic challenges, often producing a "resource curse", or a "staples trap" (Haley, 2014; Pineault, 2014; Shrivastava, 2015). The literature finds that reliance on oil exports may lead to revenue unpredictability, while also undermining efforts to diversify the economy's productive base (Laxer, 2015b). Importantly, fossil fuel production is highly capital-intensive, meaning that employment in the sector is slight in relation to other industrial sectors and relative to output and emissions (Albo and Yap, 2016).[2] Through advancements in technological productivity, carbon firms have been able to steadily increase production levels, while employing fewer and fewer workers (Hussey, 2020).

Structural dependence on fossil fuel revenues (combined with distinctive political-institutional configurations and policies[3]) has also produced negative political impacts, with troubling implications for democracy (Adkin, 2016a;

---

2   The oil economy has also been profoundly gendered and booms have not created nearly as many jobs for women as they have for men (O'Shaughnessy and Dogu, 2016).
3   While pointing to reliance on oil revenue as an explanation for "democratic deficits", the authors cited here recognize the crucial importance of policy and governance directions in "petro-state" formation. They point to the need to avoid undue focus on the commodity of oil itself, in favour of more complex explanations that include a focus on royalty and taxation regimes, as well as public ownership frameworks in accounting for state-society relations (see especially Carter, 2016; Shrivastava, 2015). Studies here often point to Norway's success in overcoming some of the challenges of resource revenue dependence, citing the political-institutional context undergirding the government's ability to reap economic and political benefits and achieve comparatively better environmental records.

Carter and Zalik, 2016; Shrivastava, 2015). In the Alberta context, research points to the heightened deterioration of the link between the state and citizens, as oil rents release the state from reliance on tax revenue, contributing to its privileging of corporate interests over democracy and environmental sustainability (Shrivastava, 2015).

States or regions suffering from a resource curse may also experience a "carbon trap" or policy deterioration due to the "institutional molding effects" of oil revenue dependency (Carter, 2014, p. 26). Here government reliance on fossil fuel revenues combined with royalty regimes and tax structures geared to carbon-extractive interests are argued to obstruct progress on carbon emissions reduction and environmentally progressive policies, making future climate adaptation and post-carbon transition all the more difficult (Adkin, 2016b; Adkin and Miller, 2016; Carter, 2014; Carter and Zalik, 2016; Nikiforuk, 2010).

2   Corporate Power and Carbon Capital

Work examining the political inertia that characterizes fossil fuel dependent economies is complemented by a recent literature that combines the sociology of corporate power with the political economy and ecology of fossil capital (Adkin et al., 2017; Carroll, 2017, 2020b; Carroll et al., 2018a; Carter and Zalik, 2016; Graham, 2017; Graham et al., 2020).

Corporate power, as we have seen, is rooted in capitalist production relations – is the power that accrues to enormous concentrations of economic resources, or to corporations in the later modern world (see also Carroll, 2016; Carroll and Sapinski, 2018). As Marx argued, control over means of production, enables the dominant class (those who own and/or control big capital) to appropriate the economic surplus produced by a subordinate class that depends on the dominant class for access to the means of production and subsistence. Within capital's competitive dynamics, each firm must grow or die and thus the surplus that capital appropriates from labour gets re-invested on pain of extinction. Therefore, as Carroll and Sapinski (2018) suggest corporate control over the social surplus gives capitalists power not only within current economic practices, but over the future.

The project of climate capitalism reflects and does not seek to challenge this power. It centres market-mechanisms aimed at incentivizing an energy transition, while not disrupting profitability or the concentration of economic power in the hands of a relatively small group of major investors and corporate executives. Meanwhile, the suggestion that oil and gas firms will play a key role in energy transition, points not only to their control over capital and investment decisions, but also to their monopolization of knowledge, capacities and skills, many of which are highly pertinent to for energy transition. As Fatih Birol, executive director of the International Energy Agency, remarked at the 2020 Davos Global Energy Challenge Panel: "Looking at Aramco, Siemens, many companies who are here, they have all the skills, all the engineering knowledge to run large-scale projects. Why don't we get them on board and make them part of the solution?" (Lewis and Defterios, 2020).

However, corporate power, as Carroll (2016) explains, is "janus-faced", and includes not only economic, but also cultural-political facets. The latter speaks to corporate "reach" into political and civil society, as dominant fractions of capital bring leadership into public domains and promote the virtues of one or another aspect of corporate capitalism (Jamie Brownlee, 2005). Where carbon extraction comprises a leading sector, corporate power invests deeply in maintaining conditions for the accumulation of fossil capital (i.e., blocking or slowing energy transition). Studies have extensively examined the reach of carbon capital into political and civil society and at regional, national and international scales. In the political field, research has focused on corporate lobbying (Carter, 2016; Elsner and Kasper, 2015; Graham, 2017; Graham et al., 2020; N. Klein, 2014), political party donations (Graham, 2017), and "revolving door" relations or close personal ties between the corporate community and the state apparatus (Adkin and Miller, 2016; van Apeldoorn and de Graaff, 2012; de Graaff, 2012b; de Graaff and van Apeldoorn, 2017; Taft, 2017). Such avenues of influence allow carbon capital to shape the so-called policy planning process, erecting barriers to the development of robust environmental regulations, including policies aimed at carbon emissions reduction and pro-clean energy policies.

In circumstances of increased public criticism and robust social movement opposition, carbon capital's "accumulation strategy" – its growth model, including the various "extra-economic" supports and preconditions for its realization (Jessop, 1983) – demands careful ideological legitimation. Therefore the power of the sector reaches into civil society, as carbon-capital fractions and their allies participate in the governance and funding of organizations such as policy-planning groups, think-tanks, media outlets (Bonds, 2016; Brulle, 2014; Elsner and Kasper, 2015; Carroll et al. 2018), as well as research institutes and universities (Adkin and Stares, 2016; Carroll et al., 2018b; Gustafson, 2012).

Business influence over such sites of knowledge production and dissemination helps institutionalize a "new climate denialism" – a disjuncture between scientific knowledge and political action (Derber, 2010; S. Klein and Daub, 2016).

According to Klein and Daub, industry and political leaders "assure us that they understand and accept the scientific warnings about climate change – but they are in denial about what this scientific reality means for policy and/or continue to block progress in less visible ways" (2016, para. 4). The new denialism centres technological fixes that thinly green productive forces (e.g., greater efficiency in carbon extraction and consumption), as well as market-based policies (e.g., carbon taxes) aimed at incremental change (Derber, 2010).

3   Post-carbon Futures and Corporate Strategy

The various modalities of corporate power discussed above together comprise a "regime of obstruction" (Carroll, 2020b) and are a key factor in the chasm between climate science and climate action. However, while carbon capital is actively supressing a rapid process of decarbonisation, its tactics of delay and of new denialism are potentially supported by a longer-term strategy of participating in a slow and "managed transition" to more climatically benign sources of energy. As suggested in existing literature, the fossil fuel sector, certain organizations, or key individuals within it, may support a drawn-out transition to climate capitalism, as a project which gradually transforms the energetic basis of capitalism towards hydropower, solar, wind, tidal, wave and nuclear, while leaving its class structure untouched, including the concentration of economic power in the hands of a relatively small group of major investors, executives and corporate directors (Adkin, 2017; Derber, 2010; Lohmann, 2011; Muller, 2013; Sapinski, 2015, 2016). The research here focuses on the Canadian context, asking *in what ways the fossil fuel sector in Canada is shaping and controlling the development of renewable energy and conversely, and how has the development of renewables shaped the fossil fuel industry itself?*

4   Sample and Data

To investigate this question, I examine the extent to which the top ten Canadian fossil fuel companies (based on 2016 revenues) are diverting capital into renewables. This includes wind, solar, hydro, tidal, geothermal and biofuels.[4]

---

4 I include companies broadly involved in renewable power development, operation and transmission, as well as energy products, services and power storage. Nuclear energy, which provides 14 percent of Canada's electrical power in addition to that from renewables, is excluded (Laxer, 2015b). Studies have found that nuclear power stations may use more useful

These large companies are the most likely to be investing given that they have the capital to hedge. Information on the capital expenditures of these "majors" is obtained from annual reports covering 2012–2016. This five-year period allows us to consider short-term trends in capital investment and includes both the highest years for recorded profits in the sector in 2013 and early 2014, and the relative decline of profits due to falling oil and gas prices beginning in late 2014 and into 2015.

Next, I analyze inter-sectoral relations via a social network analysis of interlocking directorate relations between the fossil fuel sector and the renewables industry. To represent the carbon-extractive corporate sector, 238 corporations in this industry were selected, all based in Canada with 2014 assets of at least $50 million. The renewables industry sample includes 51 publicly traded Canadian companies and five Crown corporations.[5] I also include energy "hybrids" – companies (both private and Crown) with a mixed energy portfolio consisting of at least 20 percent renewables assets,[6] or diversified corporations with renewable energy divisions alongside their other operations. In total, the sample includes seven private or independent hybrids and eight Crown hybrids.[7]

Subsequently, I investigate the Canadian fossil fuel sector's participation on the boards of key Canada-based civil society organizations that emphasize accelerating renewable energy development in Canada and transitioning to a low-carbon future. This includes nine Canadian renewable industry associations. Industry associations are governed almost exclusively by corporate directors from the renewables sector, allowing the industry to define issues of common importance and to organize strategies for advancing its interests. They are effectively part of the green energy sector; they form its political arm

---

energy over their life cycle (in mining, transportation, decommissioning the power stations and managing waste) than is generated over the power station's lifetime (Laxer, 2015b).

5   Also included are foreign controlled multinationals with a Canadian subsidiary company or division (including Canada-based corporate directors). There were eight such companies. The sample is intended to capture the renewable industry in Canada as a whole, but comprehensive listings are lacking. To identify companies I drew from governmental listings (Foreign Affairs, Trade and Development Canada, 2014), as well as renewable industry association reports. Several companies listed in these reports are either private or do not have boards of directors (or publicly available information). They were dropped from the sample.

6   In cases where renewable asset figures were not available, I used total power generation capacity (from renewable and non-renewable sources) as a proxy measure.

7   Data on the directors and top executives of the 238 carbon-extractive corporations, is gathered as of yearend 2016. The database was constructed by a team of researchers at the University of Victoria, as part of the Corporate Mapping Project. Sources included online business databases (ORBIS and FP Infomart), as well as company websites and annual reports.

and reach into political and civil society by creating and circulating policy briefs, research reports, and lobbying different levels of government.

Further, I include seven advocacy organizations, whose remit centres on advancing a green, or "clean" capitalist vision.[8] These organizations bring together multi-sectoral business leaders, non-government organizations, policy experts and unions in an effort to advance green capitalism as a "hegemonic project". A hegemonic project, as Jessop (1983) defines it, involves the mobilization of support behind a concrete program that brings about a coalition of different interests. They aim to cultivate the passive and active approval of various groups and extend to the whole field of civil-society relations and the state.[9] Concomitantly, hegemonic projects are densely linked to the formulation of an appropriate accumulation strategy, as a vital component of a project's bid for hegemony centres on its perceived economic viability and desirability (Jessop, 1983). More than lobby organizations, the above groups participate in the creation of the discourses and practices of climate capitalism, and mobilize them by reaching out to economic, political and other elites (Sapinski, 2016).

Together, these methods provide insight into the relations between Canadian fossil corporations and renewable energy firms. They allow us to investigate strategies employed by the carbon-extractive sector aimed at asserting controlling over the energy field, while simultaneously keeping fossil fuels in the "energy mix" for the foreseeable future.

5   Renewable Energy Development in Canada

A "wave" of global investment in renewables, including by fossil fuel firms, began in the late 1990s and early 2000s, as momentum built around reaching a global climate agreement (Switzer, 2013). However, in the immediate aftermath of the financial crisis of 2007–2008, political support for renewable energy waned and investment levels decelerated and even fell in some regions (Sweeny and Treat, 2017). Since 2010, investment in renewable power and fuels have made a steady recovery globally, and reached a record $348.5 billion in 2015

---

8   The civil society associations reflect a judgement sample of the key organizations in the field.
9   In its effort to gain approval and support from sectors of civil society such as from environmental non-government organizations and unions, the climate capitalist project can be read as engendering a form of what Antonio Gramsci (1971) referred to as "passive revolution". This consists of an elite engineered process of social transformation, that partially and selectively satisfies oppositional demands from below, while simultaneously denying subaltern groups the initiative and ability to engage in self-leadership (Sassoon, 1982; Thomas, 2011). By contrast, their intellectuals are absorbed into the power bloc (Candeias, 2013a).

(Frankfurt School-UNEP Centre, 2016). There was a relative decline in 2016, with investments falling to $287.5 billion (Bloomberg New Energy Finance, 2016).

Canada, for its part, is the 4th largest renewable power generator in the world (National Energy Board, 2016). Close to 60 percent of this comes from hydropower, which accounts for 17 percent Canada's total energy consumption. Most of it already constructed in the form of large "legacy" dam projects, with Crown corporations playing an important role (Laxer, 2015b). These provide a tremendous base from which to transition to a low carbon future through the expansion of wind and solar power, as well as hydro from run-of-river turbines and tidal turbines.

Investment in renewable energy in Canada (by both private and Crown corporations) reached a high point of $12 billion 2014, but dropped slightly in 2015 to $10 billion (its second highest level) (Clean Energy Canada, 2016). Solar and wind investments fell again in 2016 by 46 percent, leaving Canada out of the top ten largest renewable investing nations (Frankfurt School-UNEP Centre, 2016). Reflecting on the overall growth of green energy, recent work has cited the carbon-extractive sector's prominent role as both producer and investor (Adkin, 2017; Bakx, 2016; M. Smith, 2016; Wedding, 2016). Considering only their Canada-based assets, Clean Energy Canada (2016) finds both Enbridge and Suncor to be among the five largest corporate renewable electricity operators and developers in Canada for 2015. However, the extent of carbon-capital's investments in renewables and whether they reflect an emerging and core accumulation strategy, or a modest, yet profitable hedge, remains unclear. While the existing research on climate capitalism suggests that a process of "transition capture" may be underway, this work is largely theoretical and informed by anecdotal evidence. It can be enriched through a more detailed empirical analysis.

6   Carbon Capital and Renewables: An Emerging Accumulation Strategy?

Of the top ten Canadian fossil fuel companies, six have invested in or hold significant renewable energy assets since 2012. As seen in Table 3, these companies are investing in and developing a range of renewables including hydro, solar, wind, geothermal and biofuels (ethanol).

Enbridge currently has assets in wind, solar and geothermal energy in Canadian Provinces of Quebec, Ontario, Saskatchewan, Alberta, as well as in the US in Colorado, Texas, and in the United Kingdom, France and Germany.

TABLE 3   Top ten fossil fuel companies and investments in renewables

Company name	Main operations	Renewables investment	Renewable type
Enbridge	Oil/gas pipelines	Yes	Wind, solar, geothermal
Imperial	Integrated oil	No	N/A
Suncor	Integrated oil	Yes	Wind, ethanol
Husky	Integrated oil	Yes	Ethanol
TransCanada	Oil/gas pipelines	Yes	Wind, solar, hydro
Cenovus	Integrated oil	No	N/A
CNRL	Integrated oil	No	N/A
Teck	Divers. mining	Yes	Wind, hydro
Fortis	Electric utilities	Yes	Solar power, hydro
Parkland Fuel	Fuel supplier	No	N/A

SOURCE: INVESTMENT INFORMATION IS DERIVED FROM EACH FIRM'S ANNUAL REPORTS FROM 2012–2016.

TransCanada operates three wind farms in Canada and the US, and has interests in nine Ontario-based solar projects, and a hydro project. Fortis owns six hydroelectric generating facilities in Canada and three in the Caribbean, and has an interest in US-based solar power. As of 2016, Suncor's renewables business includes investments in five operating wind facilities throughout Canada, as well as an ethanol plant in Ontario. Husky is the largest ethanol producer in western Canada, with plants in both Saskatchewan and Manitoba. Before selling its shares in 2016, Teck was a partner in the Wintering Hills wind power facility in Alberta and continues to be a majority owner of Waneta hydroelectric dam.

Table 4 compiles power generation capacity from all renewables from these six companies from 2012–2016. With 2,500 Megawatts of power capacity, Enbridge is, based on the level of capacity, the largest player in renewable energy, followed by TransCanada.

Analyzing the data in Tables 3 and 4, together with associated statements on climate change and renewable energy found in annual reports, we can place the majors into three categories. In the first category are Imperial, Cenovus, Canadian Natural (CNRL) and Parkland Fuel, which did not invest in renewable energy development or hold significant renewable energy assets during this period. Imperial explicitly recognizes a growing market for renewable power, but maintains its decision to focus on oil and gas. In its strategic discussion on renewables, it draws on its parent firm Exxon Mobil's *Long-Term Outlook for Energy*, which anticipates a growth in global energy demand (especially in the Global South), and expects that oil will continue to be the largest source of energy until at least 2040, with natural gas forecasted to grow precipitously and overtake coal in the same period (Imperial Oil, 2017). Neither Parkland, Cenovus nor CNRL directly discuss the growth of renewable energy in their annual reports, while the latter two highlight the need to address emissions and other environmental concerns by "greening" the carbon-extractive process. Cenovus is particularly forthright about the need for the industry to take responsibility for the challenge of climate change, but remains focused on becoming a leader in the areas of "energy efficiency, developing oil sands technology to reduce GHG emissions and carbon dioxide sequestration" (Cenovus Energy, 2015, p. 54).

In a second category, we find significant investments in non-fossil fuel energy by Suncor, Teck, TransCanada and Husky. However, investments by these companies have either remained flat or declined from 2012 to 2016. In fact, at the end of 2016, companies tended towards shedding renewable assets. In 2016, Suncor announced the sale of one of its six wind farms (Cedar Point wind facility) for gross proceeds of $291 million. With declining revenues since 2014, the sale of the wind farm was cited as part of a decision to continue to "streamline our portfolio through a divestment program of non-core assets" (Suncor Energy, 2017, p. 4). In January 2017, Teck also announced that it had entered into an agreement to sell its interest in its sole wind power facility – Wintering Hills – for $59 million. It made near simultaneous investments of $640 million in the Fort Hills oil sands project (Teck, 2017). Among majors, TransCanada boasts the second largest generation capacity from renewables, but its large investments were made prior to 2012, and therefore the overall share of power generated from its solar, wind and hydro assets remained consistent at 9–10 percent from 2012 to 2016. Moreover, in November of 2016, the company announced the sale of Ravenswood, Ironwood, Ocean State Power and Kibby Wind projects for US$2.2 billion and TC Hydro for US$1.07 billion (TransCanada, 2017). This reduces TransCanada's renewable generation capacity to 441 Megawatts, less than half of its 2016 capacity displayed in Table 4. This divestment from renewables enabled TransCanada to acquire Columbia Pipeline Group for US$13 billion, expanding its natural gas business in the US market (TransCanada, 2017).

In a third category are Enbridge and Fortis, which as seen in Table 4 have steadily increased total renewable energy capacity since 2012. While Enbridge continues to grow its renewable stock, the company's rate of expenditure on renewables has remained relatively consistent over the last five years. Annual

TABLE 4   Power generation/net capacity of all renewable energy assets

Company	2012	2013	2014	2015	2016
Enbridge	1,280 MW	1,280 MW	1,616 MW	1,997 MW	2,500 MW
Suncor	N/A	255 MW	327 MW	287 MW	187 MW
TransCana-da	1167 MW	1161 MW	1156 MW	1156 MW	1156 MW
Fortis	402 MW	402 MW	442 MW	612 MW	596 MW
Teck	88 GWh	85 GWh	83 GWh	136 GWh	0
Ethanol					
Husky (thousand litres/day)	721.2	742.4	780.7	794.9	820.6
Teck (thou-sands of m^3)	413	415	412	418	N/A

SOURCE: Compiled from each firm's annual reports from 2012–2016. Capacity is the maximum amount that a facility can produce, while generation refers to the amount actually produced. Reports of Megawatts (MW) reflect capacity, while gigawatt hours (GWh) reflect the amount of energy produced over the course of a year.

reports indicate that Enbridge has invested 2.8 billion since 2012, averaging just over half a billion per year, while its expenditure of $0.9 billion in 2013 was a high, followed by $0.7 billion in 2016. In addition to increasing renewable power generation capacity, Fortis increased the percentage of the power it generates from renewables from 11.53 percent in 2014 to 16.03 percent in 2016 (Fortis, 2017).

Virtually all the majors recognize climate change as a growing problem and acknowledge the need to respond to public demands to reduce emissions. Overall, however, we find relatively little evidence of a move into renewables energy as an accumulation strategy. Four majors have not diversified their investments into renewables, focusing instead on enhancing energy efficiency and the use of new technologies to improve the carbon intensity and environmental footprint of the extractive process. While TransCanada and Suncor have made significant and sizeable investments into wind, solar and hydro production, as well as biofuels, their recent shedding of renewable assets marks a continuation of a fitful relationship between fossil fuel companies and renewables that reaches back almost two decades (Derber, 2010; Switzer, 2013).

Enbridge and Fortis, on the other hand, continue to grow renewable capacity and Enbridge is now a major player within the field. Notably, however, renewables remain a minor component of both companies' overall energy assets, earnings and expenditures. Fortis, for its part, still generates close to 84 percent of its power from gas, coal and oil (and power generation is a minor component of its business, which is mainly focused on transmission).[10] While Enbridge is an outlier in the sample in terms of the scale of its renewable investments, its $2.8 billion in spending amounts to approximately 7.6 percent of total capital expenditures from 2012 to 2016 and renewables represent 5.3 percent of the company's total before income tax earnings, from 2014 to 2016 (Enbridge Inc., 2017, p. 80). Such levels of investment may indicate an orientation towards climate capitalism in the very long-term. However, they can equally be interpreted as a (relatively low-cost) legitimation effort made by a company that has faced intense public scrutiny and social movement opposition, particularly surrounding its proposed Northern Gateway pipeline from the Alberta tar sands to the British Columbia coast. Without foreclosing the possibility of efforts at "transition capture" in the future, Enbridge's interest in positioning itself as a significant player in renewables compared to other fossil fuel majors may stem from a more immediate concern to improve its public image in an effort to legitimate its primary revenue stream – oil and gas production and transport.

So far, I have looked at investments in renewable energy by the ten largest Canadian fossil fuel corporations. I now examine directorate interlocking between the fossil fuel sector in Canada and Canadian renewable energy firms, as well as the sector's participation on the boards of renewable industry associations and climate-capitalist civil society organizations.

7   Interlocking Directorates

As mentioned above, sociologists have long mapped the social relations that link across corporations – in particular, the practice of two or more corporations sharing directors or top managers. These interlocking directorates serve

---

10   The fact that Enbridge, as well as Suncor and TransCanada are key renewable energy players in Canada and also fossil fuel majors, may partly reflect the export-oriented nature of their operations. Indeed, the majority of oil and gas produced in Canada is exported (Laxer, 2015). This points to how countries in the global North, such as Canada, may green their energy consumption first, while continuing to be fossil fuel exporters. Yet, this conclusion is premature: most of Canada's energy still comes from oil, natural gas and coal, and Canada is also a major importer of fossil fuels.

many purposes. At an organizational level, they help put boards in contact, serving as information channels and providing corporate managers with a broad scan across sectors of the business community (Mizruchi, 1996). They also allow for the coordination of economic activity and business strategy within an interlocked group, and at times enable the influence or control of one firm over another (Carroll and Sapinski, 2011; Mizruchi, 1996). As a system, interlocks form an extensive network linking large corporations, demonstrating the institutionalized relations between firms, and thereby between the different forms or fractions of capital – industrial, commercial, financial and so on (Carroll, 1986, 2010). This provides evidence that corporations are embedded in and construct a network of social relations that reach beyond the firms themselves (de Graaff, 2012a).

In an innovating and competitive emerging sector, such as renewable energy, interlocks at the firm level (and between ostensible competing sectors such as between carbon and renewable corporations) are likely to be relatively sparse (Mizruchi and Koenig, 1988). The absence of extensive board interlocks with competitors would not necessarily point to the absence of a strategic orientation towards energy transition by fossil fuel firms. In contrast, the participation of carbon capital directors (especially senior executives) on the boards of renewable industry associations and also climate capitalist civil society organizations, would both strengthen the strategic capacity of oil companies to shape and control the alternative energy field, and further represent "signposts" of stakes in expanding the renewable sector and planning for energy transition, or transition capture.

Table 5 presents our sample and displays overall levels of network participation (network participation indicates the number of organizations within each institutional category that have board interlocks with other firms in the sample).

In all, we find 27 fossil fuel corporations in the network. This includes four majors (Enbridge, Suncor, Teck, CNRL) as well as Fortis BC, a subsidiary of Fortis Inc. Figure 1 displays the network. For simplicity of presentation, the individuals carrying the ties are excluded and only organizational ties are displayed.

As we see in Figure 1, direct corporate interlocks between the carbon sector and renewable companies are fairly sparse. In total, there are seven in this data set. Naikun Wind (NAIK_WIND), for example, is connected to Enmax, a natural gas and power utility, via Dave Rehn, who is sits on the board of directors at both companies. TransAlta renewables (T-ALTA_RENEW) interlocks with Precision Drilling (PREC_DRIL) via Allen Hagerman, while Don Seaman is on the boards of both New Energy (NEW_EN), a small-scale hydro power firm, and Trinidad Drilling (TRIN_DR). On the board of directors at Alterra, a diversified renewables

TABLE 5   The sample of organizations and network participation

Sample stratum	Overall sample	Network participant	Rate of participation
1. Carbon-capital firms	238	27	0.11
2. a. Renewable firms	51	20	0.39
b. Crown renew- able firms	5	4	0.8
3. a. Hybrid firms	7	5	0.71
b. Hybrid Crown firms	8	5	0.63
4. Renewable associations	9	7	0.77
5. Climate-capitalist orgs.	7	5	0.71

SOURCE: BASED ON MY OWN CALCULATION OF NETWORK PARTICIPATION.

company, is David Cornhill who is also Chairman of Altagas and a board member at Painted Pony Energy (P-PONY_PET). Annette Verschuren, who is Chair and CEO of NRstor, a renewable energy storage firm, also sits on the board of directors at CNRL (CAN_NAT). Sky Power Global (SKY_PWR_GLOB), a solar energy producer, is connected to oil and gas firm Dundee, which has ownership stakes in Windiga, a solar and renewable energy producer in West Africa. While solar firms Sky Power Global, SkyFire Energy (SKY_FIRE_EN) and the Canadian Solar Industries Association (CAN_SOL_ASSOC) are interlocked, this segment of the renewables sector is disconnected from the dominant component. (The segment is the set of nodes that link to all others in the set and form a complete sub-graph, running from the top left of Figure 1 to bottom right.)

Crown renewable corporations BC Hydro (BC_HYDRO) and Manitoba Hydro (MN_HYDRO) also interlock with Sprott Resources (SPROT_RES) and Strad Energy Services (STRAD_EN) respectively, while Hydro Quebec and Columbia Power (COLUM_PWR) do not have corporate interlocks, but are integrated into the larger network component through their representation on the board of Canadian Hydropower Association (CAN_HYDRO_ASSOC). Both Crown and private hybrids, especially electricity power generators, are central to the network. Of the Crown corporations, electricity transmission firm Hydro-One

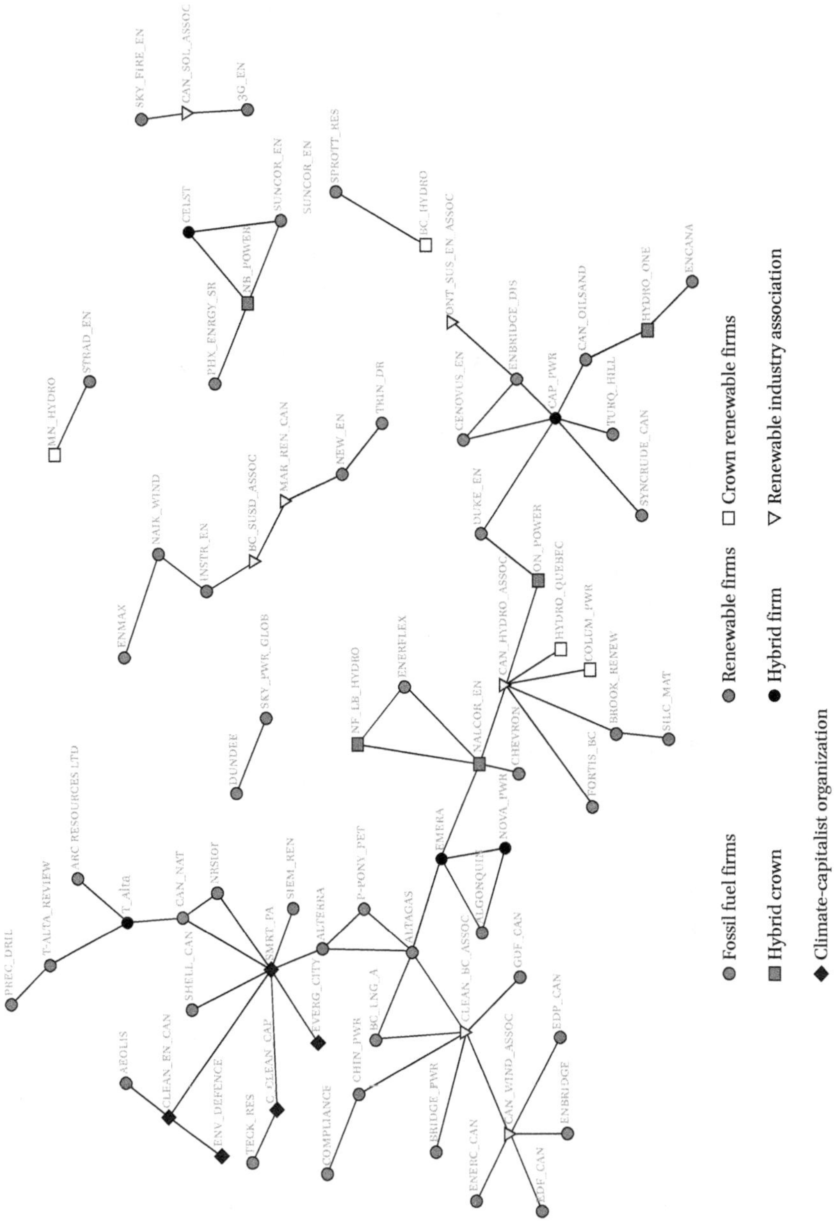

FIGURE 1   Directorate interlocks between fossil fuel and renewable energy sectors
SOURCE: CREATED BY THE AUTHOR, USING NETDRAW SOFTWARE.

- ● Fossil fuel firms
- ■ Hybrid crown
- ◆ Climate-capitalist organization
- ● Renewable firms
- ● Hybrid firm
- □ Crown renewable firms
- ▽ Renewable industry association

and power producers Nalcor Energy (NALCOR_EN) and New Brunswick Power Corporation (NB_POWER) have multiple interlocks with fossil fuel firms. Capital Power (CAP_PWR), a private power generation firm with coal, gas and wind assets, has a prolific six fossil fuel firms represented on its board.

By dint of their investments in renewables, fossil fuel firms are well represented on the boards of renewable energy associations. Mary Sye, program director at Enbridge Gas Distribution (ENBRIDGE_DIS), is on the board at Ontario Sustainable Energy Association (ONT_SUS_EN_ASSOC), while Rocco Vita, Director of business development at Enbridge Inc., sits on the board of Canadian Wind Association (CAN_WIND_ASSOC). Executive Director of Fortis BC, Doyle Sam, also sits on the board Canadian Hydro Association (CAN_HYDRO_ASSOC). Also intriguing is Clean Energy BC (CLEAN_BC_ASSOC), whose board of directors includes Dan Wosnow, director at both Altagas and at the BC LNG Alliance (BC_LNG_A). While Altagas has modest investments in wind power, Wosnow's directorship at Clean Energy BC may help explain the association's positioning of gas as a renewable fuel and its efforts to advocate for its development as part of the "clean economy" (Clean Energy BC, 2016).

Three of seven climate-capitalist organizations participate in the network. Among them Smart Prosperity (SMRT_PA) plays a key role in integrating the network and bringing renewable and fossil fuel firms together. It links Alterra, Siemens Canada Renewables (SIEM_REN) and Nstor together with Shell Canada (SHELL_CAN) and CNRL. This is consistent with its mandate to bring together leaders in business and to forge a consensus around a green capitalist vision. Meanwhile, the representation of CNRL on its board (which, as noted above, does not have significant investments in renewables) is indicative of the organization's version of climate capitalism. Smart Prosperity makes energy transition appealing to a wide number of corporations, including many fossil fuel firms, by emphasizing efforts aimed at reducing the carbon footprint of fossil fuels, while promoting a gradual, market-based approach to decarbonisation (McCartney, 2018). This approach maintains the supply of fossil fuels in the medium term, while pricing carbon to incentivize and support a slow, "stable" energy transition.

This vision for transitioning to a low-carbon economy is advanced through both public-facing reports, as well as via public appearances by high profile CEO's, such as Annette Verschuren, co-chair of Smart Prosperity. It has gained national relevance, as similar policies are found within the Trudeau government's Pan-Canadian Framework (McCartney, 2018). Indeed, Smart Prosperity's (re)launch in 2016 coincided with Prime Minister Trudeau's announcement of his government's climate policy program, and Trudeau himself was an enthusiastic guest speaker at the event (Gutstein, 2018, p. 207).

The above interlocks signal the strategic capacity of carbon capital, or certain key firms and individuals within it, to exert political influence in shaping the field of alternative energy development. Given existing investments, fossil fuel firms have some stake in seeing these markets slowly expand and linkages with renewable firms and industry associations can help to advance that line of business. By participating on the boards of industry associations and climate-capitalist organizations, carbon capital also gains information on the latest policy developments.

Extensive directorate interlocks between "hybrid" electrical power generators and transmitters and "core" fossil fuel firms speak, in part, to the fossil fuel industry's appetite for electrical power. In Alberta, this relation is especially pronounced. Electricity is an essential input to tar sands extraction, and the industrial sector accounts for over half of electricity consumption in the province (Weis et al., 2016). The province is also unique in that (unlike most other provinces), power generation and transmission are not owned or managed by Crown corporations. Through interlocks, carbon capital is able to influence electricity planning and development.

More generally, the presence of Alberta-based private hybrids in our sample speaks to the increasing share of electricity generated by renewable sources, following from policy frameworks aimed at the phase-out of coal-fired electricity in the province. While it remains somewhat unclear who will provide the power, large predominantly coal firms such as Capital Power, Emera and TransAlta have steadily increased their share of non-fossil fuel assets (now producing between 25–30 percent of their power from renewable sources) and have proposed several further large renewable electricity projects (Steward, 2017). This suggests that what little energy transition is taking place in Alberta is oriented primarily towards large-scale private electricity producers, rather than towards community and co-operative energy projects, or towards Crown corporations. In this context, the aforementioned firms may be a harbinger of the fossil fuel sector's renewed efforts to move slowly "beyond carbon" once a clear sunsetting policy decision on oil and gas has been made.

However, it is important to recognize that the vast majority of electrical power previously generated by coal has been replaced by natural gas, rather than renewables (D. Hughes, 2018; Witt, 2018). Moreover, consistent with the petro-politics literature, the political viability of building a low-carbon electricity sector is linked to the small role electrical power plays in the economy and its relative insignificance as an export.[11] By contrast, phasing out tar sands

---

11   Only 10 percent of power generation is exported – all to the US – while close to two thirds of oil and gas is exported. This is not meant to diminish the challenge and importance of

and fracked gas development and moving away from reliance on exports are in combination a much more difficult task, one that carbon capital will not easily accommodate.

Broadly, the findings point to a certain level of coordination and cooperation between the renewable and carbon sectors, rather than opposition. However, as noted above, relatively few direct corporate interlocks join the carbon sector and renewable companies. Further, while carbon capital is represented on green energy associations, those tying the organizations together are overwhelmingly lower level managers (such as program directors or vice presidents of a corporate division) rather than CEO's or top executives. In fact, Dan Wosnow is the only director or executive on the board of renewable industry associations. This is consistent with findings that investment in renewables by Canada-based fossil fuel majors continues to constitute a minor component of their accumulation strategy. As we see in Figure 1, climate-capitalist organizations like Smart Prosperity play important integrative role, pulling the dominant component together, but overall, linkages between carbon capital and the renewables sector are sparse, with a small number of individuals and firms carrying a thin network that could easily devolve into a set of dispersed groupings.

8   Conclusion

This chapter began by discussing research on the political economy and ecology of fossil capitalism, which has identified social and political barriers to a just energy transition. As observed, much of this resistance comes from fossil capital fractions, who are deeply invested in maintaining a carbon-powered social metabolism. However, while carbon capital is actively engaged in supressing a rapid process of decarbonization, recent literature considers how the sector's strategic attempts at self-preservation may be supported by a longer-term strategy of participating in a slow and "managed transition" towards a climate capitalist project built on green energy. Indeed, it is an increasingly commonplace assertion that energy system transformation is well underway and that fossil fuel companies have seen the "writing on the wall".

As Lohmann (2011) suggests, such a strategy would allow for the short-term valorization of the large sums of capital invested in fossil fuel energy

---

decarbonizing electricity as the backbone of energy system transformation. Moreover, with close to 40 percent of electricity coming from fossil fuels and nuclear, there is still a long way to go in achieving it.

production, while simultaneously leaving business to establish control over energy substitutes (such as wind, solar, biofuels), as well as the land that is required to maintain them. Going further, Muller (2013) argues that fossil capital's tactic of delaying energy transitions can be understood as a short-term strategic move allowing oligopolistic energy companies and the finance industry to gain dominance in an emerging new energy system, subsuming renewables under their centralized control. Such an accumulation strategy, as Adkin notes (2017), runs counter to the vision shared by many on the green-left, for whom a largely decentralized energy system, based on a diversity of sources under collective control, is seen to provide the foundation for a wider transformation of patterns of production and consumption, gender relations, and relations with First Nations communities.

We observe some "signposts" of a strategic (re)orientation by large Canadian fossil fuel firms towards a future climate capitalism. I found that fossil fuel firms have some stake in seeing the slow expansion of renewables and their linkages with renewable firms and industry associations can help to advance that line of business. This development sits in some tension with the idea of fettering advances in forces of production. Overall, however, our findings point to a carbon-extractive sector without plans for energy transition or transition capture.

Directorate interlocks show carbon capital's efforts to shape the field of alternative energy development and are further indicative of the sector's stake in expanding renewable energy markets. Meanwhile, the presence of several private "hybrids" in our sample, especially in the electrical power sector in Alberta, speaks to the increasing share of electricity generated by renewable sources and to the prominent role played by large private fossil fuel firms in that development. This development suggests that transition capture may be carbon-capital's response, once a clear sunsetting decision (a muscular policy aimed at declining, weaning off and retiring) has been made. For oil and gas, no such framework exists in Canada (or is in the works) and consequently the sunsetting of coal remains mostly a boon to natural gas. While the findings point to a degree of coordination and cooperation between the sectors, rather than outright opposition, carbon-renewable linkages are relatively sparse overall, with a small number of firms (represented mostly by lower-level managers and directors from carbon-capital firms) carrying a thin network. Evidence that oil and gas firms are orienting themselves towards a climate-capitalist project is therefore only very tentatively supported at the level of corporate networks.

In examining investments, I found that four of the ten largest fossil fuel firms in Canada have not diversified their investments into renewables, focusing instead on developing other features of productive forces, especially technology to achieve greater efficiency in carbon extraction and reduce the carbon footprint of fossil fuels. While this development in the productive forces has practical benefit for the environment, the effectiveness of this approach is strictly limited: these initiatives are not intended to reduce, nor capable of reducing, hydrocarbon dependence. In the absence of parallel investments in renewable energy they signal the continuation of fossil capitalism as a project of "business as usual".

Suncor and TransCanada (and to lesser extend Teck and Husky) have made significant investments in renewables, but we observed a significant recent trend among these firms of shedding such assets. These findings help explain some of the year-to-year volatility and recent overall reductions in Canadian investments in renewable energy noted above. A likely reason for this recent shedding of assets, is that renewables struggle to compete (generate profits on par) with oil and gas investments (Wood Mackenzie, 2018), while the short-term profit seeking of capitalist firms discourages investigation of alternative paths of development.

Andreas Malm (2016, pp. 368–373) argues that the qualities and "spatio-temporal profile" of renewable energy "flows" simply do not allow for the kind of profits generated by the primitive accumulation of fossil capital. In effect, he suggests that because such flow is not concentrated in underground stores and is instead more like a fruit that can be widely picked, there is much less profit attached to its appropriation. As sunshine and wind cannot be extracted and sold on the market, profit through surplus value is primarily found in the manufacturing of the technologies for capturing, converting and storing the energy of the fuel. This argument may help explain the curious situation whereby reductions in the price of solar panels and wind turbines, actually leads to divestment from them (see also Miller, 2013). Therefore, as prices on solar panels or wind turbines plummet, profit from already installed solar or wind capacity is squeezed in a manner that is without equivalent in carbon-capital's core business. Malm captures the contradiction succinctly, arguing that (carbon) capital is not investing in renewables at the rate that might be expected, "because energy flow lost so much of its exchange-value at the very same time as its social use-value – slowing down climate change – rose towards priceless heights" (2016, p. 371).

While increased investment in renewables by Fortis and especially Enbridge suggests the possibility of a more strategic (re)orientation towards a climate capitalist vision that could buck this trend, this can at present only be interpreted as a very long-term alignment, and one that is consistent with the notion of relative (developmental) fettering. Even among these firms, renewables account for only a small fraction of overall investments, as these majors are also simultaneously expanding oil and gas operations (as witnessed in Chapter 5). Along with the contradiction between the use and exchange-value of renewables noted by Malm, it is vital to again recognize the contradiction between the quest to valorize massive fixed capital investments and the requirement to decarbonize energy in a rapid and socially just manner.

While fossil fuel corporations like Enbridge have made significant investments in renewables, the benefits of some green initiatives can be outweighed by misleading conclusions that these corporations are green saviours. Coupled with dubious yet increasingly common pronouncements that energy system transformation is now well underway, these relatively minor investments can justify inaction.

The case study has several limitations. Further work could examine the investment strategies of large Canada-based firms beyond the top ten majors, as well as those of non-Canada based corporations operating in its oil and gas sector (such as the subsidiaries of Shell, Total, Chevron, Nexen CNOOC and ConocoPhilips). This would enable comparisons between Canada-based, Europe-based, United States-based, Asian and Middle-Eastern and other carbon corporations in regard to their investment strategies, as well as a consideration of factors that help explain any differences. Additionally, it would be helpful to address the financial sector's role in both the ownership and funding of renewables – considering the extent to which major banks may be slowly shifting investments towards green energy – as well as the sector's interlocks with renewable energy firms and linkages into climate-capitalist organizations. This would help deepen the concrete-complex analysis of fettering within fossil capitalism, producing increasingly comprehensive and detailed explanations.

It remains an open question whether capitalism can decarbonize. What is clearer, however, is that a capital-centric approach will not suffice to catalyze a green energy transition within our current carbon budget. While we have seen growing volumes of installed capacity, this development is fettered. In the context of the climate emergency, this carries catastrophic implications and demands political intervention.

Policies are needed that constrain and strategically shape energy development in a manner that assists in effecting a rapid transition to renewable energies. This will require muscular leadership – presumably by the state. Higher royalties on hydrocarbon extraction, taxes on carbon usage, and controls on overall emissions (including through polluter-pays provisions) can raise funds to facilitate a planned transition to alternatives, including the creation of "green jobs". These short-term and ameliorative measures are an important component of climate change mitigation and reforms that are conceivable within the system to slow climate change are needed.

Regulatory reforms aimed at facilitating a rapid and just transition to alternative energies must simultaneously be accompanied by more radical measures that enhance democratic control over new energy projects and over investment decisions more broadly. Novel forms of public ownership that allow for participatory and decentralised control are needed, as are robust social and ecological mandates that substitute the pursuit of exchange-value with the aim of meeting ecological and social ends. In this manner, rapid energy transition is intimately linked to the radical anti-capitalist question of the basis of corporate power, which is a problem not defined by or restricted to the carbon sector.

CHAPTER 7

Science, Ecology and the Greening of Carbon-Extractive Development

In 2012, Canada's Oilsands Innovation Alliance (COSIA) – a collaboration of thirteen of Canada's largest tar sands companies, which pools resources, shares new technologies and funds research to lessen the ecological impacts of tar sands development – was formed. Recognizing that the extraction and combustion of fossil fuels account for the majority of global carbon dioxide emissions, COSIA seeks to advance industry-wide climate mitigation strategies and efforts, while also working to cleanse the industry's public image. It subsequently presents tar sands producers as forward-thinking innovators who will play a key role in advancing solutions to climate change, assuring us that as "science and innovation have been constant companions of oil sands development for the last century" the COSIA idea is but a "new a chapter in a history of innovation" ... "enabling responsible and sustainable development of Canada's oils sands, while delivering accelerated improvement in environmental performance" (COSIA 2012, pp. 2–3). In addition to prominent Canadian tar sands producers, COSIA's "associate members" include government agencies, academic bodies, and other companies that "share the COSIA vision" and have apparently joined the alliance to "ensure their strategic planning efforts are aligned with industry priorities" (COSIA, 2020).

Beyond COSIA, a host of interlinked corporate, government and university research and development (R&D) institutes seek to shrink the ecological footprint of fossil fuels, through technologies and innovations such as carbon capture and storage (CCS), the injection of CO_2 for enhanced oil recovery (EOR), and improved tailings management and water treatment. In the process, which I term "greened extractivism", components of ecological science are incorporated into the carbon-extractive process.

Through a social network analysis, in this chapter I map the social and institutional architecture behind this "clean tech" knowledge, highlighting its production in a cluster of networked industry–university–state research institutes and centres. The analysis considers how research and development (R&D), including that which is ecologically oriented and public funded, is directed towards the needs of carbon capital. Indeed, carbon-capital's representation on governing boards of university and public research institutes enables corporations to shape their agendas and priorities in ways that mesh with corporate business strategies. At the same time, through these networks, prominent actors in the sector are able to cultivate relations with a cadre of scientifically minded policy and decision makers (themselves often past carbon elites) and develop shared perspectives and rationalities.

While such technologies have a practical environmental benefit, they are not intended or capable of reducing hydrocarbon dependence. By lowering the carbon intensity of each barrel of oil, they legitimate a business of usual expansion of fossil fuels. Thus, they function primarily to maintain conditions for the accumulation of fossil capital. This process suggests a fettering in both the use and the development of ecological knowledge itself: the co-optation and harnessing of earth-science insights into the carbon-extractive process is a drastic underutilization of its potential in the context of the climate crisis, while extensive institutional support for fossil fuel-related knowledge undermines the potential for re-directing public research towards robust sustainability, including energy transition.

To provide historical and strategic context for the analysis, I start with a broad overview of the growth of science as a productive force, tilting the analysis towards fossil capitalism and observing the nexus of science and fossil fuels. I begin with Marx, followed by a discussion of the historically shifting relationship between science and capitalism. This extends into the neoliberal present, including the growth of technoscientific research in unconventional oil and gas development.

1   Marx and Science as a Force of Production

As we saw in Chapter 3, Marx was among the first to analyze how capitalism systematically incorporates natural science as a force in the productive process. Through a process of real subsumption, science is harnessed to capitalism to increase the productivity and output of industrial capitalist production. Marx noted that the development of large-scale industry (including the application of "natural forces" (fossil fuels) to power production) and the creation of infrastructures for the circulation of commodities both required natural scientific knowledge. Large-scale industry he wrote, "raises the productivity of labour to an extraordinary degree by incorporating into the production process both the immense forces of nature, and the results arrived at by natural sciences" (Marx, 1976b, p. 509). In Marx's time, this knowledge was appropriated as a "free gift" (not typically produced as commodity under its own labour processes) and pressed into the service of capital.

Moreover, Marx recognized that capitalism's generation of an ever-greater mass of commodities, required an ever-larger quantity of "inputs" to production, whether of wood, fiber, metals, water or energy. The heightened productivity that capital achieves, combined with its need to expand constantly the circle of production and consumption, leads to the development of new branches of production, based on discovering and appropriating objects and forces in the rest of nature. Hence, it promotes, on an expanded-scale, "The exploration of the earth in all directions, to discover new things of use as well as new useful qualities of the old; such as new qualities of them as raw materials etc". (1993b, p. 409). It follows from this that capitalists engage in an ever-widening pursuit of new sources of resources, working to ceaselessly to discover, develop and subject to capital all aspects of nature that are conducive to accumulation. In the process, it provokes steady developments in the extraction and processing of materials, as well improvements in the means and methods of search and discovery of inputs to production, another form of technoscientific "progress".

While Marx saw capital promoting the general growth of sciences, he also saw it placing important constraints on that development. The constraints, as we saw in Chapter 3, inhibit both the development of ecological knowledge and its application (use) in production. At the same time, Marx argued that with its increasingly intensive appropriation of nature and environmental dysfunctions, capitalism cannot help producing new and also more universal forms of ecological consciousness, knowledge and science. More noted that aspects of this knowledge are applied to production to cope with ecological problems, insofar as the latter jeopardize the conditions for profitability and growth. For example, in *Capital Volume III*, he noted the development soil chemistry and agronomy, and its application to agriculture in response to severe crises of soil fertility wrought by capitalist industrial techniques. Despite his enthusiasm for this growth in knowledge, he noted that such insights could be applied to production in only a highly circumscribed fashion and "in so far as this is at all possible within the conditions of private property" (Marx, 1993a, p. 754).

2   The Scientific-Technical Revolution and Growth of Fossil Capitalism

As Harry Braverman suggests (1998), Marx's reflections on capitalism's application of science to production were mostly anticipatory – prescient observations of a process that had only just begun. While the routine integration of science within the production process begins with the advent of large-scale industry, it is under conditions of monopoly capitalism, beginning in the last two decades of the 19th century, that science came to occupy a central place in the forces of production. Braverman refers to capital's increased organization, harnessing and funding of science beginning in the late 19th century and progressing through the 20th as the scientific-technical revolution.

In his reflections on the scientific-technical revolution, Braverman points to the vital fusion of science, fossil fuels and large-industry. He writes:

> The old epoch gave way to the new during the last decade of the nineteenth century primarily as a result of advances in four fields: electricity, steel, coal-petroleum and the internal combustion engine. Scientific research along theoretical lines played enough of a role in these areas to demonstrate to the capitalist class, and especially to the giant corporate entities then coming into being as a result of the concentration and centralization of capital, its importance as a means of furthering the accumulation of capital. This was particularly true in the electrical industries, which were entirely the product of nineteenth-century science, and the chemistry of the synthetic products of coal and oil.
>
> 1998, p. 111

Indeed, new methods of organizing production and dramatic increases in labour productivity witnessed at the end of the nineteenth century and into the early twentieth, were made possible through the growing electrification of industrial operations. As Huber details (2013), this transformation ushered in a transition away from the heavy machinery of the early nineteenth century (e.g., steam engines powered by coal) to the compact power of electric motors and assembly-line production, most emblematically in the production of automobiles in Henry Ford's factories. As Huber reports, total electricity generation in the United States skyrocketed in the opening decades of the twentieth century, while fuel for the generation of electric power came from multiple sources – coal, oil, natural gas, hydroelectricity, and eventually nuclear fission.

As suggested by Braverman, the nexus of big business and science was pronounced in the field of industrial chemistry, which was developing entirely new products made from by-products of oil and coal refining, or that required the high levels of energy that only oil could provide. In the 1930s, chlorofluorocarbons for refrigeration, air conditioning, aerosol sprays and a host of electrical appliances for the home, were introduced by giant manufacturers like General Motors and General Electric (Angus, 2016).

As fossil fuels were progressively incorporated into the production process throughout the last two centuries, the means and methods of search, discovery, and extraction also simultaneously grew. Numerous innovations in geological exploration (growing geo-spatial knowledge) and engineering field development enabled the extraction and mining of coal in the mid eighteenth century, and oil and gas in the early nineteenth (Frehner, 2016).

Along with the creation of networks of corporate research laboratories and the extensive hiring of research scientists by large firms in the inter-war period, Braverman notes that this growth of science and engineering was supported by new or expanded university departments, as well as a growth of government research institutes. While these institutions (especially the former) retained substantial autonomy from industry and often pursued "pure" science, in the inter-war period, as Werskey (2007) argues, technical scientific knowledge, including occasionally the academic science establishment, became more effectively linked to needs of both private industry and empire,[1] while important networks and research projects spanning academic, industrial and state scientific bodies were established.

3   Science in the "Golden Age"

While the scientific-technical revolution began in the late 19th century and progressed in the early 20th, in the post-war era of state organized monopoly

---

[1] Through the notion of a "treadmill of destruction," Hooks and Smith (2005) show that the twentieth century has witnessed an unprecedented growth in the research, testing and employment of both conventional weaponry and weapons of mass destruction, which have profound environmental impacts. They point out that this treadmill expresses or is bound up with a statist logic (including geopolitical rivalry), which cannot be reduced to capitalism. Werskey (2007) meanwhile examines the establishment of state-directed "military industrial complexes" in numerous advanced capitalist countries during the inter-war period, linking technical scientific knowledge to the production of scientific weaponry and other imperialist pursuits. In the process, important networks and research projects spanning academic, industrial and state scientific bodies were thereby established, while public funding of R&D became weighted towards military pursuits, especially in the US and Britain (Edgerton, 2005). Cathryn Carson (2015) analyzes the science-based weaponry of the Second World War, as well as the extensive R&D infrastructural networks that enabled the further "scientization" of war. As she suggests, R&D systems that had been built up in the early 20th century and through the First World War were extended and intensified during the Second World War, while linkages between large industrial firms, academia and centres of state power carried into the post-war context. An account of the militarization of scientific knowledge and policy is important to discussions of how science could be "re-made" in its organization, prioritization and application, yet it is beyond the scope of this study.

capitalism, science became more directly and thoroughly enrolled in production (Reynolds and Szerszynski, 2012). Growing in-house corporate R&D centred the production of petrochemicals and synthetic substances (J.K. Smith, 1998). US chemical companies, such as DuPont and Dow Chemical, developed artificial fibers such as nylon, rayon, as well as a host of industrial chemicals, fertilizers and pesticides. Their production, which is typically based on converting natural gas and the by-products of oil, greatly accelerated our consumption of fossil fuels. Indeed, the whole petrochemical industry, and the associated production of prodigious waste grew exponentially in the so-called "golden age" of capitalism (Angus, 2016).

As O'Connor details (1974), beginning in the post-war era, the role of the state in supporting, funding and directing science also grew precipitously. Through funding of universities, especially in science, technology and medicine, along with corresponding increases in basic and applied scientific research, and the construction of new government research and development facilities, science was progressively converted into a more social and "organized" productive force (O'Connor, 1974). While government continued to fund basic research and university scientists retained substantial autonomy from state and industry through their control of funding, growing state intervention effectively socialized production costs (especially the training of a scientific labour force), and created a vast pool of "free" technical and scientific workers, whose knowledge and inventiveness became available to capital to be appropriated and applied to production.[2] Meanwhile, as Werskey (2007) shows, "big-science" projects based on private-public partnerships expanded, and a cadre class of scientifically minded policy and decision makers grew to direct "mission-oriented" R&D and harness scientific knowledge towards perceived national interests.

While science became more enmeshed in production, the growing environmental destructiveness of the post-war production process also encouraged the growth and deepening of ecological science. Allan Schnaiberg (1977) captured this dialectic through his broad but helpful distinction between the "Impact" and "technological-production" sciences. He argued that paralleling the post-war growth of technological-production science – science aimed at

---

2   This is not to suggest that all or even a majority of education is based on or emerges from corporate capital's drive to socialize these costs. Theoretical, "pure" and "basic" research exceeds this dynamic, while here are many "traditional" and social purposes of education (the structuring of subjectivities, thoughts and behaviours, the creation and maintenance of social prestige and status) that accord with the establishment of social order more broadly. Furthermore, public and free higher education was won through social movement struggles.

increased productivity and output of industrial capitalist production – was the advancement of the impact sciences – sciences oriented to identifying the negative social and environmental impacts associated with high-technology production.

The growth of the impact sciences also spurred the rise of "Radical Science" movements in the late 1960s and 1970s (see Werskey, 2007). These movements, which involved coalitions of social and natural scientists, pointed to the ecological destructiveness of post-war industrial growth and to the role of science in such development. They subsequently aimed to transform and "re-make" science in its organization and prioritization.

4   Science and Neoliberalism

The neoliberal period has seen a transformation in the processes of scientific knowledge generation and in the means and methods of its appropriation and enclosure. Since the 1980s there has been a concerted effort by corporate capital to externalize the costs of research by appropriating both university and state research infrastructures, resources, skills and knowledge (Brownlee et al., 2018; Brownlee, 2015; Carroll and Beaton, 2000).

While corporations have for many years exercised influence within universities, in neoliberal times their influence has broadened and deepened, and universities have become more directly integrated into capitalist production (Noble, 1998). In a process of university "corporatization", universities have become both more integrated with, and operate more like, private firms (Brownlee et al., 2018).

As Reynolds and Szerszynski (2012) detail, alongside trends in declining state funding, universities themselves began a process of reorganization to fit it ever more closely to the needs of industry and tropes of competitiveness. A legal infrastructure of patents and intellectual property laws, joint ventures with business and training courses for industry, have all meant that the scientific spaces of universities became increasingly like those of corporations. Simultaneously, industry's influence over university operations has proceeded through means such as the growing presence of corporate-affiliated board members and increased corporate funding of academic research (Brownlee, 2015). A "university-industrial complex" (Kenney, 1986) was subsequently consolidated, involving novel couplings of public and private and increasingly dense linkages between universities and corporations.

Corporate capital, has long had a powerful voice in setting the agenda of state agencies, including in scientific R&D. In the Canadian context, Nelles describes the prominence of a form of "state-enterprise capitalism" with government enterprises, including research centres "run by businessmen and for businesses" (as cited in Brownlee, Hurl, and Walby 2018, p. 7). Meanwhile, Leo Panitch (1977) identifies a longstanding "confraternity" of power in Canada – an ideological hegemony emanating from the state and economic elites, cultivating the view that national interests and business interests are one and the same. At the same time, neoliberalism has entailed a deepening of processes of "state–corporate symbiosis" – an increased integration of public sector organizations with private/corporate firms and a thickening of ties between private and public agencies (Jaimie Brownlee et al., 2018; O'Reilly, 2010). This process reflects the increasingly entrepreneurial role of the state in the neoliberal era and its renewed role in facilitating the accumulation of capital (Jessop, 2002b; Reynolds and Szerszynski, 2012).

In the next section, I point to the extraordinary amounts of capital and scientific resources that have been mobilized in an effort to profitably develop the tar sands in Canada and to the extensive industry–university–state collaborations this involves.[3] We then turn to a consideration of how the climate crisis and growing resistance to carbon-extractive development is forcing carbon capital to attempt to harness science to the production process to cope with ecological degradation.

5   Fossil Knowledge and the Corporate Colonization of R&D

Former Canadian Prime Minister Steven Harper indicated the huge amount of resources required for tar sands development in clear terms:

---

3   While I focus here on tar sands, producing fracked shale gas as a commodity with exchange-value, takes tremendous amounts of capital, labour and scientific resources (Bridge, 2004). While it has long been recognized that shale rock basins, as well as low-permeability sandstone reservoirs (or "tight gas" sands) contain gas, no feasible and profitable means of developing them were available. However, by combining hydraulic fracking (the injection of tonnes of sand, water and chemicals at high pressure to shatter rock) with horizontal drilling (drilling wellbores down vertically, as well as out in horizontal reaches to expose more of a gas bearing formation), major technical barriers to exploiting vast unconventional shale and tight gas deposits have been removed. A further limitation on natural gas usage is the difficulty of its transportation in gaseous form, particularly overseas and over long distances (Bridge, 2004). As we saw in Chapter 5, the development of a global market in natural gas is therefore also heavily dependent on the growth of the liquefied natural gas (LNG) industry, which must be extensively "engineered" via the production of a series of networked infrastructures and techno-scientific complexes that surround extracted gas and entail the further "reworking" of nature.

Digging the bitumen out of the ground, squeezing out the oil and converting into synthetic crude is a monumental challenge. It requires vast amounts of capital, Brobdingnagian technology and an army of skilled workers. In short, it is an enterprise of epic proportions, akin to the building of pyramids or China's Great Wall. Only bigger.

as cited in CARTER, 2014, p. 23

While Harper describes the dynamics of today's extractive processes, earlier research laid the ground work for this development.[4] In the depths of the oil scarcity crisis in the 1970s, oil company R&D departments and university labs began investigating drilling methods and specialized techniques to extract bitumen located deeper in the ground. The government of Alberta established the Alberta Oil Sands Technology and Research Authority (AOSTRA) in 1974, with a $100 million budget (nearly half a billion dollars in today's money) to develop new technologies for extracting bitumen (Turner, 2017). In the mid-1980s, AOSTRA began a pilot test project for the development of what came to be known as steam-assisted gravity drainage – an oil recovery technology used to extract heavy crude oil and bitumen. AOSTRA's field tests of SAGD overlapped with advances in horizontal drilling developed by the oil industry, and was first tested commercially by Encana Corporation in 1996 at Foster Creek just southwest of Fort McMurray. The first commercial production facility was developed at this same site by Encana in 2001 (Turner, 2017). SAGD has since been widely adopted by industry players like Suncor and ConocoPhillips, and is reported to have unlocked over 170 billion barrels of previously inaccessible oil from the tar sands (Turner, 2017).

Research on the production of fossil knowledge has emphasized the important contemporary role played by universities and public institutes

---

4   In fact, the "technics" of tar sands reach back over a hundred years and involve dense ties to private and public agencies. The first full geological mapping of the region's potential for oil development, for example, was conducted in 1913 by an engineer from the Federal Department of Mines (Wilt, 2018). Hot water separation, the process vital to the commercializing bitumen, was developed beginning in the late 1920s by research scientist Karl Clark when he worked for the provincial government. Following the perfection of the technique, the province of Alberta hosted a sizeable conference in Edmonton that attracted oil companies from around the world to hear about the region's prospects. The process was only later put into commercial production in 1967 by Great Canadian Oil Sands Limited, now Suncor Energy (Wilt, 2018). While a contemporary version of this process has enabled the mining of bitumen just below the boreal forest floor, the vast majority of bitumen is buried much deeper below the earth's surface.

(Adkin, 2020; Adkin and Stares, 2016; Carroll et al., 2018a; Gustafson, 2012; Tretter, 2019). In a tangible sense, universities offer access to expert information tailored to corporate interests through funded and directed research projects. By embedding itself in the university, industry externalizes the costs of research, appropriating the institution's resources and talent at a fraction of what they would incur on their own. Gustafson (2012) subsequently documents the immense pressures put on higher education organizations in Alberta, pointing to a situation nearing that of research and university "capture" by the fossil fuel industry. Similarly, Carroll, Graham, and Yunker (2018) have used network analysis to examine the reach of the fossil fuel industry into universities and public policy research institutes. Examining the connected network of academic and research organizations that interlock with carbon capital, they find a "carbon-centred scientific-industrial complex" – a densely connected network of research institutions (both state and academic), based primarily in Alberta, that are significantly influenced by the fossil fuel industry.

Tretter (2019) documents the paradoxical situation whereby carbon-extractive development has become increasingly knowledge-intensive, alongside declining levels of "in-house" industry spending on R&D. He attributes this shift to the increasingly broad range of expertise that is required today to profitably exploit unconventional fossil fuels. Oil firms, he argues are often unwilling to build and maintain expensive in-house labs to support knowledge advances made in a wide array of earth science fields. As a result, he suggests that external research centres, including universities, which offer access to expert information tailored to corporate interests through funded and directed research projects, are of growing significance for global oil production.

Drawing from literature on petro-states and a "resource curse", Adkin (2020) and Adkin and Stares (2016), consider how a carbon-intensive economic structure and heavy reliance on oil rents (especially in Alberta but also nationally), has far reaching implications for the production of knowledge, powerfully shaping state research infrastructures and funding priorities in accordance with interests of carbon capital. In an impressive empirical examination of funding flows between major government innovation agencies (both federal and provincial) and the Universities of Calgary and of Alberta over a 15-year period from 2000 to 2016, Adkin (2020) reveals the heavy public subsidization of fossil fuel-related research, including that focused on "clean fossil fuels". Importantly, she points to the comparative failure to invest in the production of knowledge that is critical to advancing a transition to a post-carbon economy, such as that related to renewable energy development, low-carbon transport and sustainable agriculture.

6   The Greening of Fossil Capitalism

While current trajectories in fossil capitalism threaten to breach key ecosystem tipping points within the next two decades (D. Hughes, 2018; Le Quéré et al., 2013; Muttitt, 2016), widespread evidence shows that unconventional fuels are yet more ecologically damaging that conventional sources. Given the energy intensive extraction process and extensive processing, upgrading and refining required to transform bitumen into commodified energy, recent studies have found that the lifecycle emissions (from extraction, upgrading, pipeline or tanker transport, refining and use) of bitumen from the tar sands ranges from eighteen to twenty-five percent higher than conventional crude (Grant et al., 2013). As discussed in Chapter 5, protagonists promoting development of natural gas often characterize it as a "bridge" fuel, capable of aiding in the transition to renewable sources of energy. However, several recent studies on the greenhouse gas (GHG) emissions of shale gas and LNG have challenged the evidence for this characterization (Howarth, 2014; Hughes, 2015).

Facing a protracted crisis, industry R&D efforts are increasingly trained on the development of "environmental" or "clean technologies" which reduce the environmental impacts of fossil capital development and lower costs. Examples include carbon capture and storage intended to capture emissions from coal-fired plants, fracked gas wells, and oil sands upgraders, the injection of CO_2 for enhanced oil recovery (EOR), using solvents rather than steam to produce bitumen (cyclical solvent technology), along with improvements in ecological remediation.

The effectiveness of such efficiency-enhancing carbon-extractive technologies in mitigating climate change is highly limited. Indeed, such measures are extensively supported by carbon capital as they allow the industry to protect its vast sunk carbon investments, expand oil and gas operations in the medium-term, while rendering each barrel of oil less "carbon intensive". Meanwhile some in the industry cling to the hope of discovering a technological "silver bullet" that is capable of achieving near-zero emissions across the carbon-extractive life cycle at commercially viable price levels (Rathi, 2020).

Such "clean growth" development is also extensively supported by governmental policy frameworks. This includes the Trudeau Liberal's 2016 Pan-Canadian Framework on Clean Growth and Climate Change, which offers a policy of slow domestic and market-based energy transition, to be funded by expanding capacity for bitumen production and transport in the short to medium term, alongside the taxation of those same resources when used domestically. Therein the ecological footprint of new extractive developments and pipelines that will purportedly finance the needed transition to a low carbon

economy are reduced through government support for technological innovations. Such an approach simply does not square with the scientific consensus
on the scale and time frame for transition beyond carbon. It reflects a new
climate denialism – a disjuncture between scientific knowledge and political
action.

7   Networks of "Green" Fossil Knowledge in Canada

In the following section, I provide a network analysis of the cluster of research
institutes in Canada (and directors and researchers within them) producing,
funding and coordinating fossil fuel-related R&D, and their ties to carbon capital. By mapping interlocks among these institutes and between them and carbon capital, I identify the formation of industry–university–state collaborations
and networks – revealing a process of state–corporate symbiosis – and the extensive social architecture through which R&D is directed towards fossil fuel-
related clean tech innovation. In the concluding sections, I point to the need
for and outline broad political strategies aimed at transforming ecological and
earth science research in its organization and prioritization as an important
component of just energy transition and broader green transformation.

To represent the carbon-extractive corporate sector, I selected 238 corporations in this industry, each based in Canada with 2014 assets of at least $50
million as well as 21 industry associations. The sample of research institutes
includes thirty-four research and technology organizations and institutes
whose remit extends to fossil fuel-related research.[5] Fifteen of these institutes
are located in universities and receive funding from industry partners. Seven
are housed at the University of Calgary, six at the University of Alberta, one at
the University of Regina, and one at The Northern Alberta Institute of Technology, near Edmonton.

Twelve institutes are government research and technology organizations.
While these organizations often conduct their own research, for the most part
their function is to fund and facilitate science and technology research and innovation that is applied to industry (including, though in most cases not

---

5   These institutes were identified through a review of existing literature (Adkin and Stares,
    2016; Adkin, 2020; Canadian Association of University Teachers, 2013), and through searching
    university and government websites. I included state and university research centres that
    have an advisory board and which include corporate directors/officials and/or state manag-
    ers (i.e., university–industry–state research collaborations). Research parks, now a corpora-
    tizing feature of many universities, were not included, although future research could benefi-
    cially trace these parks' linkages to corporate capital.

exclusively, fossil fuel production). They bring together industry, university researchers and state representatives and provide further structural support for corporate-university linkages, in the form of funding. The seven remaining institutes are industry–created innovation associations or collaborations (such as COSIA) that concentrate and coordinate R&D centred on "clean technology", while also including academics, state managers and corporate directors from other industries on their governance boards.[6] To carry out the analysis, data was gathered on the names of the directors, or governors of these thirty-four research organizations and the directors, technical advisors and executives of the 238 carbon-extractive corporations, as of March 2018.[7]

Fully twenty-nine of the thirty-four research organizations/institutes belong to a single connected network that includes twenty-eight carbon-capital firms. This indicates that interlocks create a basis for elite cohesion among carbon capital leaders and others involved in university and state research-institute governance. On average, each research institute is linked to four other organizations, while some are far more integral to the network than others. Seven research institutes have only one interlock and five have two, while ten have at least six. This is seen in Figure 2 where node size is proportional to centrality within the network.

Particularly central is Ottawa-based Sustainable Development Technology Canada (SDTC), as well as Canada's Oilsands Innovation Alliance (COSIA), each of which has 9 interlocks. The Petroleum Technology Alliance of Canada (PTA_CAN), a non-profit industry collaboration that facilitates research and technology development for the petroleum industry has eight interlocks, as does the Sharp Research Consortium at the University of Calgary. The Centre for Oil Sands Sustainability (COSS), a university–industry collaboration at

---

6 Some organizations are "hybrid" private-public partnerships that could be categorized as either industry collaboration or state agencies. For example, the Petroleum Technology Research Centre, coded as an industry collaboration, is a non-profit founded by Natural Resources Canada, the Government of Saskatchewan, University of Regina and the Saskatchewan Research Council, as well as industry partners Nexen, Husky, and CNRL. Similarly, CMC Research Institutes, while also coded as an industry collaboration is founded through grants from the government of Alberta, as well as seven industry supporters and is housed at the University of Calgary. These organizations are a harbinger of what may come if the trend towards corporatization and state–corporate symbiosis continues on its current path.

7 Information on top executives and directors was gathered by the Corporate Mapping Project, via online business databases (ORBIS and FP Infomart), as well as company websites. The database was expanded here by including senior research directors and other corporate technical advisors, officers and managers. Sources for research organizations were mainly organization websites and annual reports. Unless otherwise indicated, all findings in this chapter refer to the situation at the beginning of 2018.

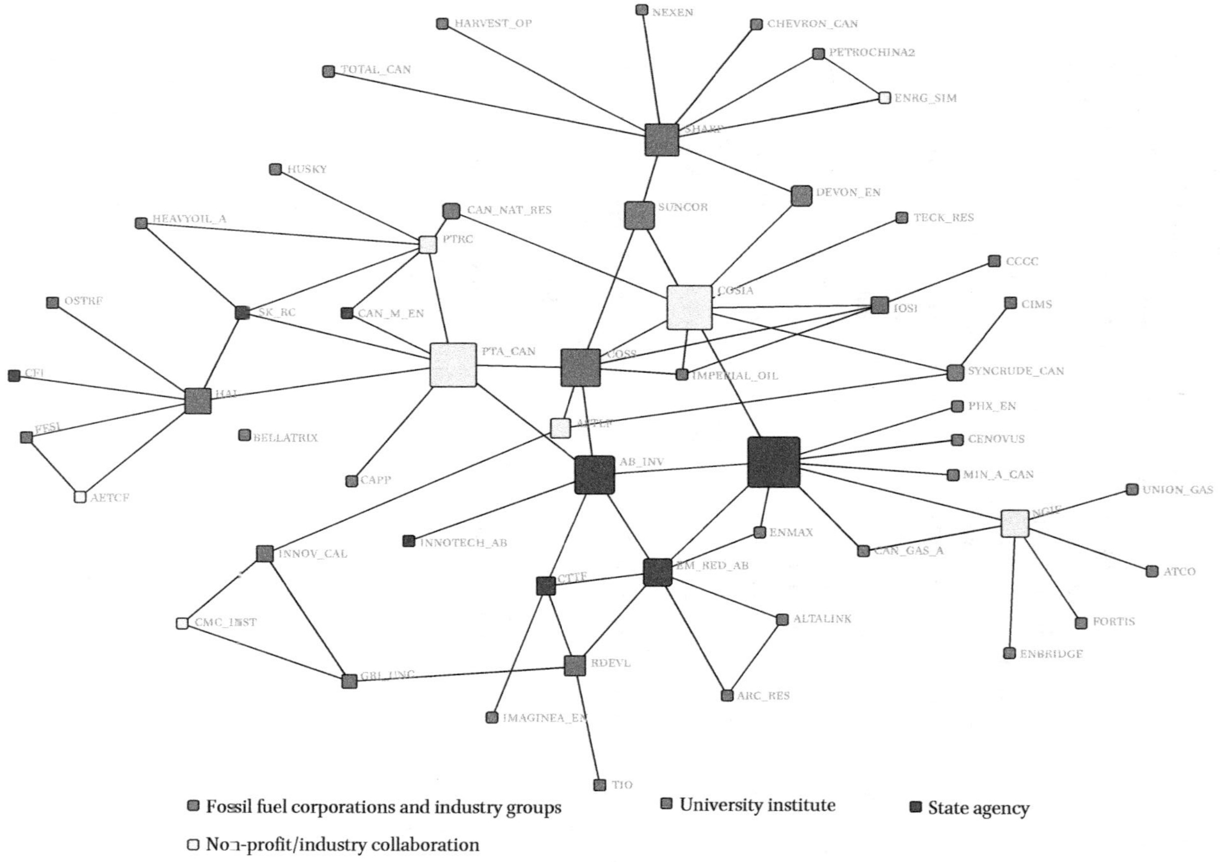

FIGURE 2   Interlocks between green tech research institutes and carbon-capital firms (organizations only)

SOURCE: CREATED BY THE AUTHOR, USING NETDRAW SOFTWARE.

- ■ Fossil fuel corporations and industry groups
- □ Non-profit/industry collaboration
- ■ University institute
- ■ State agency

The Northern Alberta Institute of Technology, and the recently created Emissions Reductions Alberta (EM_RED_AB) each have seven. Alberta Innovates (AB_INV), Helmholtz-Alberta Initiative (HAI), Petroleum Technology Research Centre (PTRC) and the Natural Gas Innovation Fund (NGIF) have six interlocks.

Illustrating their integrative role, when five organizations at the centre of the network diagram – Alberta Innovates, Sustainable Development Technology Canada, The Centre for Oil Sands Sustainability, the Petroleum Technology Alliance of Canada and Canada's Oilsands Innovation Alliance, are removed, the network breaks into six pieces, the largest of which contains 14 organizations (nine research institutes and five fossil fuel firms). Given that Alberta is far and away the heaviest emitter in Canada, it is not surprising that eight of nine institutes, which heavily network with carbon capital, are based there. In the context of the crisis of fossil capitalism, the latter's reach into focal sites of knowledge production indicates a strategic attempt at self-preservation.

Below, I investigate further by focusing on the elite individuals who carry the network and their affiliations with the three types of organizations (industry–state–university). I pay particular attention to organizations that are central to the network and bear numerous ties to the fossil fuel sector.

7.1   State Research Institutes and Carbon Cadres

The main function of state research institutes, which are created by government but operate at arms-length, is to fund and facilitate applied research and development. Several of these research institutes interlock with each other, as well as with the carbon-extractive sector, helping to form an elite governance and R&D network. As noted above, prominent in the network are Sustainable Development Technology Canada (SDTC), Emissions Reductions Alberta (EM_RED_AB) and Alberta Innovates (AB_INV).

The SDTC is an Ottawa-based government institute established in 2001 to "demonstrate new technologies to promote sustainable development, including technologies to address issues related to climate change and the quality of air, water and soil" (Sustainable Development Technology Canada, n.d.-a). These clean technologies are developed through public–private partnerships with SDTC acting as a public funder. It has funded numerous projects carried out by carbon corporations. These include

- a $1 million grant to Suncor in 2008 for research on carbon sequestration and enhanced methane production,
- $2,673,652 to Teck Resources for developing a "green approach" to copper and coal recovery in 2016, and
- $10 million to MEG Energy in 2018 for innovation to lower the costs and GHG emissions intensity of bitumen production that uses SAGD.

SDTC also contributed over 3 million in 2010 to the Petroleum Technology Research Centre research (a hydrocarbon industry association that facilitates collaborative R&D, seen in Figures 1 and 2), aimed at developing an environmentally sensitive and energy-efficient enhanced oil recovery (EOR) process for heavy oil reservoirs in Western Canada and $5 million to the organization in 2015, for research investigating the potential of CO_2 capture and storage in deep saline aquifers (Sustainable Development Technology Canada, n.d.-b).

Emissions Reductions Alberta (EM_RED_AB) is an Alberta-based government organization that works as a research funding steering committee directing funds to support the discovery, development and deployment of technology aimed at reducing emissions. Formerly Climate Change and Emissions Management Canada (CCEMC), the organization pools funds from carbon taxes levied on large-emitting companies. Under the Alberta government's "Specific Gas Emitters Regulation" emitters are required to pay carbon taxes if they fail to reduce their emissions intensity according to a given benchmark. Through a network of institutional arrangements, major tar sands companies and industry associations that represent them, such as COSIA, receive grants paid for by carbon taxes, for projects aimed at reducing emissions. They therefore effectively re-appropriate the taxes paid on carbon. For example, Emissions Reductions Alberta has recently funded Suncor to a tune of $1.6 million for its Oil Sands Energy Efficiency and Greenhouse Gas Mitigation Study, $5 million for a study by CNRL (in partnership with the Southern Alberta Institute of Technology) to improve detection, monitoring and quantification of methane emissions from mine faces and has supported a COSIA project that aims to draw on low-grade waste-heat to generate clean electricity (Emissions Reduction Alberta, n.d.).

Both SDTC and Emissions Reductions Alberta are governed by boards of directors that participate in the allocation of funding and, as seen in Figure 3, are interlocked extensively with the fossil fuel sector.

Kathleen Sendall (K_Sendall), who is a corporate director at coal and gas firm Enmax and former board chair of the Canadian Association of Petroleum Producers, sits on the governance boards of both of SDTC and Emissions Reductions Alberta. Former president of CAPP, and current director at Arc Resources and AltaLink, David Collyer, (D_Collyer) is chair of Emissions Reductions Alberta. Collyer also co-chaired the Oil Sands Advisory Group that helped inform Alberta's Climate Leadership Plan, and in 2016 was inducted into the "Canadian Petroleum Hall of Fame". In addition to Sendall, SDTC's board of directors and members council include four other carbon-capital elites. These are Judy Fairburn (J_Fairburn), executive vice president at Cenovus and past chair of Alberta Innovates, Pierre Lapointe (Lapointe_Pierre), director at the

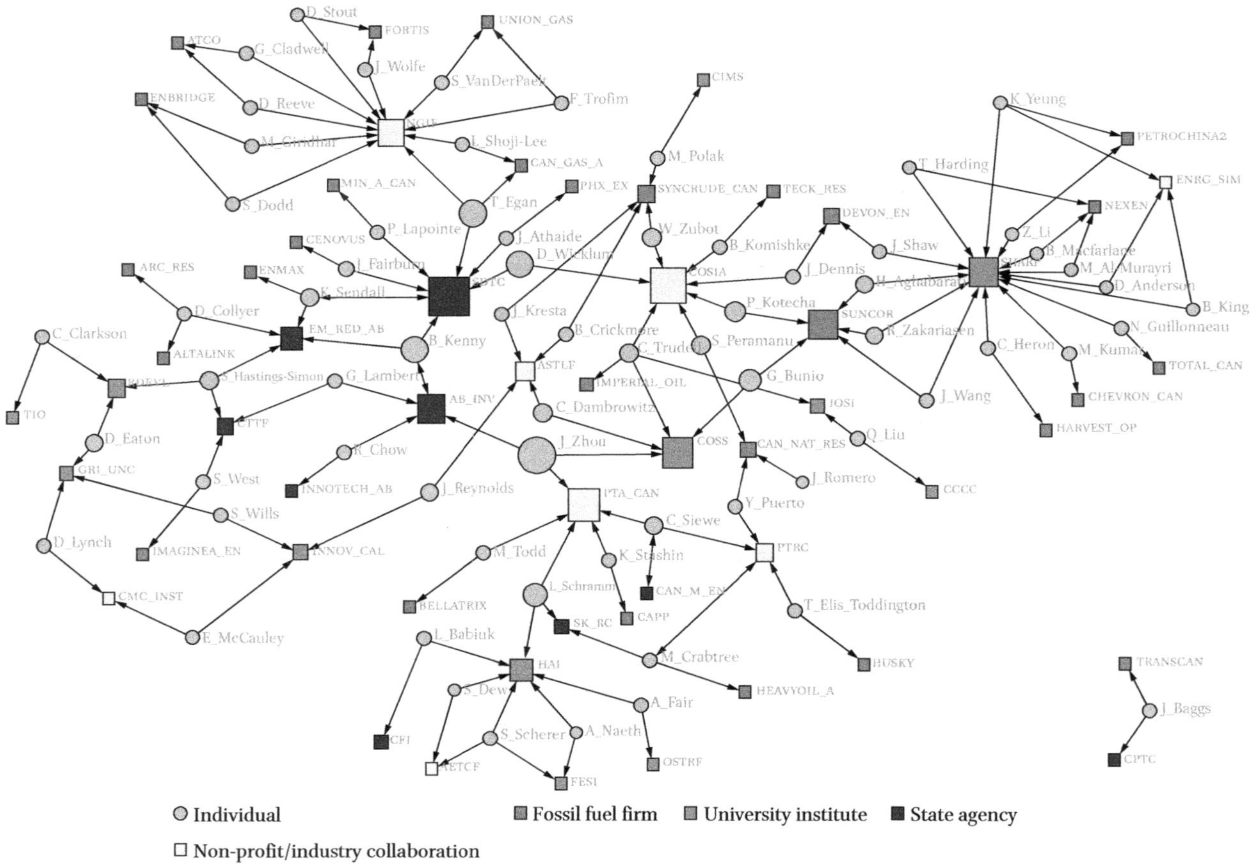

FIGURE 3   Interlocking between clean tech institutes and carbon-capital firms (including individuals)
SOURCE: CREATED BY THE AUTHOR, USING NETDRAW SOFTWARE.

○ Individual   ■ Fossil fuel firm   □ University institute   ■ State agency

□ Non-profit/industry collaboration

Mining Association of Canada, Judith Athaide (J_Athaide), director at Phoenix Energy and Timothy Egan. Egan is president and CEO of the Canadian Gas Association – an industry association representing Canada's natural gas distribution sector – and also director at the Natural Gas Innovation Fund (NGIF).

Also helping to stitch the network together is Alberta Innovates (AB_INV), an organization that was initially created in 2010 by the government of Alberta, with the aim of funding and facilitating applied research and development and to assist in commercializing research discoveries. While formerly composed of four separate Innovates corporations (Technology Futures, Bio Solutions, Energy and Environment Solutions, and Health Solutions) in 2017 it was consolidated into one corporation called Alberta Innovates, and is now managed by a single board of directors. The board does not include current carbon capitalists, but it is populated by prominent past players in the industry, acting as revolving door between industry and (quasi-)state institutions. For example, the current chair of Alberta Innovates, Brenda Kenny (who replaced Judy Fairburn in 2018), is the past president and CEO of the Canadian Energy Pipeline Association – a group representing Canada's transmission pipeline companies – and also director of SDTC and Emissions Reductions Alberta. Also on the board at Alberta Innovates, is Gordon Lambert, who is former vice president at Suncor and currently Suncor Sustainability Executive in Residence at the Ivey School of Business. Lambert also played an influential role in the creation of COSIA.

By participating in the governance of state research institutes, carbon capital is strategically positioned to direct public funds for research and innovation. In a process that is consistent with (and further entrenches) "petro-state" priorities and imperatives, interlocks enable the fossil fuel sector to cultivate close relations with scientific policy makers and to develop shared priorities. They create a platform through which a consensus is built in favour of clean tech as a solution to climate change.

7.2   *University Institutes and Corporate Elite*

In comparison to state research agencies, university research centres bear less extensive directorate ties to carbon capital. Important exceptions to this are the Centre for Oil Sands Sustainability (COSS) and the Sharp Research Consortium (SHARP). COSS is a research centre at Edmonton's Northern Alberta Institute for Technology that carries out applied research "designed to meet the needs of Alberta's oil sands industry" (Centre for Oil Sands Sustainability, n.d.). It was established through a $1.5 million endowment from Ledcor Group, as well as key additional funding from industry partners such as Suncor, along with both federal and provincial finding. It convenes university researchers with industry and government directors to conduct applied research on tailings management and water treatment, as well as developing technologies to reduce the emissions intensity of oil sands operations. Its "management advisory board" includes Cheryl Trudell (C_Trudell), who is a Vice President at Imperial Oil. Trudell is a member of the steering committee at COSIA and the Institute for Oil Sands Innovation (IOSI), a research centre at the University of Alberta, also seeking to reduce the environmental footprint of tar sands operations. Meanwhile Dr. John Zhou (J_Zhou) who is a vice president of clean energy at Alberta Innovates, member of the advisory board at the Centre for Oil Sands Sustainability and board member of Petroleum Technology Alliance of Canada, is an example of a highly networked research scientist in the field of "clean" petroleum technologies.

The Sharp Research Consortium, as we see in Figure 3, has extensive ties to carbon capital. The Consortium was established in 2008 at the University of Calgary, with the aim of helping industry develop economically sustainable heavy oil and bitumen recovery processes that are less energy intensive and more environmentally friendly. Specifically, it is dedicated to developing solvent based bitumen extractive processes, such as vapour extraction and hybrid processes involving steam and solvents (solvent enhanced steam assisted gravity drainage), which hold the promise of reducing the energy intensity, water usage and treatment, and CO_2 emissions of current practices. Its industry advisory committee contains representatives from numerous partnering corporations including Chevron Canada, Suncor, Nexen, PetroChina Canada, Devon Energy and Total Canada. Representatives on the advisory committee are senior advisors and directors of research at fossil fuel corporations, rather than members of boards of directors or top executives. For example, Bill Mcfarlane (Mcfarlane_B), is Senior Research Advisor at Nexen, Jerry Shaw (J_Shaw) is Senior Technical Advisor at Nexen, Hossein Aghabarati is Engineering Advisor at Suncor and Zhaowen Li is Director of Resources at PetroChina Canada. These organic intellectuals bring technical expertise and help direct research tailored to the needs of industry, but do not themselves have significant influence over the direction of the corporations they represent.

While we find less extensive interlocks among universities research centres and carbon capital, this is partly due to the lack of publicly available information pertaining to them. For example, the University of Alberta's Canadian Centre for Clean Coal, is reported to be directed by a "Management Advisory Board" and a "Scientific Advisory Committee", with the former including industry representatives drawn from its partnering firms including Teck Resources, Nexen Energy, Glencore Canada, and Capital Power, but information on the individuals who make up these boards is not publicly available. Despite being a public institution, it refused formal requests for this information. Similarly, the University of Calgary's Tight Oil Consortium is reported to be governed by an external advisory committee, the details of which are not available.[8]

Other university research centres and institutes in the sample did not have oil representatives on their boards, but receive extensive funding from industry. This is seen, for example, at the University of Calgary's Consortium for Heavy Oil Research by University Scientists. The consortium is an "oil industrial sponsored program", located in the Geology/Geophysics/ Petroleum Engineering Departments. It conducts research on the geological aspects of reservoir production, engineering, and simulation, and aims to develop technologies that simultaneously maximize the production and energy efficiency of extraction from heavy oil fields. Industry sponsors include ConocoPhillips, Nexen Energy, Shell Canada, British Petroleum, Japan Oil and Gas, Chevron Canada, and Kuwait Oil. Similarly – and also at the University of Calgary – the Hydrocarbon Metagenomics Lab conducts exploratory research surrounding the potential to harness naturally occurring organisms and bioprocesses present in Canada's tar sands, oilfields, and coal beds in an effort to decrease the environmental impact of carbon extraction. While not governed by an advisory board, it also receives funding from a host of fossil fuel companies, including ConocoPhillips, EnCana, Nexen, ARC Resources, Quick Silver Resources, Shell Canada, Suncor, Syncrude, and Trident Exploration.

While some research funding for the development of reputedly "clean technologies" comes directly from industry, as noted above, it is also publicly subsidized. The Hydrocarbon Metagenomics Lab and The Centre for Oil Sands Sustainability, for example, receive funding from the Canada Foundation for Innovation – a research institute and funding body created by the government of Canada, but which operates as an independent, non-governmental entity. Alberta Innovates is also listed as a sponsor/funder for the Canadian Centre for Clean Coal and The Centre for Oil Sands Sustainability. Meanwhile, the Centre for Intelligent Mining Systems (CIMS) and the Helmholtz-Alberta Initiative (HAI) receive funding from the government of Alberta.

By funding and participating in the governance of university-based institutes, private corporations are able to direct and appropriate research and knowledge, while the public again helps foot the bill. The university has an important role to play in knowledge production for ecological transition, but

---

8 The same goes for the University of Alberta's Institute for Oil Sands Innovation, which is directed by an Executive Management Committee, whose composition is unknown and not publicly available. Trudell's position on the board of IOSI was only discovered through her online profile at the Centre for Oil Sands Sustainability.

this potential is obstructed and foreclosed upon as university-based resources and capacities are oriented towards the greening of the carbon sector.

7.3   *Industry Collaborations*

Not surprisingly, industry-led green innovation institutes and collaborations are extensively governed by carbon-capital elites. They also interlock with state and university research institutes, helping to form a networked research infrastructure supporting carbon extraction, especially in Alberta, but also Canada more broadly. Below I focus on the three most central organizations in the network, the Natural Gas Innovation Fund, Canada's Oilsands Innovation Alliance and the Petroleum Technology Alliance of Canada.

The Natural Gas Innovation Fund (NGIF) was created in 2017 by the Canadian Gas Association to support clean technology development across the natural gas production chain. It works to bring the clean fuel characterization of natural gas (at least in comparison to coal) closer to reality. As a result, the NGIF places significant emphasis on supporting research aimed at reducing methane emissions. Its focus on this front is currently on capture and storage of fugitive emissions (leaks in fracking and production) and in gas venting mitigation technologies (Natural Gas Innovation Fund, n.d.). NGIF's investment advisory committee includes ten carbon-capital representatives, drawn from prominent natural gas producers and distributors. These include Doug Stout and Jason Wolfe who are respectively Vice President and the Director of Energy Solutions at Fortis BC, Dan Reeve, Senior Vice President at Atco, Scott Dodd, director at Enbridge and Leigh Shoji-Lee and Timothy Egan, who are respectively Vice Chair and President of the Canadian Gas Association. As mentioned, Egan is also director at Sustainable Development Technology Canada.

As discussed above, Canada's Oilsands Innovation Alliance (COSIA), formed in 2012, is a collaboration of thirteen of Canada's largest tar sands companies, which pools resources, shares new technologies and funds research to lessen the ecological impacts of tar sands development. Its green technology efforts are focused in four "Environmental Priority Areas" of land, water, tailings and greenhouse gases. COSIA members launch projects related to these priority areas, share and assess results and implement technology to improve environmental performance. Most projects are joint endeavours involving one or more producers, as well as "third parties", such as university research centres and state innovation agencies.

The organization has a CEO and six directors (one director per each of four Environmental Priority Areas), as well as an advisory and steering committee. As seen in Figure 3, COSIA is governed by representatives from large capital firms, and also interlocks with government and university research centres. Dan Wicklum (D_Wicklum), who is president and CEO of COSIA is also director at SDTC. Wicklum has also previously held senior positions at Environment Canada and Natural Resources Canada. Meanwhile, COSIA's funding of projects at University of Alberta's Institute for Oil Sands Innovation and NAIT's Centre for Oil Sands Sustainability (COSS), are accompanied and supported by the strategic direction of Cheryl Trudell (C_Trudell), who is a Vice President of the steering committee at COSIA, and an industry advisor at both University Centres.[9]

The Petroleum Technology Alliance of Canada (PTA_CAN) also plays an important role in stitching the network together and linking industry–state–university organizations in the development of fossil fuel R&D. The Alliance, which is headquartered in Calgary, was established in 1996, to promote collaborative research and technology development for the hydrocarbon energy industry, broadly defined. Its vision is to "help Canada become a global hydrocarbon energy technology leader", and its projects span a number of priority areas, including: managing industry's environmental footprint, improving oil and gas recovery, creating operating savings and finding ways to create value-added products (Petroleum Technology Alliance Canada, n.d.).

While the organization pursues a broad mandate, beginning in 2010, it redefined its strategy and direction, so as to focus more closely on technology development and innovation related to unconventional oil and gas. In this area, it is focused on addressing what it views as the unique challenge facing the industry today: the effort to "recover increasingly challenging deposits while reducing costs" and at the same time meeting the demand "that hydrocarbon production have significantly less environmental impact... [and] significantly higher energy efficiency" (Petroleum Technology Alliance Canada, 2010). In 2015, the organization launched 59 research and development projects (by far the most since its inception in 1996), 41 of which address "high-priority environmental and social issues" pertinent to Western Canada's oil and gas industry. A key priority area that it identified is to "create the lowest environmental footprint in multi-stage hydraulic fracturing"... "while establishing the best economic performance for Tight Oil and Shale Gas operations throughout Western Canada" (Petroleum Technology Alliance Canada, 2015). In 2018, along

---

9 COSIA is listed a corporate contributor and funder at IOSI (Institute For Oil Sands Innovation, n.d.) and the organization funds projects at COSS, including a $200,000 donation in 2018 for tar sands water treatment (Canada's Oil Sands Innovation Alliance, 2018).

with the Canadian Association of Petroleum Producers and the Explorers and Producers Association of Canada, it launched the Fugitive Emissions Management Program Effectiveness Assessment (FEMP EA) project, focused on methane leak detection, quantification and repair. The project has funding support from over 400 oil and gas producers and is described as "immense in scope" (JWN Energy, 2018).

The Alliance is governed by a twenty-person board that extensively links together carbon-capital elites and state and university officials. The former include Kevin Stashin (K_Stashin), who is chair of PTA_CAN and member of the board of directors at the Canadian Association of Petroleum Producers (as well as CEO of private oil and gas producer NAL Resources) and Murray Todd (M_Todd) director at Bellatrix Exploration (BELLATRIX). The latter include Laurier Schramm (L_Schramm), president and CEO of Saskatchewan Research Council (SK_RC) – a Crown corporation conducting applied research on behalf of the Saskatchewan provincial government – and Cecile Siewe (C_ Siewe), a director at CanMet energy (CAN_M_EN), a Government of Canada research laboratory focused on addressing the environmental impacts of fossil fuel extraction, processing and use. The board also includes high ranking environmental state regulators such as Paul Jenkins, Vice Chair of the Canadian Oil and Gas Commission; Jim Ellis, President and CEO of the Alberta Energy Regulator; Mike Ekelund, former assistant Deputy Minister in the Department of Natural Resources Canada and former CEO of the Canadian Gas Association; and the Dean of Engineering at the University of Calgary, William Rosehart.

The centrality of fossil fuel industry innovation organizations in the network reflects the sector's strategic focus on "clean fossil fuels". Playing a role in the direction of these organizations are prominent carbon-capital elites, including CEO's and directors of firms that dominate much of the sector and the industry associations that represent them. Meanwhile, the thick ties between industry innovation organizations and carbon-capital firms and key university and state research bodies are indicative of the way that government and university R&D priorities in Alberta and Canada more broadly align closely with the current interests and needs of the industry. Corporate innovation organizations thereby allow industry to define sectoral strategies and are a basis for developing social relationships with governmental cadre in key institutions that support and help advance sectoral interests. The highly integrated character of the network contrasts with the carbon-renewable linkages seen in Chapter 6, which as we saw are overall relatively sparse, involving a small number of firms (represented mostly by lower-level managers from carbon-capital firms).

8   Greened Extractivism and Fettering of Ecological Knowledge

Through an analysis of interlocking directorates, I provided an overview of networked industry–university–state research institutes and centres that provide the foundation for clean tech research, while demonstrating the centrality of carbon-extractive industries in these networks. Interlocking directorates enable economically dominant fractions of capital to define and advance their interests, while also promoting elite cohesion and unity. The above network analysis thereby reveals the pathways through which carbon capital priorities and strategies penetrate into academic and public research organizations that are often assumed to be independent of big business. They facilitate the appropriation and indeed colonization of scientific research processes. Interlocks observed across sectors (corporate, academic and state) are also a means of creating and sustaining a common sense in favour of greening the fossil fuel sector as a "solution" to climate change.

The architectonic network analysis provided here is limited in explaining causality and demonstrating how carbon capital instrumentally operates within these networks to advance its agenda. Interlocking directorates are best understood as "traces of power" (Carroll and Alexander, 1999). More in depth and focused case studies, such as those undertaken by the Canadian Association of University Teachers (2013) and by Washburn (2010), have demonstrated that the corporate funding of research, as well as industry representation on governance boards of academic institutes, centres and schools, profoundly influences the direction and scope of research undertaken within them. When industry directs scientific research, knowledge that may portend alternative futures is diminished.

The ascendency of a clean tech approach to ecological sustainability and the fusion of carbon-extractive industries with government and universities surrounding this development, has far reaching implications for those working to challenge existing models of fossil-based economic development and advance alternatives. In this process, knowledge and research vital to ecological and energy transition is fettered. This fettering of research and knowledge takes two forms. It involves, on the one hand a sub-optimal or ineffective *use* of existing productive capacities. Therefore, while "greened extractivism" involves limited objectifications of ecological knowledge and impact science, any application of this potential beyond profit-making is strategic and sharply constrained. In the development of reputedly clean fossil fuel technologies, ecological science is *underutilized* – appropriated, enclosed and employed only in half-hearted processes of ecological modernization that do not halt, but instead measure, monitor, and mitigate some of the environmental impacts of ecological debasement.

In addition to the underutilization of this existing productive capacity, by focusing on carbon-capital's reach into universities and the state and the institutional architecture that supports greened extractivism, the research points to how transforming scientific research in its organization and prioritization would encourage the further *development* of ecological knowledge. Indeed, as Adkin argues (2020), these institutes take up resources that might be utilized for other research initiatives. Ending the colonization and harnessing of the scientific research process itself to fossil fuel-related R&D, while re-directing funding and institutional support for various forms of sustainable earth science, pursued on the basis of their broad ecological or metabolic use-value, would generate new knowledge vital for energy transition and for a sustainable economy more broadly.

Corporations powerfully shape which knowledge is produced, how is produced and for whom. Universities and governments have become increasingly oriented towards research that is of strategic value to business. However, the fettering in the *development* of ecological knowledge that ensues from this process, appears to be subordinate to (or nested within) its broader *underutilization*. That is, even if public knowledge production processes were reconfigured to emphasize sustainability research, such knowledge would continue to find limited application, so long as production is fundamentally guided by exchange-value and capital.

9   Conclusion

I began this chapter by noting with Marx that science is a crucial component of the productive forces, harnessed to capitalism to transform the rest of nature in commodity production and to cope with ecological problems, insofar as the latter jeopardize the conditions for profitability and growth. It has played a vital role in the making of fossil capitalism since the 18th century and has enabled the development unconventional sources, into the 21st century.

In the face of the current climate crisis, which is simultaneously a crisis of fossil capitalism, carbon capital is engaged in a strategic effort to "green" its operations, or at least the public perception of them, in order to maintain conditions for the accumulation of fossil capital. Development of reputedly clean fossil technologies is a crucial component of industry's accumulation strategy (and its efforts at strategic self-preservation). It is also extensively supported by state policy frameworks. In such innovations, components of ecological and impact science, such as conservation and restoration ecology, climatic and atmospheric science, which have grown in the context of the deepening climate crisis, are now harnessed (back) into fossil capital development. In this process, I argued that knowledge and research vital to ecological and energy transition is itself fettered – constrained, shackled and blocked.

Network analysis identified the social form of this knowledge – its production in and through a host of interlinked industry–government–university centres and organizations. It thereby revealed the architecture through which carbon capital exerts continuous pressure on and works together with higher education, state and civil society research organizations to appropriate scientific capacities and direct the process of scientific discovery itself. The fusion of carbon-extractive industries with government and universities in a process of neoliberal state–corporate symbiosis is consistent with (and further entrenches) "petro-state" priorities and imperative.

The situation in Canada is troubling but not exceptional. A recent study of carbon-capital's influence over leading American universities concludes: "Fossil fuel interests – oil, gas, and coal companies, fossil-fueled utilities, and fossil fuel investors – have colonized nearly every nook and cranny of energy and climate policy research in American universities, and much of energy science too" (Franta and Supran, 2017).

Carbon capital's reach into academic and public research organizations and the shaping of science infrastructures around fossil fuel R&D is a barrier to challenging existing models of fossil-capital development and demands political intervention. At the level of policy and political strategy, Werskey's (2007) recollection of past efforts (especially in the 1960s and 70s) to radicalize science politically are helpful. While these efforts ended in failure, visions of a "public interest science" model have merit. Such a model confronts the long-standing yet deepening processes of corporatization and state–corporate symbiosis, surrounding R&D. It seeks to overturn the increased integration between public sector organizations and private firms, and the blurring of lines between public/academic and private/corporate spheres regarding the goals of knowledge production witnessed in this study. Concertedly, as universities and state innovation agencies continue to express a commitment to the production of knowledge and research for the public good, it is important to expose the limitations of "clean fossil fuel" technology and the parochial interests driving their development.

In addition to "reclaiming" public institutions, Werskey (2007) calls for the formation and revival of Radical Science movements akin to those of the

1960s/70s. These sought to transform science in its organization and prioritization and also in its application. The climate crisis, as he suggests, may provide a unique opportunity for such a development, based on a vision that various branches of earth science, indeed science at large, needs to serve society in new and better ways. The crisis provokes politics aimed at, as Marx put it, "converting science from an instrument of class rule into a popular force" (as cited in Perelman, 1978, p. 868).

The Future of Productive Forces: Towards Green Socialism

In 2015, the World Meteorological Organisation reported that the amount of carbon dioxide in the atmosphere exceeded 400 parts per million and that planetary temperatures had reached a 1 degrees Celsius increase since preindustrial averages (Connor 2015). The halfway point towards a 2 degrees Celsius increase in planetary temperature, which is considered to be the threshold of catastrophic climate change, had been broken. According to the United Nations Intergovernmental Panel on Climate Change, we now have a decade to reduce greenhouse gas emissions by half and get on target to reach zero emissions by 2050 (Intergovernmental Panel on Climate Change, 2018). Failing that, global temperatures will exceed a 1.5 degrees Celsius increase. Despite increasingly urgent warmings, emissions are growing fast.

The implications for human lives are dire. These are already witnessed as extreme weather events, such as droughts, heatwaves, drier conditions enabling fires and floods, are becoming more commonplace. Sea levels are also rising, placing many low-lying communities, populous coastal cities and island states in jeopardy. Moreover, climate change on this scale within the earth system is not expected to unfold in a linear way. Instead, it can potentially happen abruptly or through feedback loops further accelerating run-away climate change. Anthropogenic climate change, driven primarily from the production and consumption of fossil fuels, represents the greatest existential peril of our time and demands immediate action.

In a widely cited essay in *Dissent* (2013), Christian Parenti argued that the compressed time frame for reducing emissions forces us to approach the climate crisis in a pragmatic, short-term, and reformist fashion. We are in an emergency and the window to address climate change is so short that we must recognize that "it is *this society* and *these* [existing] *institutions* that must cut emissions. That means, in the short-term, realistic climate politics are reformist politics, even if they are conceived of as part of a longer-term anti-capitalist project of total economic re-organization" (Parenti, 2013, second section). Anyone who suggests otherwise, who proposes that the "existing economic system must be totally transformed before we can deal with the impending climate crisis is delusional" (Parenti, 2013, final para.). For Parenti, a transition to a post-capitalist society will entail a long and drawn-out, maybe even multigen-erational, struggle.

He goes on to assert that while capitalism may ultimately be incapable of "accommodating itself to the limits of the natural world ... that is not the same question as whether capitalism can solve the more immediate climate crisis" (Parenti, 2013, third para.). Capitalism has been successful in the past in ad-dressing "specific environmental crises" and this may well be the case with re-spect to climate change. He outlines several immediate measures to mitigate carbon emissions, focusing on the US context. These include using govern-ment purchasing to buy clean energy, electric vehicles, and retrofit buildings for energy conservation. This would achieve economies of scale, lower clean energy prices, and thus aid a transition in the private sector. He also suggests demanding that the Environmental Protection Agency (EPA) impose a de facto carbon tax.

Parenti points to the need for state action and seeks to valorize the state as a force for climate mitigation. The creation of government agendas and spending programs geared toward a zero-carbon economy, he recognizes, pre-supposes well-organized, tactically and strategically radical social move-ments pressing for climate policy. Reformist state-led climate mitigation and adaptation actions, undergirded by social movements, would thereby gener-ate changes that do not produce an alternative to capitalism, but in the short-term vastly reduce emissions and possibly "solve" the climate crisis. This "buys time" for a longer-term project to address the whole planetary ecologi-cal crisis.

Parenti's essay provokes a debate on socialist strategy in the context of the climate emergency and on the purpose of present inquiries into the climatic destructivity of capital accumulation. The left today, as he asserts, needs realis-tic assessments of obstacles to green transition and credible proposals for deal-ing with the climate crisis, while also having a systemic critique and vision of long-term change.

In this book I have aimed to contribute to existing systemic critiques, as well as to more concrete-complex analyses of barriers to green transition. Part 2 an-alyzed the deepening of fossil-fuelled productive forces and a process of fetter-ing in both renewable energies and in the development and application of eco-logical knowledge. Within relations of production, I emphasized modalities of corporate power, particularly the power of carbon capital, as a crucial obstacle to their advancement and use. Case studies considered carbon-capital's liminal efforts to incorporate green productive forces into its accumulation processes and strategies– witnessed through some investments in renewable energy, in ecological efficiencies, and through the application of ecological knowledge to industry in the pursuit of "greened extractivism".

This more concrete analysis limited the study to the Canadian context. Yet as I have suggested, how contradictions between the forces and relations of production (particularly here the fettering of ecological knowledge and renewable energy technology) are resolved, will not be decided in the abstract, but through the formulation–realization of specific strategies and projects at various economic and political scales in specific spatio-temporal contexts. From a "pragmatic" and historical materialist angle, I also argued that transforming and transitioning away from existing productive networks, infrastructural configurations and built environments entails some inevitable "compromise" with the forms of productive organization and social relations that produced them.

Parenti is right to argue that climate mitigation must entail reformist politics and that reforms that are conceivable within the system to slow climate change are needed. However, to suggest that climate change can be solved without systemic change, misunderstands the relationship between capital and carbon emissions and the drive to accelerate fossil fuel extraction. The climate crisis is the most dangerous and threatening of contemporary ecological crises, but it is deeply interlinked with other metabolic rifts, and it is a product of a systemic logic and deep historical trajectory.

Through a green-dialectical framework, Part 1 of this work analyzed capital's appropriation of productive forces and their development in pursuit of maximum exchange-value and surplus value. Through Marx, I examined how the transition to large-scale fossil powered industry and machinery, activates the potential for relative surplus value, and completely transforms the competitive dynamics of the economy. Under the "whip of competition", competing capitals, in an oligarchy of corporations, are compelled to increase the productivity of production processes. This entails and presupposes rising matter and (at a system level) energy throughput. With the continuous expansion of fossil powered and compounding economic growth since the 18th century, the rift in the Earth's carbon metabolism has steadily widened and has now spun out of control.

"Realistic" climate politics must entail reformist efforts, but it is not conceivable to resolve climate change (and ecological crises as a whole) without deep incursions into and in part superseding relations of production. Part 1 of this book thereby pointed to how relations of production inhibit true ecological transformation, as exchange-value seeking continually trumps social and ecological use-value criteria. It indicates that broad structural change is required to mend the climate rift.

At the level of strategy, this suggests that concrete and urgent emissions reducing reforms and measures to be fought for and implemented right now, must oppose the logic of capital, while working towards the long-term effort of superseding relations of production. A world not centred on capital accumulation, but based on human flourishing within sustainable ecosystems may take generations to fully achieve. This is a horizon to work towards. Yet, as the notion of the "transition society" suggests, it is helpful to think of socialism less as a destination, or as something to be achieved either before or after we deal with the impending climate crisis, but as a process of continual and revolutionary transformation that works towards and removes barriers to this flourishing.[1] Urgent reforms right now can help instigate the growth of green productive forces and reduce emissions, while also pursuing longer-term goals by consciously transforming productive forces in ways that better accord with egalitarian social relations and facilitate a restorative metabolic relation to nature. This means detaching them from capital's growth imperative, opposing the logic of exchange-value and quantitative growth, substituting this with the qualitative logic of ecological and social use-value in their development, at every turn.

In the remaining sections of this work, I develop the practical implications of a more dialectical, green-Marxist approach to forces of production. I seek to bring together the framework of Part 1 with the more empirical account of Part 2 in outlining programmatic efforts towards green socialism. I do not provide a "blueprint" or an elaborated set of policy proposals, but rather suggest broad first measures for a transition society aimed at, to paraphrase Marx, governing the human metabolism with nature in a rational way, bringing it under collective control and accomplishing it with the least expenditure of energy. The actions involve concrete and immediate reforms and more radical measures based on collective decision making and ownership of production, sustaining a longer-term perspective. While I emphasize control over productive forces (and especially energy resources, infrastructures, technologies, and associated skills and knowledge), the transformations necessarily extend to the sphere of reproduction and everyday life. The vision is tilted towards Canada, but maintains an eye towards the international and the global.

Key Measures:
- Rapidly and comprehensively phasing out fossil fuels, while transitioning to a clean energy system based on sources such as wind, hydro, solar, wave and geothermal.
- Restructuring existing extraction, production and distribution systems, including eliminating the production of useless and harmful goods, reducing

---

1 A critical response to Parenti from the editors of Monthly Review (2014), made a similar point, referring to socialism as a "movement of the present reality".

the length of commodity chains and the amount of transport where feasible and desirable.
- Halting the colonization of knowledge by industry and "remaking" science in its organization, prioritization and application.
- Planning the transition at all levels in a democratic and participatory manner.

Taken in isolation, these measures appear somewhat compatible with a renovated capitalism. Braiding them together into a coherent plan achievable within the next few decades will require deep incursions into relations of production. The transition is not based on short-term profit, but rather necessitated in large part by the urgent threat of carbon-based fuels to the long-term viability of ecosystems that support human life and the life of other species. It will require new forms of planning and different forms of social property, opening paths for deep and radical democratization. The measures aim to break from the logic of private accumulation and the reign of exchange-value, moving towards what Burkett (2005) calls "sustainable human development". They also seek to provide common ground for converging agendas across what Candeias (2013b) calls a "mosaic" and transformative left.[2]

1   **Rapidly and Comprehensively Phasing out Fossil Fuels, While Transitioning to a Clean Energy System**

Despite increasingly common pronouncements that energy system transformation is now underway, and that carbon corporations are helping lead the transition, there is little evidence that current capital-led approaches can produce a timely energy transition, or that carbon capital or financial fractions will act as "green saviours".

An analysis of the fossil-fuel sector's investments in both renewable energy and efficiency-enhancing carbon-extractive technologies in Canada revealed "signposts" of a strategic orientation some oil and gas firms have taken toward "climate capitalism". However, the carbon sector's main priority is efficiency enhancement, not renewable energy technology. Investments by large firms in renewables can at most be interpreted as a very long-term vision of renewable

---

2 While a mosaic of left agencies/movements can form the basis of such a fundamental transition, this does not preclude the role, indeed the likely imperative of, political parties struggling over the space of the state in conjunction with and alongside left movements. For discussion and debate on the form of such a party or political organization might take, see Albo et al. (2010, pp. 89–121) and Dean (2016).

THE FUTURE OF PRODUCTIVE FORCES

energy transition, which simply does not square with the scientific consensus on climate change. A climate capitalist model of energy transition portends ecological disaster.

In examining the relative-developmental fettering of renewable energy, I pointed to a basic contradiction between the use-value and exchange-value of renewables: they possess tremendous metabolic worth, but struggle to attract capital investment, as they are less profitable than fossil fuels. I also pointed to the contradiction between carbon capital's (and financial institution's) quest to valorize massive fixed capital investments and the requirement to decarbonize energy in a rapid and socially just manner.

Carbon capital and its allies are not only protecting vast sunk carbon investments, but are doubling down on the fossil fuel regime in the context of ecological overshoot, developing new methods to extract the dirtiest deposits and pushing hard to create vast new infrastructural complexes that would enable the heightened accumulation of fossil capital. Both the material lock-in of infrastructures and the power of carbon corporations and other "enablers" of carbon-extractive development, are key blockages to a rapid and comprehensive transformation to a sustainable post-carbon economy.

Eroding power in and around this sector is therefore an urgent and pressing task. An enforced and managed wind-down of fossil fuel production is needed, alongside a planned process of development in renewable energy. Robust regulatory policies can help constrain and strategically shape energy development in a manner that assists in effecting a rapid transition to renewable energies. Higher royalties on hydrocarbon extraction, taxes on carbon usage, and controls on overall emissions (including through polluter-pays provisions) can raise funds to facilitate a planned transition to alternatives. However, regulatory reforms must be accompanied by more radical measures. As Carroll puts it, rapid energy transition requires that we "shift power, in both senses of the term: from fossil-fuel power to renewables (decarbonization) and from corporate oligarchy to public, democratic control of economic decisions (democratization)" (2017, p. 256).

Establishing democratic control requires public ownership of the energy sector. This can take different forms – state, community-based, worker-led operations and co-ops – which in different ways challenge commodification and the drive towards growth and private profit. A combination of different forms of organization could be used, yet public ownership does not merit blanket, uncritical endorsement. In terms of state ownership, much is wrong with traditional Crown corporations, which often function much like private corporations; they frequently operate with a profit-maximization mandate, encourage little public involvement in decision-making and maintain extensive ties to private industry. As Thompson and Newman (2009) suggest, it is therefore vital to provide such institutions with robust social and ecological mandates, while also democratizing their governance. From an ecological use-value perspective, a public interest mandate means that renewable firms would induce consumers to buy less of what they sell, reducing energy demand and promoting conservation, while curtailing expanding production. Such strategies are incompatible with and substitute the private sector's growth and profit imperative, with social and ecological value seeking.

In the Canadian context, close to 60 percent of Canada's current renewable power comes from hydropower, most of it already constructed in the form of large dam projects, with Crown corporations playing an important role (Laxer, 2015a). There is still a need for new large-scale development,[3] but this provides a strong base from which to transition to a low carbon future through the expansion of small-to medium-scale renewable energy projects, including wind and solar power, as well as hydro from run of the river turbines and tidal turbines. Since the 1970s, many pioneering initiatives in renewables have taken the form of co-operative and community-ownership, with emphasis on local control (Abramsky, 2010).

First Nations in Canada have been playing a leading role in community-scale development (Shaw et al., 2017). Such projects have provided a platform for energy autonomy, food self-sufficiency and the resurgence of cultural practices (A. Bhattacharya, 2018). Some projects simultaneously sell renewable power back to the grid, serving as a means of community economic development, while contributing to a wider process of renewable energy transition. Other communities, especially in rural areas, could also be encouraged on this path, while Indigenous Peoples should be first to receive public support for their own clean energy projects.

In addition to different forms of public ownership and interest in renewable energy, which can facilitate a bottom-up process of development with built-in

---

3 In left approaches to energy transition, such as those outlining "two paths" discussed in the Chapter 6, a binary is often made in the literature surrounding the "scale" of renewable energy development, with a climate capitalist political economic project involving large-scale installations (such as Desertec – a proposed string of concentrated power plants in the Northern Sahara exporting electricity to Europe via underwater cables) and a green-left project consisting of small-scale, local and community level developments. While small-scale developments are often most desirable, both from an ecological perspective and in view of the democratization of energy, such a binary or "scaler determinism" can prove unhelpful in some cases. As I have suggested, planning, including the coordination of energy flows, even at a global level, will be required in some instances and is integral to green socialism. Despite the failures of command-style state socialism, and what neoliberalism tells us, large-scale installations could be publicly owned and democratically managed.

social and ecological value seeking, it is important to consider forms of planning aimed at comprehensive phase-out of fossil fuels. As is the case globally (York and McGee, 2017), non-fossil fuel sources have been added to Canada's "energy mix" incrementally and on top of a net expansion in the consumption of fossil fuels (D. Hughes, 2018). The yearly ebb and flow of renewable energy development, along with the fact that clean energy capacity can continue to grow along with an expanding bed of fossil fuels, points to fettering that follows from an inability to develop productive forces systematically and comprehensively, on a prolonged basis (rather than temporarily, fleetingly and erratically) and according to a plan.

In the transition, as Abramsky (2010) points out, there is a need for continued use of fossil fuels, but these must be used in a rational and collectively planned way, rather that through wasteful competitive market allocations. In Alberta, the recent decision by the New Democratic Party government to impose a nearly 10 percent cut on the production of bitumen (in an effort to reduce excess supply and increase price per barrel, thereby maximizing profit across the sector), unwittingly points toward the clear feasibility of progressively downsizing and even sunsetting of the tar sands (see Acuña, 2018).

Laxer's (2015) "ecological security plan" for Canada combines a number of these measures. He advocates using existing conventional resources in the short-to medium term, with their planned phase out in a transition towards renewables. Moreover, as a component of the plan and drawing on Thompson and Newman (2009), Laxer points to the potential merits of transforming some segments of the existing oil and gas industry to public interest ownership models. As he argues, some public interest ownership in this sector, along side a broader "power down plan" would mandate non-profit entities to buy less of what they sell and could simultaneously wean users off carbon and onto renewables. His plan thereby helpfully combines strong regulatory measures with a shift away from private, for-profit ownership and control, as energy companies are converted to or displaced by such public-interest, not-for-profit entities.

1.1   *Transforming and Democratizing the State*
A number of the above measures recognize that the state, through government regulation and public spending, can intervene directly in the climate crisis. The state, as Parenti suggests, is a necessary force in robust climate mitigation. Of course the state is only *relatively* autonomous from capital and is biased in favour of the capitalist class in general and dominant fractions in particular.

In regions with high levels of carbon extractive development, states are structurally dependent on revenue from gas and oil production and this

212   CONCLUSIONS

reliance is inextricably intertwined with and reinforced by carbon capital's active reach into political society. As discussed, this reach occurs through means such as political party donations, political lobbying and "revolving-door" relations or close personal ties between the corporate community and the government, as well as the regulatory and advisory boards and commissions that make up the state apparatus. Together these multiple means of influence help stitch together corporations and economic elites with state leaders and managers in a "state-capital nexus" that portends deepening ecological degradation (Graham, 2017).

While revenue dependency and more direct means of influence exert strong pressure on the state to defend corporate interests, they in no way ensure that it will always do so. The state, as Jessop suggests (2007) is an ensemble of many relations that offers a contradictory terrain of struggle. It should not be doubted that popular organization and social activism from below can significantly shape the organization and priorities of the state in capitalist society. Democratizing and decisively transforming the state at various scales (from the local, regional, national, and international) must be a critical facet of the struggle to decarbonize energy in a rapid, democratic, and socially just manner.

Novel forms of public ownership that allow for participatory and decentralised control are themselves part of the radical democratization of the state (see Angel, 2017). There are addition short-term reforms that should be undertaken. These include banning corporate donations to political parties, including the purchase of tickets to fundraising events and donations (Graham, 2017). Changes to the practice of lobbying can also limit the exertion of direct corporate influence on government policy. Policies could proactively support more equal access to political influence, balancing against industry's direct overrepresentation in shaping policy. This could be accomplished through increased support for public interest or public advocacy lobbying (see Graham, Carroll and Chen, 2019). Having corporate executives sit on regulatory boards, universities or other public bodies should be strictly limited. As a general rule, they should be guided by labour, academics, students and informed community members who have public interest at heart (Carroll and Sapinksi, 2018).

Energy transition can begin nationally, but it must ultimately be achieved at the global level through cooperation and ideally based on collectively agreed pace and priorities.

1.2 *Control over Finance*

Castree and Christophers (2015) point to the possibility of regulatory practices and reforms that can re-route private finance capital towards more ethical and ecological ends. Short-term reforms and regulation of markets, as they suggest, can help provoke private, ecologically oriented financing. Such reforms may be helpful, but as these author's admit, they are yet to come close to unlocking capital at the scale that is required. As we have seen in the Canadian context, the financial sector maintains a very close relationship with the fossil fuel industry and has a strong vested interest in valorizing its massive investments in fixed fossil capital. Financial fractions continue to be resolutely "dirty and brown" and "short-termism" continues to dominate institutional investment (Zadek, 2013). Moreover, as Castree and Christophers (2015) recognize, given that much of the needed infrastructural development (transportation and built environment reconstruction for green energy) will not be revenue generative, it will not be pursued on capitalist criteria. Corporate allocative power, the control of the financing of energy and infrastructure is a powerful obstacle to dealing effectively with the ecological and economic challenges we face today.

As Carroll and Sapinski (2018) argue, a timely transition requires bringing banks and other sectors of allocative power under greater democratic control, including through public ownership. The socialization of banks has been long been an aim of the left, but as they make it clear, public ownership alone is not sufficient. As with energy Crowns, banks need to be thought of as a service delivered in the public interest (mandated to support socially and ecologically healthy investment), and also democratized in their governance. In contrast to the allocative power of today's financial institutions, Carroll and Sapinski point to a financial system organized as a network of public banks, whose governance is democratized through participatory budgeting. While participatory budgeting has been successfully practiced at the local and municipal level, the challenge is to scale it up and think of how it could apply to economic decision making broadly.

1.3 Worker Control

Workers currently employed either directly or indirectly in fossil and nuclear sectors and other energy intensive sectors have a key role to play in energy transition. Mobilizing and "redirecting" their skills and knowledge is vital to green transformation (while re-training may be needed in some cases). As Abramsky (2010) suggests, in a drawn-out energy transition on the model of the market, every effort will be made to accomplish the shift on the back of workers. Having renewables out-compete fossil fuels in costs does not only mean technology advancements, it means reducing labour costs across the (global) renewable commodity chain. Public forms of ownership in the sector and across the chain (in manufacturing, installation, maintenance) provides an opportunity for not only good working conditions and wages, but also for worker participation in and democratization of workplaces in the establishment of these new industries. This is a vital part of collectively reclaiming and taking control over means of production. The combination of decarbonization and economic democratization has been endorsed by the international trade union movement, including Canada's largest unions and the Canadian Labour Congress, through Trade Unions for Energy Democracy.[4]

1.4 Land-Based Struggles, Indigenous Resurgence and Renewable Transition

Indigenous peoples, as we have seen in the Canadian context, have been on the frontlines of protecting lands from extractive development and blocking the further expansion of the fossil economy. As Coulthard argues (2014), Indigenous resistance is at once negation *and* affirmation. Resistance actions are often a prelude to and an affirmative gesture of resurgence, with the latter involving the renewal and reinvention of Indigenous ways of being, knowing and doing, as well relationship with other First Nations.

Land-based resistance and sovereignty are foundational for the futurity of Indigenous people and Coulthard sees such resistance as having greater revolutionary potential than the left has recognized. He argues that land-based struggles of Indigenous peoples are struggles "not only *for* land in the material sense, but also deeply *informed* by what the land *as system of reciprocal relations and obligations* can teach us about living our lives in relation to one another and the natural world in nondominating and nonexploitative terms" (2014, p. 13). In a similar manner to Ariel Salleh, he points to how the land-connected practices and associated forms of knowledge of peoples that have not been swept into the current of capitalist industrialization, have much to teach in forging alternatives. By pointing to land not just as a material resource, but as a source of ethical teachings, he indicates a deep reciprocal and relational dimension in the relation to nature and a robust sense of the natural world's intrinsic value.

This book has been somewhat "anthropocentric"; I have emphasized the transformation of nature through human means and practices and argued for the importance of ecological integrity and flourishing, primarily for human ends and needs. Intrinsic values, as Foster and Burkett suggest (2016, pp. 34–56), can be considered as a part of use-value, which is not restricted to "utility" as it is in bourgeois conceptions. In a society no longer dominated by exchange-value, intrinsic value, including concerns for non-human creatures, and

---

4   TUED was formed through the roundtable of trade unionists in 2012, and currently includes 47 unions in 17 countries. See http://unionsforenergydemocracy.org/.

aesthetic criteria (such as beauty) could play an essential role guiding the practices and processes by which we are linked to nature. While I have only gestured
to such considerations in this study, such lines of theorizing are important for
deepening eco-socialism and connecting its praxis with Indigenous anticolo-
nialism and anticapitalism.

The process of energy transition could be an opportunity for re-claiming
and asserting control of land by Indigenous communities, creating space for
the construction of Indigenous alternatives to capitalism. The primitive accumulation of fossil capital entails extensive land grabs, through which carbon
capital appropriates and controls huge swaths of land for both carbon-
extractive exploration and production. In addition to land held for the process
of "search and discovery", Jacobson et al. (2018) show that oil and gas development actually requires a much larger land footprint than renewables would.
This counters the common claim that alternative energy systems require huge
amounts of space and territory to generate the equivalent energy from buried
sunshine (Huber, 2015; Laxer, 2015b). This is because fossil fuel energy production entails much more that extracting fuel from a single "hole". As we saw in
Chapter 5, oil and gas production involves numerous wells and fields, as well as
extensive networked infrastructures (associated roads and local storage facilities, vehicle fueling stations, large refineries, and processing plants, pipelines
for import and export, long distribution networks and so on). This is dedicated
fossil-fuel land and little of this land footprint can be used for other purposes.
Giving substantial amounts of land back to Indigenous peoples currently held
by carbon firms (and other large producers) and dedicated to fossil fuel use
during the transition could contribute to decolonization and resurgence.

Moreover, much of the land for renewable development (where much renewable energy development is likely to be located and where renewable energy resources are located) is in rural and (unceded) Indigenous territories. In
Canada, First Nations are themselves advancing community level projects,
while securing or asserting control over land formerly held by or used in service to fossil fuel development can help ensure real decision-making power.
Further to this, a largely publicly owned and democratically managed sector,
built through organizations with strong social and ecological mandates, would
help ensure robust consent for any new and large-scale projects.

1.5   *Geographies of Reproduction and Everyday Life*
Throughout the study, I have focused primarily on the process of industrial
energy transformation, while energy transition must include a transformation
of the energy system as a whole – energy that powers production, as well as
(public) transportation, communities and homes. Within this view, free and

efficient public transport networks built on renewable electricity, along with urban planning schemes that increase walkability and reduce the need for private trucks and cars, as well as the retrofitting of homes and buildings for energy efficiency, are important aspects of green transformation. Such a shift, as Huber (2013) suggests, involves a radical transformation in the geographies of social reproduction and everyday life. As he shows, the New Deal resurrected capitalism through not only the reorganization of production, but also the reproduction of material life built around private cars and suburban homes, dramatically reshaping the way people consumed oil and other forms of energy.

Deep structures of feeling associated with regimes of energy consumption are a critical barrier to movements for a just transition. Yet, as he writes, "the cars, homes, roads and countless petroleum products that make up so much of American life are products not of atomized individuals but broader social relations, public investments and legacies of social and environmental injustice" (2013, p. 69). Within this understanding, an energy transition is viewed as a political struggle to "produce new spatialities of social life" (2013, p. 168). It is situated within a broader struggle to control and remake various aspects of life and conditions of production (patterns of housing, transport, leisure, education, health), bringing them under social and democratic control against the abstract forces of the market and the private appropriation of wealth.

Moreover, just as an energy transition implies a radical transformation in what Huber refers to as geographies of social reproduction and everyday life, it can form the basis for, or be a component of, broader processes of democratic transformation in the productive forces. Energy transition is a central component of green transformation, but it will not be enough to mend the climate rift. A sustainable alternative must go beyond replacing an industrial energy system built on fossil fuels with one based on cleaner and renewable fuels, grid for grid, pipe for pipe. A renewable energy system, organized to mend and restore the metabolic relation with the rest of nature would need to look quite different. It would be constructed around a broader system of sustainable production for use and would be much more decentralized.

2   Transforming and Restructuring Existing Extraction, Production, Distribution Systems

In the 19th century, Marx did not yet broadly question the use-value of growing material output and maintained that in its propensity to advance technical productivity, capitalism helped produce material conditions for socialism. From a perspective of relative scarcity, he suggested that socialism may yet be more productive than capitalism. Yet he considered productivity advances (especially reductions in labour time) in light of their potential to enable qualitative changes, including new richer forms of human development, rather than unlimited and ever-expanding material abundance. Moreover, Marx did not blindly endorse the total development of the productive forces; through the notion of metabolic rift, he recognized the wastefulness and ecological destructiveness inherent in capitalism's development of the productive forces and viewed ecological sustainability as a central goal of socialism.

Building on this recognition, while reflecting on new ecological issues accompanying capitalism beginning in its monopoly phase (including through the scientific-technical revolution of the late 19th and early 20th century) and into the post-war period, Ernest Mandel (1999) along with thinkers like and Rachel Carson (2002), Herbert Marcuse (1991) and Barry Commoner (1971) pointed to the proliferation of environmentally destructive technologies and the role of planned (capitalist) science in these developments. For these thinkers, it had become clear that capitalist production no longer conformed to basic human needs and instead often consisted in negative use-values in the form of the growing output of superfluous, wasteful and harmful commodities. For Mandel, any "objective material conditions" of socialism had long been established, while in the post-war era he recognized that "growing productive forces, with growing commodity-money relationships can in fact move a society farther from the socialist goal instead of bringing it closer" (1974, pp. 20–21).

Recent sharp outsourcing trends mean that large swaths of materialized productive forces that provision the "overdeveloped world" are now located in the Global South. This adds complexity to a recognition that the socialist alternative must involve in some respects a "retreat" in material processing of goods (and in some cases a decline in the productivity of labour). Nevertheless, as this outsourcing remains heavily focused on Global North consumption, we can acknowledge that the productive forces dedicated to the output of goods which service the Global North have been developed too far. Along with decarbonization and the construction of a new energy system, a transition towards green socialism that mends the climate rift requires substantially transforming and in some cases sunsetting high energy and polluting industries beyond the fossil fuel sector, such as in transport, automobiles, petrochemicals, mining construction, factory farms and monocrop agriculture.

In shutting down or substantially scaling back such industries there is an opportunity for the conversion of firms and workers in them to become "green service" providers. Those in the automotive, steel and transport industry, for example, possess vital skills and knowledge for developing and facilitating public transport and public mobility. Efforts to realize such a process of green conversion are witnessed in Canada, at the General Motor's (GM) plant in Oshawa, Ontario. Following GM's announcement of a number of plant closures in North America, the largest of which was in Oshawa, rank and file workers, joined by community allies, have mobilized in an effort to realize a just transition of the plant (see Socialist Project Toronto, 2020). While such struggles are ongoing, a fulsome conversion of such industries and capacities to ecological ends again requires a broader national plan that creates the social demand for such a transition. The short and medium-term interests of workers must be a priority in such transition and tangible jobs must be identified to win over unions and non-union workers suspicious of anything green after years of environmental scapegoating. There are difficulties and conflicts that cannot be glossed over, however. As the energy transition cannot be joule for joule, it also would not, in the long-run, directly be job for job.

Supporting farmers to convert to ecological agriculture – more local food production on the basis of agroecology, while eliminating factory farms and high-polluting agribusiness – is also an important feature of green transformation. As Tanuro (2014) points out, this conversion provokes questions surrounding labour productivity. While growing the productivity of labour as a means of reducing work time has often been considered a central goal of socialism (and broad reductions of work time can have positive ecological effects), the need to move away from large-scale, one-crop farms to more integrated, organic agriculture and farming implies some decline in productivity. Marx's vision that we govern the human metabolism with nature rationally and with "the least expenditure of energy", is suggestive, yet he was likely referring to reducing the amount of human energy devoted to arduous human labour. In our times, it should be taken to refer firstly to a reduction in the use and squandering of "buried sunshine", to be largely replaced by solar flow, while the amount of human energy and work – that is, of people power – devoted to fields of production such as agriculture, may need to increase.

2.1   *Reducing Transport and Shortening Commodity Chains*

For Marx the metabolic rift is exacerbated and becomes irreparable due to the spatial disjuncture in production and in the antagonism between the city and the country. Already in the 19th century, he recognized that production chains were overstretched and wasting resources. While their predecessors were already staggeringly large in Marx's time, today's continent spanning "megacorridors" (Hildyard, 2017) that facilitate and structure the flow of goods and the associated re-engineering of ecologies and geographies they entail, dwarf those he could have possibly imagined. Today, lessening the spatial disjuncture between production and consumption must be a feature of sustainable transition. This is echoed in calls on the left for partial de-globalization, including the shortening of commodity chains, the re-municipalization of infrastructure, and a re-focusing on domestic and local production (Candeias, 2013b; N. Klein, 2011). Within domestic spaces or regions, efforts must simultaneously be made to mend a rift between the city and the country. For a model of the environmentalist city, one could look to Havana for inspiration. During the special Period in the 1990s, organic low-input agriculture was developed both in countryside, as well as in the island's capital, through urban farms. Urban agriculture covers large expanses within and at the outskirts of the city, where rich land is located (Koont, 2009).

Such shifts could contribute towards ending the "imperial mode of living", enabling spaces for independent development in the Global South (Candeias, 2013b). A move away from the export orientation of domestic corporations and a process of renationalization, could also allow firms to begin to develop their own strategies, moving away from whims of global market and choices taken by corporate controllers.

While supporting perspectives advocating forms of localization and re-nationalization, and in some instances the replacement of "dead" by "living" labour, it is worth sounding a cautious note around this shift. Such a transition would need to be complemented by extensive redistributions (including at the global level) addressing reproductive needs. A re-centring of activity upon the local and domestic economy would need to proceed simultaneously through an association of connected locales.

2.2   *Shift to a Caring Economy*
Marx considered there to be progressive potentialities associated with large-scale industrialization. He pointed to forms of human development and freedom enabled by the transformation of work away from human muscles. As we have seen, Marx's views surrounding reductions of work time have often been interpreted in an anti-ecological fashion.

By reading his arguments around free time through a productivist lens, critics miss an opportunity to think of increased free time as a possible means of *reducing* the pressure of production on the environment (see Rosnick, 2013). Indeed, reducing work time is an important means of reducing energy and matter throughput (and thereby emissions), while increases in free time could also help institutionalize subsistence practices and a "do it yourself" ethos, with positive environmental effects. Under conditions of present ecological overshoot, such a shift might reduce the quantities of objectified labour we surround ourselves with (leaving us poorer in terms of this capital-logic criterion) yet open up more free time for various social and cultural pursuits, while also enabling richer human relations. Reducing work time provides material conditions for the population broadly to engage in effective political participation, providing time to read, think and learn, to attend meetings and events, and to take part in strategizing.

In his reflections on the realm of freedom in *Capital Volume III*, Marx problematically excluded friendly unalienated relations with other human beings from the sphere of labour and pointed to the goal of reducing all labour for the basic maintenance of one's life (see Mies, 1986, pp. 212–213). However, today in reducing work dedicated to the production of "things", more time and energy could also be devoted to forms of labour that centre reproductive needs. This would mean substantially shifting from carbon intensive forms of labour, based on the production of commodities and goods, towards not only "cleantech jobs", but also towards expanding sectors of the economy based on social provisioning and in areas such as caregiving, teaching, social work, the arts and public interest media, which create small ecological footprints (Stanford, 2008). These too are "green jobs", whose growth is critical to projects aimed at sustaining and rehabilitating the metabolism between humanity and the rest of nature. Together with reductions of work time, the shift to a caring economy is part of an *ethico-political* re-definition and re-visioning of that which is valued and considered to be "socially necessary labour".

Moreover, as most reproductive labour is performed by women, it points to their central role among the "associated producers", in sustainable transformation.[5] Concomitantly and from a global perspective, we can point to the central role of women in peasant agriculture and subsistence farming practices, which meet the needs of much of the world's population (Bennholdt-Thomsen and Mies, 2000; Shiva, 2016). Indeed, as Shiva reports (2016, p. 16), the world's peasantry, mainly women, produce almost 70 percent of the world's food. As Salleh (2010) argues, peasant subsistence farming and reproductive provisioning have established a good "metabolic fit" – they produce concrete use-values, while maintaining ecological integrity. Subsistence farmers continue to resist enclosure of their commons and collectively maintain Indigenous knowledge and food production, offering alternatives to fossil fuel and petrochemical reliant food systems. Meanwhile, peasant-based land reclamation and food

---

5   The need to shift from the production of ever-increasing quantities of things to an enhanced production of services in a "caring economy" has resonances with ecofeminist work which points to the *regenerative* nature of reproductive work and social provisioning, and is also found in recent green left alternative visions in Canada such as the Leap Manifesto: https://leapmanifesto.org/en/the-leap-manifesto/.

sovereignty movements, such as Via Campesina,[6] mobilize for the remaking of the global food system, promoting sustainable forms of food production and distribution and women's democratic control (La Via Campesina, 2018; McMichael, 2007).

3   Halting the Colonization of Knowledge by Capital and "Remaking" Science in Its Organization, Prioritization and Application

Since the real subsumption of labour to capital, science has been systematically appropriated and harnessed to capitalism. While this process began in the early 19th century, we considered transformations, throughout historical capitalism, in the processes of scientific knowledge generation and in the means and methods of its appropriation and enclosure. In our neoliberal times, corporate–state–university linkages have broadened and deepened while publicly funded and generated research has become more directly integrated into capitalist production.

Chapter 7 pointed to how scientific and ecological knowledge is increasingly co-opted and harnessed as a means of greening the production and consumption of fossil fuels. Through a network analysis I considered how research and development (R&D), including that which is ecologically oriented and public funded, is directed towards the carbon extractive-industry. The case study is but one (albeit an important) example of the appropriation and colonization of science and ecological insights by industry and one case of the drastic underutilization of such knowledge in the context of the ecological crisis. Corporate reach into academic and public research organizations and the shaping of science infrastructures around fossil fuel R&D, is a barrier to addressing urgent ecological challenges and demands political intervention.

At the level of policy, visions of a "public interest science" model have merit and renewed purchase (Hamlin, 2007; Werskey, 2007). Such a model confronts and challenges the way industry–state–university relations are organized and the various practices and programs (private funding to support industrially oriented research, university/industry partnerships, having corporate executives direct higher education and government research bodies), through which control over these organizations is ceded to industry. By contrast, reorienting them to serve more public purposes (especially ecological sustainability and energy transition), could begin by encouraging greater openness, consultation and

---

6   Via Campesina is a coalition of 182 organisations in 81 countries across Europe, Latin America, Asia, North America, Central America and Africa. See https://viacampesina.org/en/.

partnerships with labour, academics, students, community and public interest groups, in the development of a bottom-up mandate and vision (Atkinson-Grosjean, 2006; Polster, 2018). As intimated above, this is also a component of democratizing the state, working towards its absorption into civil society (Candeias, 2013c).

Moreover, as Werskey suggests, the climate crisis offers a unique opportunity for Left coalition and alliance formation, based on a vision that ecological science, indeed science at large, needs to serve society in new and better ways. In pointing to the possible revival of "Radical Science" movements, akin to those of the 1960s/70s, Werskey revisits a long-standing question concerning the "class allegiance" of scientific knowledge producers/workers and asks if (earth) scientists might form an active component of a green socialist left. Today many scientists, especially in ecological and climate fields, express frustration due to the inadequacy of current responses to the climate crisis (see Castree 2017; Foster, Clark, and York 2010; Klein 2014). Not only individual scientist "activists", but numerous organizations and scientists coalitions, such as the revitalized Science for the People initiative, 500 Women Scientists and Collectif Scientific,[7] are today calling for a radical shift in the practice of science and scientists in responding to the climate crisis. These latter groups often explicitly criticize the limitations of clean fossil fuel technologies and have aligned themselves with left movements for socio-ecological transformation. While Veblen's belief that scientists would become the key group to move society towards post-capitalism was overstated, an organized coalition of scientists pressing for more transformative alternatives could form a powerful component of a counter-hegemonic bloc.

A public interest model of science can also be fruitfully combined with perspectives that point to the need for a greater diffusion of ecological knowledge and insights among producers or the possibilities of "lay science" (see Saed, 2011) and "citizen science" (Riesch and Potter, 2014). This more democratic

7   Science for the people, a socialist organization that emerged in the United States in the late 1960s, has experienced a revival beginning in 2014. In its current focus on climate change, it has challenged the scientific community's involvement in "false solutions" such as CCS and geoengineering (see https://magazine.scienceforthepeople.org/geoengineering/geoengineering-environmental-capitalism/). 500 Women Scientists, a non-profit made up of women scientists in STEM fields, dedicated to making science "open, inclusive, and accessible" has actively organized around the Green New Deal in the US (see https://blogs.scientificamerican.com/observations/scientists-must-speak-up-for-the-green-new-deal/). Meanwhile, the Quebec-based collective scientific is an organization comprised of social and natural scientists opposed to the expansion of fracking and has extensively debunked efforts to "greenwash gas" (see http://www.collectif-scientifique-gaz-de-schiste.com/accueil/index.php/veille-scientifique).

approach to the practice of science, is perhaps especially relevant to the field of agriculture and sharply contrasts with the big institutions of capitalist "techno-science". It is a current feature of agroecology, which involves the application of ecological knowledge to agriculture, blending traditional and Indigenous knowledge, producers' practical knowledge, and global scientific knowledge (La Via Campesina, 2016).

These approaches return us to Mao, as they encourage, in the long-term, a more bottom up approach to science, which can help alleviate inevitable tensions between "reds and experts". A greater diffusion of ecological knowledge and insights and practices of "lay science" again softens the distinction between formal ecological science and traditional and land-based knowledge, which has a vital role to play in the construction of sustainable alternatives. Yet, as I have argued, the fulsome development and expansive application of ecosystem knowledge to production is not possible within a paradigm centred on capital accumulation. It could only take place in a system devoted to human and ecosystem flourishing: a system which is based on a rational and sustainable metabolic interaction with the rest of nature.

4 Planning the Transition at All Levels in a Democratic and Participatory Manner

Throughout *Capital* Marx places emphasis on the need for the "associated producers" to freely organize and plan production on a collective basis, according to their own plan. Of course, the rational and democratic organization of production has to be the work not only of "producers" but of the whole of society, or of an "association of free human beings", working with means of production held in common (see LÖWY, 2020).

The progressive rolling back of capitalist discipline, the ending of the separation of thinking and doing (by introducing education into the workplace), the conscious organization of production on a democratic basis (through the councils' tradition, or through cooperatives, for example) is the alternative at the level of the individual enterprise (see Lebowitz, 2006). But this alternative has to be accompanied (possibly superseded) by some coordination and planning of production across the interrelated divisions of productive labour in society as a whole. Capital arrives at allocations largely through the "anarchy of the market" (particularly money flows and market processes), producing crises and great irrationality. Where it does engage in limited and partial forms of planning, these are arrived at through corporate and state hierarchies (Van der Pijl, 1998).

Planning extends to coordinating socialized labour in order to reproduce daily life at an acceptable level of material well being and in relation to conditions of ecological sustainability. It entails coordinated management or planning of associated labour with an eye to the functioning of the whole, including the restitution of the degraded natural conditions that sustain life. I have already considered how planning is vitally needed for domestic or regional energy transition, pointing to the need to develop renewables in not only a rapid, but also in a coordinated and systematic fashion, in contrast to the prolonged and chaotic market.

More broadly, as I have intimated, the geographical proliferation of productive ties allows for resource allocations that meet reproductive needs and act as insurance against local calamities. Climate change creates severe survival and livelihood challenges for many millions on a highly uneven basis. In an interdependent world, the reproductive needs of various communities require planned (global) resource flows. The contemporary left has largely avoided the issue of planning and all of the complexity of cooperation and expansive divisions of labour, likely in part because of the poor legacy and experience of communist and social democratic planning. Yet the issue cannot be ignored. Planning is crucial and as I have suggested, need not be hierarchical and centralized, or imply homogenization.

As Marx encourages us to think of it, planning is densely tied to cooperation and includes the sharing of the skills and knowledge of the collective worker. These are required to address reproductive needs and eco-metabolic problems. The right to the benefits of the "social brain and the social hand" can be seen in the technology and knowledge transfer movement. This includes a focus upon renewable energy technologies, and is seen in the practice of organizations such as the International Renewable Energy Agency.[8] As Abramsky (2010) notes, technology transfer has echoes of modernization ideology, yet it takes on a very different meaning and dynamic when it is based on a noncommercial process. Such a global movement is part of defending control and common ownership of knowledge, devoting it to common use.

5   The Future of Productive Forces

For much of today's green-left, forces of production are strictly associated with technological machinery aimed at increasing productivity and material output.

---

8   IRENA is an intergovernmental organisation founded in 2009 supporting countries in their transition to a sustainable energy future, including through knowledge sharing. See https://www.irena.org/aboutirena.

This (mis)understanding leads us to ignore the inevitable role of productive forces in a society beyond capital and forecloses the possibility of attaching political hopes to their development. By reconceptualizing forces of production as that dimension of existence by which we are purposively linked to and transform the rest of nature, the struggle for control over them is readily placed at the centre of a socio-political response to the climate crisis. Such a conceptualization, understood dialectically (and thereby through a historical and geographical lens), encourages a careful consideration of their unfulfilled potentiality, as well as the need for their creative-destructive transformation in a society moving beyond capital. Establishing democratic social control over productive forces and unfettering them from capital's profit and growth imperatives is vital for addressing the climate crisis, and for the development of a new paradigm based on human flourishing within sustainable and thriving ecosystems.

Bibliography

Abramsky, K. (2010). "Sparking an Energy Revolution: Building New Relations of Production, Exchange and Livelihood". In K. Abramsky (ed.), *Sparking a Worldwide Energy Revolution: Social Struggles in the Transition to a Post-Petrol World* (pp. 609–628). Oakland, CA: AK Press.

Acuña, R. (2018, December 6). "Seven Questions About Alberta's Oil Production Cut". *Corporate Mapping Project.* https://www.corporatemapping.ca/seven-questions-about-albertas-oil-production-cut/.

Adkin, L. (2016a). "Democracy and The Albertan Petro-State". In L. Adkin (ed.), *First World Petro-Politics: The Political Ecology and Governance of Alberta* (pp. 561–599). Toronto: University of Toronto Press.

Adkin, L. (ed.). (2016b). *First World Petro-Politics: The Political Ecology and Governance of Alberta.* Toronto: University of Toronto Press.

Adkin, L. (2017). "Crossroads in Alberta: Climate Capitalism or Ecological Democracy". *Socialist Studies/Études Socialistes* 12(1).

Adkin, L. (2020). "Petro-Universities and the Production of Knowledge for the Post-Carbon Future". In W. Carroll (ed.), *Regime of Obstruction: How Corporate Power Blocks Energy Democracy.* Edmonton, AB: Athabasca University Press.

Adkin, L., Hanson, L.L., Kahane, D., Parkins, J.R., and Patten, S. (2017). "Can Public Engagement Democratize Environmental Policymaking in a Resource-Dependent State? Comparative Case Studies from Alberta, Canada". *Environmental Politics* 26(2): 301–321.

Adkin, L., and Miller, B. (2016). "Alberta, Fossil Capitalism, and the Political Ecology of Change". In L. Adkin (ed.), *First World Petro-Politics: The Political Ecology and Governance of Alberta* (pp. 527–560). Toronto: University of Toronto Press.

Adkin, L., and Stares, B. (2016). "Turning Up the Heat: Hegemonic Politics in a First World Petro State". In L. Adkin (ed.), *First World Petro-Politics: The Political Ecology and Governance of Alberta* (pp. 190–240). Toronto: University of Toronto Press.

Agar, J. (2003). "G.A. Cohen's Functional Explanation: A Critical Realist Analysis". *Philosophy of the Social Sciences* 33(3): 291–310.

Albo, G., Gindin, S., and Panitch, L. (2010). *In and Out of Crisis: The Global Financial Meltdown and Left Alternatives.* Oakland, CA: PM Press.

Albo, G., and Yap, L. (2016, July 12). "From the Tar Sands to "Green Jobs"? Work and Ecological Justice". *The Bullet.* http://socialistproject.ca/bullet/1280.php.

Altvater, E. (2007). "The Social and Natural Environment of Fossil Capitalism". *Socialist Register* 43(1): 37–59.

Altvater, E. (2016). "The Capitalocene, or, Geoengineering against Capitalism's Planetary Boundaries". In J.W. Moore (ed.), *Anthropocene or Capitalocene?: Nature, History, and the Crisis of Capitalism* (pp. 138–152). Oakland, CA: PM Press.

Anderson, K. (2002). "Marx's Late Writings on non-Western and Precapitalist Societies and Gender". *Rethinking Marxism* 14(4): 84–96.

Anderson, K. (2010). *Marx at the Margins: On Nationalism, Ethnicity, and Non-Western Societies*. Chicago: The University of Chicago Press.

Anderson, K., and Bows, A. (2008). "Reframing the Climate Change Challenge in Light of Post-2000 Emission Trends". *Philosophical Transactions of the Royal Society A: Mathematical, Physical and Engineering Sciences* 366: 3863–3882.

Angel, J. (2017). "Towards an Energy Politics In-Against-and-Beyond the State: Berlin's Struggle for Energy Democracy". *Antipode* 49(3): 557–576.

Angus, I. (2016). *Facing the Anthropocene: Fossil Capitalism and the Crisis of the Earth System*. New York: Monthly Review Press.

Apeldoorn, B. van, and Graaff, N. de. (2012). "The Limits of Open Door Imperialism and the US State–Capital Nexus". *Globalizations* 9(4): 593–608.

Arruza, C. (2014). "Remarks on Gender". *Viewpoint Magazine* 4: 1–17.

Arruzza, C., Bhattacharya, T., and Fraser, N. (2019). *Feminism for the 99%: A Manifesto*. Brooklyn, NY: Verso.

Ashman, S. (2013). "Combined and Uneven Development". In M. Boffo, B. Fine, and A. Saad-Filho (eds.), *The Elgar Companion to Marxist Economics* (pp. 60–71). Cheltenham: Edward Elgar Pub.

Atkinson-Grosjean, J. (2006). *Public Science, Private Interests: Culture and Commerce in Canada's Networks of Centres of Excellence*. Toronto: University of Toronto Press.

Awasis, S. (2014). "Pipelines and Resistance Across Turtle Island". In S. D'Arcy, T. Black, T. Weis, and J.K. Russell (eds.), *A Line in the Tar Sands* (pp. 255–266). Toronto: Between the Lines.

Bakx, K. (2016, November). ""The Writing is on the Wall", as Oil Group Welcomes Renewable Energy Firms". *CBC News*. http://www.cbc.ca/news/business/psac-oilfield-renewables-salkeld-1.3834715.

Balibar, E. (2014). *The Philosophy of Marx*. London: Verso.

Baran, P.A., and Sweezy. (1966). *Monopoly Capital*. New York: Monthly Review Press.

Bennholdt-Thomsen, V., and Mies, M. (2000). *The Subsistence Perspective: Beyond the Globalised Economy*. New York: Zed Books.

Berman, T. (2017, November 14). "Canada's Most Shameful Environmental Secret Must Not Remain Hidden". *The Guardian*. https://www.theguardian.com/commentisfree/2017/nov/14/canadas-shameful-environmental-secret-tar-sands-tailings-ponds.

Bhattacharya, A. (2018, February 14). "T'Sou-ke First Nation: Building a Network of Clean Energy Systems". *Policy Note*. https://www.policynote.ca/tsou-ke-first-nation-building-a-network-of-clean-energy-systems/.

Bloomberg New Energy Finance. (2016). *Clean Energy Investment 2016*. Bloomberg New Energy Finance. https://about.bnef.com/clean-energy-investment/.

Bonds, E. (2016). "Beyond Denialism: Think Tank Approaches to Climate Change". *Sociology Compass* 10(4): 306–317.

Boyd, W. (2001). "Making Meat: Science, Technology, and American Poultry Production". *Technology and Culture* 42(4): 631–664.

Boyd, W., and Prudham, S. (2017). "On the Themed Collection, "The Formal and Real Subsumption of Nature"". *Society & Natural Resources* 30(7): 877–884.

Boyd, W., Prudham, S., and Schurman, R.A. (2001). "Industrial Dynamics and the Problem of Nature". *Society & Natural Resources* 14(7): 555–570.

Braverman, H. (1998). *Labor and Monopoly Capital: The Degradation of Work in the Twentieth Century*. New York: Monthly Review Press.

Bridge, G. (2004). "Gas, and How to Get it". *Geoforum* 35(4): 395–397.

Brock, D.E. (2012). "The People's Landscape: Mr. Science and the Mass Line". In D.E. Brock and C.N. Wei (eds.), *Mr. Science and Chairman Mao's Cultural Revolution: Science and Technology in Modern China* (pp. 41–117). Lanham: Lexington Books.

Brock, D.E., and Wei, C.N. (eds.). (2012). "Reasessing The Cultural Revolution". *Mr. Science and Chairman Mao's Cultural Revolution: Science and Technology in Modern China* (pp. 1–39). Lanham: Lexington Books.

Brownlee, J., Hurl, C., and Walby, K. (eds.). (2018). *Corporatizing Canada: Making Business out of Public Service*. Toronto: Between the Lines.

Brownlee, J. (2005). *Ruling Canada: Corporate Cohesion and Democracy*. Halifax: Fernwood Publishing.

Brownlee, J. (2015). *Academia Inc.: How Corporatization is Transforming Canadian Universities*. Halifax: Fernwood Publishing.

Brulle, R.J. (2014). "Institutionalizing Delay: Foundation Funding and the Creation of U.S. Climate Change Counter-Movement Organizations". *Climatic Change* 122(4): 681–694.

Burkett, P. (1996). "Value, Capital and Nature: Some Ecological Implications of Marx's Critique of Political Economy". *Science & Society* 60(3): 332–359.

Burkett, P. (2005). "Marx's Vision of Sustainable Human Development". *Monthly Review* 57(5): 34–62.

Burkett, P. (2014). *Marx and Nature: A Red and Green Perspective*. Chicago: Haymarket Books.

Burkett, P., and Foster, J.B. (2006). "Metabolism, Energy, and Entropy in Marx's Critique of Political Economy: Beyond the Podolinsky Myth". *Theory and Society* 35(1): 109–156.

Cai, H., Brandt, A.R., Yeh, S., Englander, J.G., Han, J., Elgowainy, A., and Wang, M.Q. (2015). "Well-to-Wheels Greenhouse Gas Emissions of Canadian Oil Sands Products:

Implications for U.S. Petroleum Fuels". *Environmental Science & Technology* 49(13): 8219–8227.

Canada's Oil Sands Innovation Alliance. (2018). *Support for Clean Water Technologies to Benefit the Oil and Gas Industry.* https://cosia.ca/resources/news-releases/support-clean-water-technologies-benefit-oil-and-gas-industry.

Canadian Association of University Teachers. (2013). *Open for Business on What Terms?* (pp. 1–198). Ottawa: Canadian Association of University Teachers.

Canadian Environmental Assessment Agency. (2016, September). *Review of Related Upstream Greenhouse Gas Emissions Estimates—NGTL System Expansion Project.* https://www.ceaa-acee.gc.ca/050/documents/p80099/115704E.pdf.

Candeias, M. (2013a). *Gramscian Constellations. Hegemony and the Realization of New Ways of Living and Production* (pp. 1–11). Berlin: Rosa Luxemburg Stiftung.

Candeias, M. (2013b). *Green Transformation: Competing Strategic Projects* (pp. 1–26). Berlin: Rosa Luxemburg Stiftung.

Candeias, M. (2013c, January 24). "What is 'Socialist' about 'Green Socialism'?" *The Bullet.* https://socialistproject.ca/2013/01/b765/.

Carroll, W.K. (1986). *Corporate Power and Canadian Capitalism.* Vancouver, BC: University of British Columbia Press.

Carroll, W.K. (2010). *Corporate Power in a Globalizing World.* Don Mills, ON: Oxford University Press.

Carroll, W.K. (2016). "The Changing Face(s) of Corporate Power in Canada". In E. Grabb, J.G. Reitz, and M. Hwang (eds.), *Social Inequality in Canada: Dimensions of Disadvantage* (pp. 12–23). Don Mills, ON: Oxford University Press.

Carroll, W.K. (2017). "Canada's Carbon-Capital Elite: A Tangled Web of Corporate Power". *Canadian Journal of Sociology* 42(3): 225–260.

Carroll, W.K. (2020a). "Fossil Capitalism, Climate Capitalism, Energy Democracy: The Struggle for Hegemony in an Era of Climate Crisis". *Socialist Studies/Études Socialistes* 14(1).

Carroll, W.K. (ed.). (2020b). *Regime of Obstruction: How Corporate Power Blocks Energy Democracy.* Edmonton, AB: Athabasca University Press.

Carroll, W.K., and Alexander, M. (1999). "Finance Capital and Capitalist Class Integration in the 1990s: Networks of Interlocking Directorships in Canada and Australia". *Canadian Review of Sociology/Revue Canadienne de Sociologie* 36(3): 331–354.

Carroll, W.K., and Beaton, J. (2000). "Globalization, Neo-liberalism, and the Changing Face of Corporate Hegemony in Higher Education". *Studies in Political Economy* 62(1): 71–98.

Carroll, W.K., Graham, N., and Yunker, Z. (2018). "Carbon Capital and Corporate Influence: Mapping Elite Networks of Corporations, Universities, and Research Institutes". In Jaimie Brownlee, C. Hurl, and K. Walby (eds.), *Corporatizing*

Canada: Making Business out of Public Service (pp. 58–73). Toronto: Between the Lines.

Carroll, W.K., and Sapinski, J.P. (2011). "Corporate Elites and Intercorporate Networks". In P.J. Carrington and J. Scott (eds.), *The SAGE Handbook of Social Network Analysis* (pp. 180–195). London: SAGE Publications.

Carroll, W.K., and Sapinski, J.P. (2018). *Organizing the 1%: How Corporate Power Works*. Halifax: Fernwood Publishing.

Carson, C. (2015). "Knowledge Economies: Toward a New Technological Age". In M. Geyer and A. Tooze (eds.), *The Cambridge History of the Second World War* (pp. 196–219). Cambridge: Cambridge University Press.

Carson, R. (2002). *Silent Spring*. Boston: Houghton Mifflin Harcourt.

Carter, A. (2014). "Petro-Capitalism and the Tar Sands". In S. D'Arcy, T. Black, T. Weis, and J.K. Russell (eds.), *A Line in the Tar Sands* (pp. 40–52). Toronto: Between the Lines.

Carter, A. (2016). "The Petro-Politics of Environmental Regulation in the Tar Sands". In L. Adkin (ed.), *First World Petro-Politics: The Political Ecology and Governance of Alberta*. Toronto: University of Toronto Press.

Carter, A., and Zalik, A. (2016). "Fossil Capitalism and the Rentier State: Toward a Political Ecology of Alberta's Oil Economy". In L. Adkin (ed.), *First World Petro-Politics: The Political Ecology and Governance of Alberta* (pp. 52–77). Toronto: University of Toronto Press.

Carton, W., Jönsson, E., and Bustos, B. (2017). "Revisiting the "Subsumption of Nature": Resource Use in Times of Environmental Change". *Society & Natural Resources* 30(7): 789–796.

Castree, N. (2017). "Unfree Radicals: Geoscientists, the Anthropocene, and Left Politics". *Antipode* 49: 52–74.

Castree, N., and Christophers, B. (2015). "Banking Spatially on the Future: Capital Switching, Infrastructure, and the Ecological Fix". *Annals of the Association of American Geographers* 105(2): 378–386.

Cenovus Energy. (2015). *2014 Annual Report* (pp. 1–128).

Centre for Oil Sands Sustainability. (n.d.). *What We Do*. NAIT. Retrieved November 21, 2018, from http://www.nait.ca/97473.htm.

Chakrabarty, D. (2009). "The Climate of History: Four Theses". *Critical Inquiry* 35(2): 197–222.

Chattopadhyay, K. (2014). "The Rise and Fall of Environmentalism in the Early Soviet Union". *Climate & Capitalism*. http://climateandcapitalism.com/2014/11/03/rise-fall-environmentalism-early-soviet-union/.

Chevron Canada. (n.d.). *Our Businesses—Burnably Refinery*. Chevron.Com. http://www.chevron.ca/our-businesses/burnaby-refinery.

Clark, B., and York, R. (2005). "Carbon Metabolism: Global Capitalism, Climate Change, and the Biospheric Rift". *Theory and Society* 34(4): 391–428.

Clarke, T., Stanford, J., Gibson, D., and Haley, B. (2013). *The Bitumen Cliff: Lessons and Challenges of Bitumen Mega-Developments for Canada's Economy in an Age of Climate Change* (pp. 1–101). Ottawa: Canadian Centre for Policy Alternatives.

Clean Energy BC. (2016, November 4). "Good News for B.C. Clean Energy Companies". *Clean Energy BC*. https://www.cleanenergybc.org/uncategorized/11625.

Clean Energy Canada. (2016). *A Pivotal Time for Clean Energy: Tracking the Energy Revolution Canada 2016* (pp. 1–22). Vancouver, BC: Clean Energy Canada.

Clement, W. (1975). *The Canadian Corporate Elite*. Toronto: McClelland and Stewart.

Cohen, G.A. (2000). *Karl Marx's Theory of History*. Oxford: Princeton University Press.

Commoner, B. (1966). *Science and Survival*. New York: Viking Press.

Commoner, B. (1971). *The Closing Circle: Nature, Man, and Technology*. New York: Random House Inc.

Connor, Steve. (2015, November). "Global Temperatures Have Broken Through the 1C Increase on Pre-Industrial Levels". *The Independent*. http://www.independent.co.uk/environment/climate-change/climate-change-global-average-temperatures-break-through-1c-increase-on-pre-industrial-levels-for-a6727361.html.

COSIA. (2012). *A New Chapter in a History of Innovation* (pp. 1–32).

COSIA. (2020, June 1). "Associate Member Program". *Canada's Oil Sands Innovation Alliance*. https://www.cosia.ca/about/associate-members.

Costa, M.D., and James, S. (1975). *The Power of Women and the Subversion of the Community*. Bristol: Falling Wall Press.

Coulthard, G.S. (2014). *Red Skin, White Masks: Rejecting the Colonial Politics of Recognition*. Minneapolis: University of Minnesota Press.

Council of Canadian Academies. (2014). *Environmental Impacts of Shale Gas Extraction in Canada: The Expert Panel on Harnessing Science and Technology to Understand the Environmental Impacts of Shale Gas Extraction* (pp. 1–292). Ottawa: Council of Canadian Academies.

Davis, M. (2010). "Who Will Build the Ark?" *New Left Review* 61: 29–46.

Dawson, M.C. (2016). "Hidden in Plain Sight: A Note on Legitimation Crises and the Racial Order". *Critical Historical Studies* 3(1): 143–161.

de Graaff, N. (2012a). "Oil Elite Networks in a Transforming Global Oil Market". *International Journal of Comparative Sociology* 53(4): 275–297.

de Graaff, N. (2012b). "The Hybridization of the State–Capital Nexus in the Global Energy Order". *Globalizations* 9(4): 531–545.

de Graaff, N., and Apeldoorn, B. van. (2017). "US Elite Power and the Rise of 'Statist' Chinese Elites in Global Markets". *International Politics*: 1–18.

Dean, J. (2016). *Crowds and Party*. Brooklyn, NY: Verso.

Derber, C. (2010). *Greed to Green: Solving Climate Change and Remaking the Economy.* Boulder, CO: Paradigm Publishers.

Dikötter, F. (2011). *Mao's Great Famine: The History of China's Most Devastating Catastrophe, 1958–1962.* New York: Bloomsbury USA.

D'Mello, B. (2009). "What Is Maoism?" *Economic and Political Weekly* 44(47): 39–48.

Domhoff, G.W. (1980). *Power Structure Research.* Beverly Hills, CA: Sage Publications.

Donaghy, T. (2017, May). "Tar Sands Pipelines Are Heavily Financed by 26 Key Banks". *Greenpeace USA.* https://www.greenpeace.org/usa/research/four-tar-sands-pipelines-are-heavily-financed-by-25-key-banks/.

Dyer-Witheford, N. (2004). "1844/2004/2044: The Return of Species-Being". *Historical Materialism* 12(4): 1–23.

Edgerton, D. (2005). *Warfare State: Britain, 1920–1970.* Cambridge: Cambridge University Press.

Editors. (2014). "A Reply to Parenti". *Monthly Review* 65(11): 52–58.

Ekers, M., and Prudham, S. (2017). "The Metabolism of Socioecological Fixes: Capital Switching, Spatial Fixes, and the Production of Nature". *Annals of the American Association of Geographers* 107(6): 1370–1388.

Ekers, M., and Prudham, S. (2018). "The Socioecological Fix: Fixed Capital, Metabolism, and Hegemony". *Annals of the American Association of Geographers* 108(1): 17–34.

Elsner, G., and Kasper, M. (2015). *Attacks on Renewable Energy Policies in 2015* (pp. 1–86). San Francisco: Energy and Policy Institute.

Emissions Reduction Alberta. (n.d.). *Funded Projects.* Emissions Reduction Alberta. Retrieved November 21, 2018, from https://www.eralberta.ca/projects/.

Enbridge Inc. (2017). *2016 Annual Report.*

Enbridge Inc. (2019). *Line 3 Replacement Program (Canada)—Project Overview.* https://www.enbridge.com/projects-and-infrastructure/projects/line-3-replacement-program-canada.

Engels, F. (1972). *The Origin of the Family, Private Property, and the State.* New York: International Publishing.

Estes, N. (2019). *Our History Is the Future: Standing Rock Versus the Dakota Access Pipeline, and the Long Tradition of Indigenous Resistance.* New York: Verso.

Federici, S. (2004). *Caliban and the Witch: Women, the Body and Primitive Accumulation.* Brooklyn, NY: Autonomedia.

Federici, S. (2012). *Revolution at Point Zero: Housework, Reproduction, and Feminist Struggle.* Oakland, CA: PM Press.

Fekete, J. (2012, February 10). "Harper in China: PM Attacks "Foreign Money" Behind Oil Sands Protest, Refuses to Trade Human Rights". *National Post.* http://news.nationalpost.com/news/canada/stephen-harper-pushes-for-responsible-oil-and-gas-trade-in-china-speech.

Fischer-Kowalski, M. (1998). "Society's Metabolism: The Intellectual History of Materials Flow Analysis, Part I, 1860–1970". *Journal of Industrial Ecology* 2(1): 61–78.

Fischer-Kowalski, M., and Haberl, H. (1993). "Metabolism and Colonization. Modes of Production and the Physical Exchange Between Societies and Nature". *Innovation: The European Journal of Social Science Research* 6(4): 415–442.

Flanagan, E., and Grant, J. (2013). *Losing Ground: Why the Problem of Oilsands Tailings Waste Keeps Growing* (pp. 1–6). Drayton Valley, AB: Pembina Institute.

Foreign Affairs, Trade and Development Canada. (2014). *Renewable Energy Value Proposition* (pp. 1–6). Ottawa: Foreign Affairs, Trade and Development Canada.

Fortis. (2017). *Environmental Report* (pp. 1–25).

Foster, J.B. (1998). "Introduction to the New Edition". *Labor and Monopoly Capital: The Degradation of Work in the Twentieth Century* (pp. ix–xxiv). New York: Monthly Review Press.

Foster, J.B. (2000). *Marx's Ecology: Materialism and Nature*. New York: Monthly Review Press.

Foster, J.B. (2002). "Capitalism and Ecology: The Nature of the Contradiction". *Monthly Review* 54(4): 6–16.

Foster, J.B. (2013). "Marx and the Rift in the Universal Metabolism of Nature". *Monthly Review* 65(7): 1–19.

Foster, J.B. (2016). "In Defense of Ecological Marxism". *Climate & Capitalism*. http://climateandcapitalism.com/2016/06/06/in-defense-of-ecological-marxism-john-bellamy-foster-responds-to-a-critic/.

Foster, J.B., and Burkett, P. (2016). *Marx and the Earth: An Anti-Critique*. Chicago: Haymarket Books.

Foster, J.B., and Clark, B. (2008). "Rachel Carson's Ecological Critique". *Monthly Review* 59(09): 1–17.

Foster, J.B., and Clark, B. (2016). "Marxism and the Dialectics of Ecology". *Monthly Review* 68(05): 1–17.

Foster, J.B., and Clark, B. (2018). "The Expropriation of Nature". *Monthly Review* 69(10): 1–16.

Foster, J.B., York, R., and Clark, B. (2011a). "Carbon Metabolism and Global Capital Accumulation". *The Ecological Rift: Capitalism's War on the Earth* (pp. 121–150). New York: Monthly Review Press.

Foster, J.B., York, R., and Clark, B. (2011b). *The Ecological Rift: Capitalism's War on the Earth*. New York: Monthly Review Press.

Franco, J., Martinez, A.M., and Feodoroff, T. (2013). *Old Story, New Threat: Fracking and the Global Land Grab* (pp. 1–12). Amsterdam: Trasnational Institute.

Frankfurt School-UNEP Centre. (2016). *Global Trends in Renewable Energy Investment 2016* (pp. 1–86). Frankfurt: Bloomberg.

Franta, B., and Supran, G. (2017, March 13). "The fossil fuel industry's invisible colonization of academia". *The Guardian*. https://www.theguardian.com/environment/
climate-consensus-97-per-cent/2017/mar/13/the-fossil-fuel-industrys-invisible-
colonization-of-academia?CMP=share_btn_tw.

Fraser, N. (2013). *Fortunes of Feminism: From State-Managed Capitalism to Neoliberal
Crisis*. Brooklyn, NY: Verso.

Fraser, N. (2014). "Behind Marx's Hidden Abode". *New Left Review* 86: 55–72.

Frehner, B. (2016). *Finding Oil: The Nature of Petroleum Geology, 1859–1920*. Lincoln: University of Nebraska Press.

Galbraith, J.K. (2007). *The New Industrial State*. New Jersey: Princeton University Press.

Garibaldi, L.A., Gemmill-Herren, B., D'Annolfo, R., Graeub, B.E., Cunningham, S.A., and
Breeze, T.D. (2017). "Farming Approaches for Greater Biodiversity, Livelihoods, and
Food Security". *Trends in Ecology & Evolution* 32(1): 68–80.

Gellner, E. (1980). "A Russian Marxist Philosophy of History". *Theory and Society* 9(5):
757–777.

Ghosn, R. (2010). *Flow and Its Others: Fixity, Fragmentation, and Friction*. New Orleans:
Association of Collegiate Schools of Architecture.

Gibson, R.B. (2012). "In Full Retreat: The Canadian Government's New Environmental
Assessment Law Undoes Decades of Progress". *Impact Assessment and Project Ap-
praisal* 30(3): 179–188.

Girardet, H. (1996). *The Gaia Atlas of Cities: New Directions for Sustainable Urban Living*.
London: UN-Habitat.

Gould, K.A., Pellow, D.N., and Schnaiberg, A. (2004). "Interrogating the Treadmill of
Production: Everything You Wanted to Know about the Treadmill but Were Afraid
to Ask". *Organization & Environment* 17(3): 296–316.

Government of Canada. (2016). *Greenhouse Gas Reporting Program (GHGRP)—Facility Greenhouse Gas (GHG) Data*. https://open.canada.ca/data/en/dataset/a8ba14b7-
7f23-462a-bdbb-83b0ef629823.

Graham, N. (2015). "Ecological Forces of Production". *Capitalism Nature Socialism*
26(2): 76–91.

Graham, N. (2017). "State-Capital Nexus and the Making of BC Shale and Liquefied
Natural Gas". *BC Studies: The British Columbian Quarterly* 194: 11–38.

Graham, N., Carroll, W.K., and Chen, D. (2020). *Big Oil's Political Reach: Mapping Fossil
Fuel Lobbying From Harper to Trudeau* (pp. 1–64). Vancouver, BC: Canadian Centre
for Policy Alternatives.

Graham, N., Carroll, W.K., and Chen, D. (2020). "Carbon Capital's Political Reach: A
Network Analysis of Federal Lobbying by the Fossil Fuel Sector from Harper to
Trudeau". *Canadian Political Science Review* 14(1).

Gramsci, A. (1971). *Selections from the Prison Notebooks*, edited by Q. Hoare and G.N.
Smith. New York: International Publishers.

Granoff, I., Hogarth, J.R., and Miller, A. (2016). "Nested Barriers to Low-Carbon Infrastructure Investment". *Nature Climate Change* 6(12): 1065–1071.

Grant, J., Huot, M., Lemphers, N., Dyer, S., and Dow, M. (2013). *Beneath the Surface: A Review of Key Facts in the Oilsands Debate* (pp. 1–70). Drayton Valley, AB: Pembina Institute.

Gustafson, B. (2012). "Fossil Knowledge Networks: Industry Strategy, Public Culture, and the Challenge for Critical Research". In J.A. McNeish and O. Logan (eds.), *Flammable Societies: Studies on the Socio-Economics of Oil and Gas* (pp. 311–334). London: Pluto Press.

Haberl, H. (2007). *Socioecological Transitions and Global Change: Trajectories of Social Metabolism and Land Use*, edited by M. Fischer-Kowalski. Cheltenham, UK: Edward Elgar Pub.

Haley, B. (2014). "The Staple Theory and the Carbon Trap". In J. Stanford (ed.), *The Staple Theory @ 50 Reflections on the Lasting Significance of Mel Watkins' "A Staple Theory of Economic Growth"* (pp. 75–80). Vancouver, BC: Canadian Centre for Policy Alternatives.

Hamlin, C. (2007). "STS: Where the Marxist Critique of Capitalist Science Goes to Die?" *Science as Culture* 16(4): 467–474.

Hansen, E., Mulvaney, D., and Betcher, M. (2013). *Water Resource Reporting and Water Footprint from Marcellus Shale Development in West Virginia and Pennsylvania* (p. 1–78). Durango, CO: Earthworks Oil & Gas Accountability Project.

Harlan, S., Pellow, D., and Roberts, J.T. (2015). "Climate Justice and Inequality". In R.E. Dunlap and R.J. Brulle (eds.), *Climate Change and Society: Sociological Perspectives* (pp. 127–163). New York: Oxford University Press.

Harvey, D. (1978). "The Urban Process Under Capitalism: A Framework for Analysis". *International Journal of Urban and Regional Research* 2(1–3): 101–131.

Harvey, D. (2000). "On Architecs, Bees, and "Species Being"". In *Spaces of Hope* (pp. 199–212). Berkeley, CA: University of California Press.

Harvey, D. (2001). "Globalization and the "Spatial Fix"". *Geografiska Revue* 2: 23–30.

Harvey, D. (2007). *The Limits to Capital*. London: Verso.

Harvey, D. (2010). *A Companion to Marx's Capital*. London: Verso.

Harvey, D. (2011). *The Enigma of Capital: And the Crises of Capitalism*. Oxford: Oxford University Press.

Heerema, D., and Kniewasser, M. (2017). *Liquefied Natural Gas, Carbon Pollution, and British Columbia in 2017* (pp. 1–17). Drayton Valley, AB: Pembina Institute.

Hildyard, N. (2017). *How Infrastructure is Shaping the World: A Critical Introduction to Infrastructure Mega-Corridors* (pp. 1–43). Manchester: The Corner House.

Hilferding, R. (2006). *Finance Capital: A Study in the Latest Phase of Capitalist Development*. London and New York: Routledge.

Hinton, W. (1994). "Mao, Rural Development, and Two-Line Struggle". *Monthly Review* 45(9): 1–26.

Hinton, W. (2004). "On the Role of Mao Zedong". *Monthly Review* 56(4): 51–76.

Ho, F. (2013). "A World Where Many Worlds Fit: Manifesto for an Anti-Manifest Destiny Marxism". *Capitalism Nature Socialism* 24(3): 232–246.

Holgersen, S., and Warlenius, R. (2016). "Destroy What Destroys the Planet: Steering Creative Destruction in the Dual Crisis". *Capital & Class* 40(3): 511–532.

Hooks, G., and Smith, C.L. (2005). "Treadmills of Production and Destruction: Threats to the Environment Posed by Militarism". *Organization & Environment* 18(1): 19–37.

Hornborg, A. (2010). "Uneven Development as a Result of the Unequal Exchange of Time and Space: Some Conceptual Issues". *Journal Für Entwicklungspolitik* 26(4): 36–52.

Howarth, R.W. (2014). "A Bridge to Nowhere: Methane Emissions and the Greenhouse Gas Footprint of Natural Gas". *Energy Science & Engineering* 2(2): 47–60.

Huber, M. (2009). "Energizing Historical Materialism: Fossil Fuels, Space and the Capitalist Mode of Production". *Geoforum* 40(1): 105–115.

Huber, M. (2013a). *Lifeblood: Oil, Freedom, and the Forces of Capital.* Minneapolis: University of Minnesota Press.

Huber, M. (2015). "Theorizing Energy Geographies". *Geography Compass* 9(6): 327–338.

Huber, M. (2017). "Value, Nature, and Labor: A Defense of Marx". *Capitalism Nature Socialism* 28(1): 39–52.

Huber, M. (2018). "Fossilized Liberation: Energy, Freedom, and the 'Development of the Productive Forces'". In B.R. Bellamy and J. Diamanti (eds.), *Materialism and the Critique of Energy* (pp. 501–524). Chicago: MCM'.

Hughes, D. (2015). *A Clear Look at BC LNG* (pp. 1–50). Vancouver, BC: Canadian Centre for Policy Alternatives.

Hughes, D. (2016). *Can Canada Expand Oil and Gas Production, Build Pipelines and Keep Its Climate Change Commitments?* (pp. 1–38). Vancouver, BC: Canadian Centre for Policy Alternatives.

Hughes, D. (2018). *Canada's Energy Outlook* (pp. 1–180). Vancouver, BC: Canadian Centre for Policy Alternatives.

Hughes, J. (2000). "Development of the Productive Forces: An Ecological Analysis". In M. Cowling and P. Reynolds (eds.), *Marxism, the Millennium and Beyond* (pp. 236–254). New York: Palgrave Macmillan.

Hussey, I. (2020). *Oil Sands Spending and Productivity Figures Indicate Majority of Lost Jobs Not Likely to Return* (pp. 1–36). Edmonton, AB: Parkland Institute.

Huot, M., and Grant, J. (2012). *Clearing the Air on Oilsands Emissions: The Facts About Greenhouse Gas Pollution From Oilsands Development* (pp. 1–15). Calgary, AB: Pembina Institute.

Imperial Oil. (2017). *2016 Annual Financial Statements and Management Discussion and Analysis* (pp. 1–58).

Institute For Oil Sands Innovation. (n.d.). *Partners and Contributors*. Retrieved June 8, 2020, from https://www.ualberta.ca/engineering/research/groups/oil-sands-innovation/partners-and-contributors.html.

Intergovernmental Panel on Climate Change. (2007). *IPCC Fourth Assessment Report: Climate Change 2007* (pp. 1–112).

Intergovernmental Panel on Climate Change. (2018). *Summary for Policymakers of IPCC Special Report on Global Warming of 1.5°C* (pp. 1–24).

Intergovernmental Panel on Climate Change. (2014). *Summary for Policymakers of IPCC Climate Change 2014: Impacts, Adaptation, and Vulnerability* (pp. 1–34).

International Energy Agency. (2011). *World Energy Outlook 2011: Are We Entering a Golden Age of Gas?* (pp. 1–131). Paris: IEA.

International Energy Agency. (2018). *World Energy Outlook 2018* (pp. 1–218). Paris: IEA.

Jacobson, M.Z., and Delucchi, M.A. (2011). "Providing all Global Energy with Wind, Water, and Solar Power, Part I: Technologies, Energy Resources, Quantities and Areas of Infrastructure, and Materials". *Energy Policy* 39(3): 1154–1169.

Jacobson, M.Z., Delucchi, M.A., Cameron, M.A., Coughlin, S.J., Hay, C.A., Manogaran, I.P., Shu, Y., and von Krauland, A.-K. (2019). "Impacts of Green New Deal Energy Plans on Grid Stability, Costs, Jobs, Health, and Climate in 143 Countries". *One Earth* 1(4): 449–463.

Jacobson, M.Z., Delucchi, M.A., Cameron, M.A., and Mathiesen, B.V. (2018). "Matching Demand with Supply at Low Cost in 139 Countries Among 20 World Regions with 100% Intermittent Wind, Water, and Sunlight (WWS) for all Purposes". *Renewable Energy* 123: 236–248.

Jessop, B. (1983). "Accumulation Strategies, State Forms, and Hegemonic Projects". *Kapitalistate* 10: 89–111.

Jessop, B. (2002a). "Capitalism, the Regulation Approach, and Critical Realism". In S. Fleetwood, A. Brown, and J. Roberts (eds.), *Critical Realism and Marxism* (pp. 88–115). London: Routledge.

Jessop, B. (2002b). *The Future of the Capitalist State*. Cambridge: Polity.

Jessop, B. (2007). *State Power*. Cambridge: Polity.

Johnston, A. (2015). *Canada's Track Record on Environmental Laws 2011–2015*. Vancouver, BC: Westcoast Environmental Law Association.

Jonas, H. (1984). *The Imperative of Responsibility: In Search of an Ethics for the Technological Age*. Chicago: University of Chicago Press.

JWN Energy. (2018, November 14). "Canadian Oil and Gas Associations Launch 'Immense' Joint Methane Program". *JWN Energy*. https://www.jwnenergy.com/article/2018/11/canadian-oil-and-gas-associations-launch-immense-joint-methane-program/.

Kaika, M., and Swyngedouw, E. (2000). "Fetishizing the Modern City: The Phantasmagoria of Urban Technological Networks". *International Journal of Urban and Regional Research* 24(1): 120–138.

Kenney, M. (1986). *Biotechnology: The University-Industrial Complex*. New Haven: Yale University Press.

Kiely, R. (2002). "Actually Existing Globalisation, Deglobalisation, and the Political Economy of Anticapitalist Protest". *Historical Materialism* 10(1): 93–121.

Klassen, J. (2009). "Canada and the New Imperialism: The Economics of a Secondary Power". *Studies in Political Economy* 83(1): 163–190.

Klein, N. (2008). *The Shock Doctrine: The Rise of Disaster Capitalism*. Toronto: Vintage Canada.

Klein, N. (2011, November 9). "Capitalism vs. The Climate". *The Nation*. https://www.thenation.com/article/capitalism-vs-climate/.

Klein, N. (2014). *This Changes Everything: Capitalism vs. The Climate*. New York: Simon & Schuster.

Klein, S., and Daub, S. (2016, September 22). "The New Climate Denialism: Time for an Intervention". *Policy Note*. http://www.policynote.ca/the-new-climate-denialism-time-for-an-intervention/.

Koont, S. (2009). "The Urban Agriculture of Havana". *Monthly Review* 60(08): 44–60.

Kreston, R. (2014, February 26). "Paved with Good Intentions: Mao Tse-Tung's 'Four Pests' Disaster". Discover. http://blogs.discovermagazine.com/bodyhorrors/2014/02/26/mao-four-pests-china-disease/#.XJAbNLh7k2x.

La Via Campesina. (2016). *Agroecology in Cuba: For the Farmer, Seeing is Believing* (pp. 1–4). Food and Agriculture Organization of the United Nations.

La Via Campesina. (2018). *La Via Campesina in Action for Climate Justice* (pp. 1–32). Berlin: Heinrich Boll Stiftung.

Latouche, S. (2010). *Farewell to Growth*. Cambridge: Polity.

Latouche, S. (2012). "Can the Left Escape Economism?" *Capitalism Nature Socialism* 23(1): 74–78.

Laxer, G. (2015a). "Pipelines or Pipe Dreams". *After the Sands: Energy and Ecological Security for Canadians* (pp. 159–184). Douglas and McIntyre.

Laxer, G. (2015b). *After the Sands: Energy and Ecological Security for Canadians*. Madeira Park, BC: Douglas & McIntyre.

Le Quéré, C., Andres, R.J., Boden, T., Conway, T., Houghton, R.A., House, J.I., et al. (2013). "The Global Carbon Budget 1959–2011". *Earth System Science Data* 5: 165–185.

Lebowitz, M. (2003). *Beyond Capital: Marx's Political Economy of the Working Class*. New York: Palgrave Macmillan.

Lebowitz, M. (2006). *Build It Now: Socialism for the Twenty-First Century*. New York: NYU Press.

Lee, M. (2017). *Extracted Carbon: Re-examining Canada's Contribution to Climate Change* (pp. 1–34). Vancouver, BC: Canadian Centre for Policy Alternatives.

Lefebvre, H. (1992). *The Production of Space*. Oxford: Wiley-Blackwell.

Lenin, V. (1918). *The Soviets at Work*. Marxists Internet Archive. https://www.marxists.org/archive/lenin/works/1918/mar/soviets.htm.

Lenin, V. (1920). *Our Foreign and Domestic Position and Party Tasks*. Marxists Internet Archive. https://www.marxists.org/archive/lenin/works/1920/nov/21.htm.

Levins, R., and Lewontin, R. (1987). *The Dialectical Biologist*. Cambridge, MA: Harvard University Press.

Lewis, N., and Defterios, J. (2020, January 24). "Can Oil and Gas Companies Help the Transition to Clean Energy?" *CNN*. https://www.cnn.com/2020/01/23/energy/davos-global-energy-challenge-panel/index.html.

Li, M. (2008). "Socialism, Capitalism, and Class Struggle: The Political Economy of Modern China". *Economic and Political Weekly* 43(52): 78–85.

Lohmann, L. (2011). "Capital and Climate Change". *Development and Change* 42(2): 649–668.

Lohmann, L. (2013). *Energy Alternatives: Surveying the Territory* (pp. 1–98). Sturminster Newton, UK: The Corner House.

LÖWY, M. (2020, April 29). "Ecological and Social Planning and Transition". *The Bullet*. https://socialistproject.ca/2020/04/ecological-social-planning-transition/.

Lukács, G. (1972). *History and Class Consciousness: Studies in Marxist Dialectics*. Cambridge, MA: The MIT Press.

Luke, T.W. (2006). "The System of Sustainable Degradation". *Capitalism Nature Socialism* 17(1): 99–112.

Luxemburg, R. (2015). *The Accumulation of Capital*, translated by A. Schwarzschild. Eastford, CT: Martino Fine Books.

MacNeil, R. (2014). "The Decline of Canadian Environmental Regulation: Neoliberalism and the Staples Bias". *Studies in Political Economy* 93(1): 81–106.

Magdoff, F. (2011). "Ecological Civilization". *Monthly Review* 62(08): 1–25.

Malm, A. (2012). "China as Chimney of the World: The Fossil Capital Hypothesis". *Organization & Environment* 25(2): 146–177.

Malm, A. (2013). "The Origins of Fossil Capital: From Water to Steam in the British Cotton Industry*". *Historical Materialism* 21(1): 15–68.

Malm, A. (2016). *Fossil Capital: The Rise of Steam Power and the Roots of Global Warming*. London: Verso.

Mamo, D. (1981). "Mao's Model for Socialist Transition Reconsidered". *Modern China* 7(1): 55–81.

Mandel, E. (1974). "Ten Thesis on the Social and Economic Laws Governing the Society Transitional Between Capitalism and Socialism". *Critique* 3(1): 5–21.

Mandel, E. (1995). *Long Waves of Capitalist Development: A Marxist Interpretation*. London: Verso.

Mandel, E. (1999). *Late Capitalism*. London: Verso.

Mann, G. (2013). *Disassembly Required: A Field Guide to Actually Existing Capitalism*. Oakland, CA: AK Press.

Manno, J.P., Hirsch, P., and Feldpausch-Parker, A.M. (2014). "Introduction by the Onondaga Nation and Activist Neighbors of an Indigenous Perspective on Issues Surrounding Hydrofracking in the Marcellus Shale". *Journal of Environmental Studies and Sciences* 4(1): 47–55.

Mao, T. (1947). *On Contradiction*. Marxists Internet Archive. https://www.marxists.org/reference/archive/mao/selected-works/volume-1/mswv1_17.htm.

Mao, T. (1957). *On the Correct Handling of Contradictions Among the People*. Marxists Internet Archive. https://www.marxists.org/reference/archive/mao/selected-works/volume-5/mswv5_58.htm.

Marcuse, H. (1991). *One-Dimensional Man: Studies in the Ideology of Advanced Industrial Society*. Boston: Beacon Press.

Marois, T. (2013). "Finance, Finance Capital and Financialization". In M. Boffo, B. Fine, and A. Saad-Filho (eds.), *The Elgar Companion to Marxist Economics* (pp. 138–143). Cheltenham: Edward Elgar Publishing.

Marx, K. (1853a). *The British Rule in India*. Marxists Internet Archive. https://marxists.catbull.com/archive/marx/works/1853/06/25.htm.

Marx, K. (1853b). *The Future Results of British Rule in India*. Marxists Internet Archive. https://marxists.catbull.com/archive/marx/works/1853/07/22.htm.

Marx, K. (1967). *Capital Volume II: A Critique of Political Economy*. New York: International Publishers.

Marx, K. (1976a). *A Contribution to the Critique of Political Economy*, translated by M. Dobb. New York: International Publishers.

Marx, K. (1976b). *Capital Volume I: A Critique of Political Economy*, translated by B. Fowkes. New York: Vintage Books.

Marx, K. (1992). *Collected Works of Karl Marx and Friedrich Engels, Vol. 33: Continues the Economic Manuscripts of 1861–63*. New York: International Publishers.

Marx, K. (1993a). *Capital Volume III: A Critique of Political Economy*, translated by D. Fernbach. New York: Penguin Classics.

Marx, K. (1993b). *Grundrisse: Foundations of the Critique of Political Economy*. New York: Penguin Classics.

Marx, K., and Engels, F. (1976). *The German Ideology*, D. Clemens. Moscow: Progress Publishers.

Marx, K., and Engels, F. (2004). *The Communist Manifesto*. Peterborough, ON: Broadview Press.

Mauro Di Meglio, and Pietro Masina. (2013). "Marx and Underdevelopment". In M. Boffo, B. Fine, and A. Saad-Filho (eds.), *The Elgar Companion to Marxist Economics* (pp. 206–211). Cheltenham: Edward Elgar Publishing.

McCartney, K. (2018). *Pricing Air to Starve the Fire: An Institutional Ethnography of Smart Prosperity* [Thesis]. https://dspace.library.uvic.ca//handle/1828/10001.

McCormack, G., Workman, T., and McNally, D. (2015). *The Servant State: Overseeing Capital Accumulation in Canada*. Halifax: Fernwood Publishing.

McKay, P. (2018, March 7). *The Fatal Flaw of Alberta's Oil Expansion*. National Observer. https://www.nationalobserver.com/2018/03/07/opinion/fatal-flaw-albertas-oil-expansion.

McLachlan, T., and Hatch, C. (2017, July 21). *Who's Banking on Kinder Morgan's Trans Mountain Pipeline?* National Observer. https://www.nationalobserver .com/2017/07/21/analysis/whos-banking-kinder-morgans-trans-mountain-pipeline.

McMichael, P. (2007). "Feeding the World: Agriculture, Development and Ecology". *Socialist Register*: 170–194.

McNally, D. (1981). "Staple Theory as Commodity Fetishism: Marx, Innis and Canadian Political Economy". *Studies in Political Economy* 6(1): 35–63.

Meszaros, I. (1986). *Marx's Theory of Alienation*. London: Merlin Pr.

Meyer, C. (2018, June 25). "More than $1 Billion Will Go Through Seldom-Used Canadian Account to Buy Pipeline". *National Observer*. https://www.nationalobserver.com/2018/06/25/news/more-1-billion-will-go-through-seldom-used-canadian-account-buy-pipeline.

Mies, M. (1986). *Patriarchy and Accumulation On A World Scale: Women in the International Division of Labour*. London: Zed Books.

Mikulka, J. (2018, October 25). *Why Canadian Tar Sands Oil May Be Doomed*. The Narwhal. https://www.desmogblog.com/2018/10/25/canadian-tar-sands-oil-financial-losses.

Miller, D. (2013). "Why the Oil Companies Lost Solar". *Energy Policy* 60: 52–60.

Miller, R.W. (1981). "Productive Forces and the Forces of Change: A Review of Gerald A. Cohen, Karl Marx's Theory of History: A Defense". *The Philosophical Review* 90(1): 91–117.

Minx, J.C., Baiocchi, G., Peters, G.P., Weber, C.L., Guan, D., and Hubacek, K. (2011). "A 'Carbonizing Dragon': China's Fast Growing CO_2 Emissions Revisited". *Environmental Science & Technology* 45(21): 9144–9153.

Mitchell, T. (2011). *Carbon Democracy: Political Power in the Age of Oil*. London and New York: Verso.

Mizruchi, M.S. (1996). "What do Interlocks do? An Analysis, Critique, and Assessment of Research on Interlocking Directorates". *Annual Review of Sociology* 22: 271–298.

Mizruchi, M.S., and Koenig, T. (1988). "Economic Concentration and Corporate Political Behavior: A Cross-Industry Comparison". *Social Science Research* 17(4): 287–305.

Monstadt, J. (2009). "Conceptualizing the Political Ecology of Urban Infrastructures: Insights from Technology and Urban Studies". *Environment and Planning A* 41(8): 1924–1942.

Moore, J.W. (2011). "Transcending the Metabolic Rift: A Theory of Crises in the Capitalist World-Ecology". *Journal of Peasant Studies* 38(1): 1–46.

Moore, J.W. (2014). "The Value of Everything? Work, Capital, and Historical Nature in the Capitalist World-Ecology". *Review (Fernand Braudel Center)* 37(3): 245–292.

Moore, J.W. (2015). *Capitalism in the Web of Life: Ecology and the Accumulation of Capital.* New York: Verso.

Moore, J.W. (ed.). (2016). "The Rise of Cheap Nature". In *Anthropocene or Capitalocene?: Nature, History, and the Crisis of Capitalism* (pp. 78–115). Oakland, CA: PM Press.

Moreau, J. (2012, April). *Who's Moving Oil on the Burrard Inlet?* Burnaby Now. https://www.burnabynow.com/news/who-s-moving-oil-on-the-burrard-inlet-1.413969.

Muller, T. (2013). *Of Energy Struggles, Energy Transitions and Energy Democracy* (pp. 1–8). New York: Rosa Luxemburg Foundation.

Mumford, L. (2010). *Technics and Civilization.* Chicago: University of Chicago Press.

Muttitt, G. (2016). *The Sky's Limit: Why the Paris Climate Goals Require a Managed Decline of Fossil Fuel Production* (pp. 1–60). Washington, DC: Oil Change International.

National Energy Board. (2013). *The Ultimate Potential for Unconventional Petroleum from the Montney Formation of British Columbia and Alberta—Energy Briefing Note.* https://www.neb-one.gc.ca/nrg/sttstc/ntrlgs/rprt/ltmtptntlmntnyfrmtn2013/ltmtptntlmntnyfrmtn2013-eng.html.

National Energy Board. (2015, April 30). *The Ultimate Potential for Unconventional Petroleum from the Bakken Formation of Saskatchewan.* https://www.nebone.gc.ca/nrg/sttstc/crdlndptrlmprdct/rprt/2015bkkn/index-eng.html.

National Energy Board. (2016). *Canada's Renewable Power Landscape* (pp. 1–39). National Energy Board.

National Energy Board. (2017, April 19). *NEB – Market Snapshot: Natural Gas Plays an Important Role In Alberta's Oil Sands.* https://www.neb-one.gc.ca/nrg/ntgrtd/mrkt/snpsht/2017/04-03ntrlgslbrtlsnd-eng.html?=undefined&wbdisable=true.

Natural Gas Innovation Fund. (n.d.). *Investment Focus.* Natural Gas Innovation Fund. http://www.ngif.ca/investment-focus/.

Natural Resources Canada. (2016). *Enbridge Pipelines Inc. – Line 3 Replacement Program Review of Related Upstream Greenhouse Gas Emissions Estimates* (pp. 1–28).

Natural Resources Canada. (2017, October 6). *Crude oil facts.* https://www.nrcan.gc.ca/energy/facts/crude-oil/20064.

Newell, J.P., and Cousins, J.J. (2015). "The Boundaries of Urban Metabolism". *Progress in Human Geography* 39(6): 702–728.

Newell, P., and Paterson, M. (2010). *Climate Capitalism: Global Warming and the Transformation of the Global Economy.* Cambridge: Cambridge University Press.

Newell, P., and Patterson, M. (2011). "Climate Capitalism". In E. Altvater and A. Brunnengräber (eds.), *After Cancún: Climate Governance or Climate Conflicts* (pp. 23–44). Berlin: VS Verlag Sozialwissenschaften.

Nikiforuk, A. (2010). *Tar Sands: Dirty Oil and the Future of a Continent.* Vancouver, BC: Greystone Books.

Nikiforuk, A. (2019, January 10). "Horgan Goes from Lion to Lamb on the Trans Mountain Pipeline". *The Tyee.* https://thetyee.ca/Opinion/2019/01/10/Horgan-Lamb-Trans-Mountain-Pipeline/.

Noble, D.F. (1986). *Forces of Production: A Social History of Industrial Automation.* New York: Oxford University Press.

Noble, D.F. (1998). "Digital Diploma Mills; The Automation of Higher Education". *Monthly Review* 49(9): 1–38.

O'Connor, J. (1974). *The Corporations and the State: Essays in the Theory of Capitalism and Imperialism.* New York: HarperCollins.

O'Connor, J. (1988). "Capitalism, Nature, Socialism a Theoretical Introduction". *Capitalism Nature Socialism* 1(1): 11–38.

O'Connor, J. (1997). *Natural Causes: Essays in Ecological Marxism.* New York: The Guilford Press.

Odih, P. (2014). *Watersheds in Marxist Ecofeminism.* Newcastle upon Tyne: Cambridge Scholars Publishing.

Ollman, B. (1976). *Alienation: Marx's Conception of Man in a Capitalist Society.* Cambridge: Cambridge University Press.

O'Reilly, C. (2010). "The Transnational Security Consultancy Industry: A Case of State-Corporate Symbiosis". *Theoretical Criminology* 14(2): 183–210.

O'Shaughnessy, S., and Dogu, G. (2016). "The Gendered and Racialized Subjects of Alberta's Boomtown". In L. Adkin (ed.), *First World Petro-Politics: The Political Ecology and Governance of Alberta* (pp. 263–296). Toronto: University of Toronto Press.

Panitch, L. (ed.). (1977). *The Canadian State: Political Economy and Political Power.* Toronto: University of Toronto Press.

Panzieri, R. (1976). "Surplus Value and Planning: Notes on the Reading of 'Capital'". *The Labour Process and Class Strategies* (pp. 4–25). London: Conference of Socialist Economics.

Panzieri, R. (2005). *The Capitalist Use of Machinery: Marx Versus the Objectivists.* Libcom.Org. http://libcom.org/library/capalist-use-machinery-raniero-panzieri.

Parfitt, B. (2018, August 8). "How BC's Gas Giveaway Fuels Alberta's Oilsands". *The Tyee.* https://thetyee.ca/Opinion/2018/08/08/BC-Gas-Giveaway-Alberta-Oilsands/.

Patterson, B. (2019, February 12). "Hundreds of Pro-Pipeline Protesters to Drive Cross-Country for Parliament Hill Rally". *Rabble.* http://www.rabble.ca/blogs/bloggers/brent-patterson/2019/02/hundreds-pro-pipeline-protesters-drive-cross-country.

Pauliuk, S., Majeau-Bettez, G., and Müller, D.B. (2015). "A General System Structure and Accounting Framework for Socioeconomic Metabolism". *Journal of Industrial Ecology* 19(5): 728–741.

Perelman, M. (1978). "Karl Marx's Theory of Science". *Journal of Economic Issues* 12(4): 859–870.

Petroleum Technology Alliance Canada. (n.d.). "Mission/Vision". *PTAC*. Retrieved November 22, 2018. https://www.ptac.org/missionvision/.

Petroleum Technology Alliance Canada. (2010). *Petroleum Technology Alliance Canada 2010 Annual Report* (pp. 1–20).

Petroleum Technology Alliance Canada. (2015). *Petroleum Technology Alliance Canada 2015 Annual Report* (pp. 1–20).

Pijl, K. van der. (1998). *Transnational Classes and International Relations*. London: Routledge.

Pijl, K. van der. (2004). "Two Faces of the Transnational Cadre Under Neo-Liberalism". *Journal of International Relations and Development* 7(2): 177–207.

Pineault, E. (2014). "The Panacea: Panax Quinquefolius and the Mirage of the Extractive Economy". In J. Stanford (ed.), *The Staple Theory @ 50 Reflections on the Lasting Significance of Mel Watkins' "A Staple Theory of Economic Growth"* (pp. 84–91). Vancouver, BC: Canadian Centre for Policy Alternatives.

Pineault, E. (2018). "The Capitalist Pressure to Extract: The Ecological and Political Economy of Extreme Oil in Canada". *Studies in Political Economy* 99(2): 130–150.

Polster, C. (2018). "How and Why to Change the Ways We Try to Change the Corporatization of Universities". In Jaimie Brownlee, C. Hurl, and K. Walby (eds.), *Corporatizing Canada: Making Business out of Public Service* (pp. 87–109). Toronto: Between the Lines.

Prudham, S. (2003). "Taming Trees: Capital, Science, and Nature in Pacific Slope Tree Improvement". *Annals of the Association of American Geographers* 93(3): 636–656.

Rathi, A. (2020, February 13). "BP Beefs up Carbon Capture Team in Bid to Meet Climate Goals". *BNN Bloomberg*. https://www.bnnbloomberg.ca/bp-beefs-up-carbon-capture-team-in-bid-to-meet-climate-goals-1.1389842.

Reganold, J.P., and Wachter, J.M. (2016). "Organic Agriculture in the Twenty-First Century". *Nature Plants* 2(2): 1–8.

Reynolds, L., and Szerszynski, B. (2012). "Neoliberalism and Technology: Perpetual Innovation or Perpetual Crisis?" In L. Pellizzoni and M. Ylönen (eds.), *Neoliberalism and Technoscience: Critical Assessments* (pp. 27–46). Farnham: Ashgate.

Ribes, A., Zwiers, F.W., Azaïs, J.-M., and Naveau, P. (2017). "A New Statistical Approach to Climate Change Detection and Attribution". *Climate Dynamics* 48(1): 367–386.

Riesch, H., and Potter, C. (2014). "Citizen Science as Seen by Scientists: Methodological, Epistemological and Ethical Dimensions". *Public Understanding of Science* 23(1): 107–120.

Rosnick, D. (2013). *Reduced Work Hours as a Means of Slowing Climate Change* (pp. 1–13). Washington, DC: Center for Economic and Policy Research.

Rossanda, R. (1971). "Mao's Marxism". *Socialist Register* 8(8): 53–80.

Rowe, J., Dempsey, J., and Gibbs, P. (2016). "The Power of Fossil Fuel Divestment (And its Secret)". In W. Carroll and K. Sarker (eds.), *A World to Win: Contemporary Social Movements and Counter-Hegemony* (pp. 233–249). Winnipeg: ARP Books.

Saed. (2011). "On Ecosocialism, Objectives, and the Role of the Natural Sciences". *Capitalism Nature Socialism* 22(3): 1–7.

Saito, K. (2017). *Karl Marx's Ecosocialism: Capital, Nature, and the Unfinished Critique of Political Economy*. New York: Monthly Review Press.

Salleh, A. (2010). "From Metabolic Rift to "Metabolic Value": Reflections on Environmental Sociology and the Alternative Globalization Movement". *Organization & Environment* 23(2): 205–219.

Salleh, A. (1997). *Ecofeminism as Politics: Nature, Marx, and the Postmodern*. London: Zed Books.

Salleh, A. (ed.). (2009). *Eco-Sufficiency & Global Justice: Women Write Political Ecology*. London: Pluto Press.

Sapinski, J.P. (2015). "Climate Capitalism and the Global Corporate Elite Network". *Environmental Sociology* 1(4): 268–279.

Sapinski, J.P. (2016). "Constructing Climate Capitalism: Corporate Power and the Global Climate Policy-Planning Network". *Global Networks* 16(1): 89–111.

Sassen, S. (2009). "Cities are at the Center of Our Environmental Future". *S.A.P.I.EN.S. Surveys and Perspectives Integrating Environment and Society* 2.3.

Sassoon, A.S. (1982). "Passive Revolution and the Politics of Reform". In A.S. Sassoon (ed.), *Approaches to Gramsci* (pp. 127–148). London: Writers and Readers.

Sayre, N. (2010). "Climate Change, Scale, and Devaluation: The Challenge of Our Built Environment". *Washington and Lee Journal of Energy, Climate, and the Environment* 1(1): 93–105.

Schaaf, E., Olivier, J.G.J., Guizzardi, D., and Janssens-Maenhout, D. (2018). *Fossil CO_2 and GHG Emissions of All World Countries* (pp. 1–251). Luxembourg: Publications Office of the European Union.

Schmalzer, S. (2012). "On the Appropriate Use of Rose-Coloured Glasses: Reflections on Science in Socialist China". In D.E. Brock and C.N. Wei (eds.), *Mr. Science and Chairman Mao's Cultural Revolution: Science and Technology in Modern China* (pp. 347–361). Lanham: Lexington Books.

Schmidt, A. (1971). *The Concept of Nature in Marx*. New York: New Left Books.

Schnaiberg, A. (1980). *The Environment: From Surplus to Scarcity*. New York: Oxford University Press.

Schwartzman, D. (2012). "A Critique of Degrowth and its Politics". *Capitalism Nature Socialism* 23(1): 119–125.

Schwartzman, D. (2016). "Beyond Eco-Catastrophism: The Conditions for Solar Communism". *Socialist Register* 53: 143–160.

Schwartzman, D., and Schwartzman, P. (2013). "A Rapid Solar Transition is not only Possible, it is Imperative!" *African Journal of Science, Technology, Innovation and Development* 5(4): 297–302.

Scott, D.N. (2013). "The Networked Infrastructure of Fossil Capitalism: Implications of the New Pipeline Debates for Environmental Justice in Canada". *Revue Générale de Droit* 43: 11–42.

Scott, J. (1997). *Corporate Business and Capitalist Class*. New York: Oxford University Press.

Shannon, L., Nardizzi, V., Hiltner, K., Makdisi, S., Ziser, M., Szeman, I., and Yaeger, P. (2011). "Editor's Column: Literature in the Ages of Wood, Tallow, Coal, Whale Oil, Gasoline, Atomic Power, and Other Energy Sources". *PMLA* 126(2): 305–326.

Shaw, K., Cook, D., Fitzgerald, E., and Sayers, J. (Kekinusuqs). (2017, October 12). "BC First Nations are Poised to Lead the Renewable Energy Transition". *Policy Note.* https://www.policynote.ca/bc-first-nations-are-poised-to-lead-the-renewable-energy-transition/.

Shiva, V. (2016). *Who Really Feeds the World?: The Failures of Agribusiness and the Promise of Agroecology*. Berkeley, CA: North Atlantic Books.

Shrivastava, M. (2015). "Liberal Democracy in Oil-Exporting Countries: A View from the Perspective of Staples Theory". In M. Shrivastava and L. Stefanick (eds.), *Alberta Oil and the Decline of Democracy in Canada* (pp. 31–67). Edmonton, AB: AU Press.

Smil, V. (2010). *Energy Transitions: History, Requirements, Prospects*. Santa Barbara, CA: Praeger.

Smith, J.K. (1998). "Patents, Public Policy, and Petrochemical Processes in the Post-World War II Era". *Business and Economic History* 27(2): 413–419.

Smith, M. (2016, August 12). "Is it Time for Oil and Gas Companies to Jump on the Renewables Bandwagon?" *JWN Energy.* http://www.jwnenergy.com/article/2016/8/it-time-oil-and-gas-companies-jump-renewables-bandwagon/.

Smith, N. (2007). "Nature as an Accumulation Strategy". *Socialist Register*: 16–26.

Socialist Project Toronto. (2020). *Take the Plant, Save the Planet* (pp. 1–64). Toronto: Socialist Project.

Stanford, J. (2008). *Economics for Everyone: A Short Guide to the Economics of Capitalism*. Halifax: Fernwood Publishing.

Stendie, L., and Adkin, L. (2016). "In the Path of the Pipeline: Environmental Citizenship, Aboriginal Rights, and the Northern Gateway Pipeline Review". In L. Adkin (ed.), *First World Petro-Politics: The Political Ecology and Governance of Alberta* (pp. 417–455). Toronto: University of Toronto Press.

Stephenson, E., Doukas, A., and Shaw, K. (2012). "Greenwashing Gas: Might a 'Transition Fuel' Label Legitimize Carbon-Intensive Natural Gas Development?" *Energy Policy* 46: 452–459.

Steward, G. (2017, December 4). "How Alberta's Clean Energy Transition May Actually Benefit Big Coal and Oil Players Over Small Renewables". *The Narwhal.* https://the-narwhal.ca/how-alberta-s-clean-energy-transition-may-actually-benefit-big-coal-and-oil-players-over-small-renewables/.

Stockman, L. (2013). *Petroleum Coke: The Coal Hiding in the Tar Sands* (pp. 1–44). Washington, DC: Oil Change International.

Suncor Energy. (2017). *Annual Report 2016* (pp. 1–157).

Sustainable Development Technology Canada. (n.d.-a). "About Us". *Sustainable Development Technology Canada.* Retrieved November 21, 2018, from https://www.sdtc.ca/en/about /about-us/.

Sustainable Development Technology Canada. (n.d.-b). "For Public". *Sustainable Development Technology Canada.* Retrieved November 21, 2018, from https://www.sdtc.ca/en/for-public/.

Sweeny, S., and Treat, J. (2017). *Energy Transition: Are We Winning?* (pp. 1–22). New York: Rosa Luxemburg Stiftung.

Swidler, E. (2018). "Invisible Exploitation". *Monthly Review* 69(10): 29–43.

Switzer, J. (2013, March 14). "When Renewables Meet the Oil and Gas Industry, Opposites Attract". *Renewable Energy World.* https://www.renewableenergyworld.com/2014/04/14/when-renewables-meet-the-oil-and-gas-industry-opposites-attract/#gref.

Swyngedouw, E. (2006). "Circulations and Metabolisms: (Hybrid) Natures and (Cyborg) Cities". *Science as Culture* 15(2): 105–121.

Taft, K. (2017). *Oil's Deep State: How the Petroleum Industry Undermines Democracy and Stops Action on Global Warming – In Alberta, and in Ottawa.* Toronto: Lorimer.

Tangley, L. (1988). "News Update". *BioScience* 38(8): 538–540.

Tanuro, D. (2005). *Marx, Mandel et les Limites Naturelles.* Ernest Mandel Archives Internet. http://www.ernestmandel.org/fr/surlavie/txt/colloque/tanuro.htm.

Tanuro, D. (2010). "Marxism, Energy, and Ecology: The Moment of Truth". *Capitalism Nature Socialism* 21(4): 89–101.

Tanuro, D. (2012, October 12). "A Plea for an Ecological Reconstruction of Marxism". *Europe Solidaire Sans Frontières.* https://www.europe-solidaire.org/spip.php?article27100.

Tanuro, D. (2014). *Green Capitalism: Why It Can't Work.* Halifax: Fernwood Publishing.

Teck. (2017). *Every Day. 2016 Annual Report* (pp. 1–116).

Teeple Hopkins, C. (2017). "Mostly Work, Little Play: Social Reproduction, Migration and Paid Domestic Work in Montreal". In T. Bhattacharya (ed.), *Social Reproduction Theory: Remapping Class, Recentring Oppression* (pp. 131–147). London: Pluto Press.

Therborn, G. (1980). *Science, Class, and Society: On the Formation of Sociology and Historical Materialism.* London: Verso.

Thomas, P.D. (2011). *The Gramscian Moment: Philosophy, Hegemony and Marxism*. Chicago: Haymarket.

Thomas-Muller, C. (2014). "The Rise of the Native Rights–Based Strategic Framework". In S. D'Arcy, T. Black, T. Weis, and J.K. Russell (eds.), *A Line in the Tar Sands* (pp. 240–252). Toronto: Between the Lines.

Thompson, D., and Newman, K. (2009). *Private Gain or Public Interest?* (pp. 1–36). Ottawa: Canadian Centre for Policy Alternatives.

Trainer, T. (2012). "A critique of Jacobson and Delucchi's Proposals for a World Renewable Energy Supply". *Energy Policy* 44: 476–481.

Trainer, T. (2014). "Reply to David Schwartzman on the Simpler Way and Renewable Energy". *Capitalism Nature Socialism* 25(4): 102–108.

TransCanada. (2017). *2016 Annual Report* (pp. 1–203).

Transmountain. (2017, April 20). *Scott Stoness: Expansion is in Canada's Public Interest*. https://www.transmountain.com/news/2017/scott-stoness-expansion-is-in-canadas-public-interest?

Tretter, E. (2019). "Producing Alberta's Tar Sands: Oil, Ideas, Rents, and New Enclosures". *Capitalism Nature Socialism*: 1–20.

Turner, C. (2017). *The Patch: The People, Pipelines, and Politics of the Oil Sands*. Toronto: Simon & Schuster.

U.S. Energy Information Administration. (2016). *Annual Energy Outlook 2017 With Projections to 2050* (p. 1–64).

Veblen, T. (2012). *The Engineers and the Price System*. Eastford: Martino Fine Books.

Wachsmuth, D. (2012). "Three Ecologies: Urban Metabolism and the Society-Nature Opposition". *The Sociological Quarterly* 53(4): 506–523.

Wark, M. (2015, October 15). "The Capitalocene". *Public Seminar*. http://www.public-seminar.org/2015/10/the-capitalocene/.

Wark, M. (2016). *Molecular Red: Theory for the Anthropocene*. London: Verso.

Washburn, J. (2010). *Big Oil Goes to College* (pp. 1–220). Washington, DC: Centre for American Progress.

Watkins, M. (2006). *Staples and Beyond: Selected Writings of Mel Watkins*. Montreal: McGill-Queen's Press.

Wedding, C. (2016, September). "Oil and Gas Companies' and Renewable Energy: Passing Fad or Major Trend?" *K.Nect365*. https://knect365.com/superreturn/article/365dfodf-e699-4a32-b2ed-13b0ce2cbdfb/oil-and-gas-companies-and-renewable-energy-passing-fad-or-major-trend.

Weis, T., Thimbault, B., and Miller, B. (2016). "Alberta's Electricity Future". In L. Adkin (ed.), *First World Petro-Politics: The Political Ecology and Governance of Alberta* (pp. 499–526). Toronto: University of Toronto Press.

Wendling, A. (2011). *Karl Marx on Technology and Alienation*. London: Palgrave Macmillan.

Werskey, G. (2007). "The Marxist Critique of Capitalist Science: A History in Three Movements?" *Science as Culture* 16(4): 397–461.

Wilde, L. (2000). "'The Creatures, Too, Must Become Free': Marx and the Animal/Human Distinction". *Capital & Class* 24(3): 37–53.

Wilt, J. (2018, May 16). "A Brief History of the Public Money Propping up the Alberta Oilsands". *The Narwhal.* https://thenarwhal.ca/brief-history-public-money-propping-alberta-oilsands/.

Witt, J. (2018, February 17). "Canada Is Replacing Coal With Natural Gas—And That's A Huge Problem". *The Narwhal.* https://thenarwhal.ca/canada-replacing-coal-natural-gas-and-s-huge-problem/.

Wood Mackenzie. (2018, October 5). "Oil & Gas Majors in Renewable Energy: The Hunt for the Best Returns". *Wood Mackenzie.* https://www. woodmac.com/reports/power-markets-oil-and-gas-majors-in-renewable-energy-the-hunt-for-the-best-returns-30844.

Wright, E.O. (1998). *Classes*. London: Verso.

Wright, E.O. (2015). *Understanding Class*. London: Verso.

York, R., and McGee, J.A. (2017). "Does Renewable Energy Development Decouple Economic Growth from CO_2 Emissions?" *Socius* 3: 1–6.

Zadek, S. (2013, July 26). "Greening Financial Reform". *Project Syndicate.* http://www.project-syndicate.org/commentary/integrating-the-green-growth-imperative-and-financial-market-reform-by-simon-zadek.

Zeidler, M. (2018, June 3). "Protest Camp Divides Quiet B.C. Community at Centre of Pipeline Debate". *CBC News.* https://newsinteractives.cbc.ca/longform/we-will-stand-to-the-bitter-end-trans-mountain.

Index

www.ingramcontent.com/pod-product-compliance
Lightning Source LLC
Chambersburg PA
CBHW070916030426
42336CB00014BA/2438